Ethical Aspects of Information Technology

Richard A. Spinello
Boston College

PRENTICE HALL, Englewood Cliffs, New Jersey 07632

Library of Congress Cataloging-in-Publication Data

SPINELLO, RICHARD A.
    Ethical aspects of information technology/Richard A. Spinello.
      p.   cm.
    Includes bibliographical references and index.
    ISBN 0-13-045931-3
    1. Information technology—Moral and ethical aspects.
    2. Information technology—Moral and ethical aspects—Case studies.
    I. Title.
    T58.5.S69   1994
    174'.90904—dc20

                                                          94-35323
                                                          CIP

Editorial/production supervision, interior design,
   and electronic page makeup: Kari Callaghan Mazzola
Acquisitions editor: Ted Bolen
Cover design: Tom Nery
Buyer: Lynn Pearlman

 © 1995 by Prentice-Hall, Inc.
A Simon & Schuster Company
Englewood Cliffs, New Jersey 07632

Printed in the United States of America
10 9 8 7 6 5 4

ISBN 0-13-045931-3

PRENTICE-HALL INTERNATIONAL (UK) LIMITED, *London*
PRENTICE-HALL OF AUSTRALIA PTY. LIMITED, *Sydney*
PRENTICE-HALL CANADA INC., *Toronto*
PRENTICE-HALL HISPANOAMERICANA, S.A., *Mexico*
PRENTICE-HALL OF INDIA PRIVATE LIMITED, *New Delhi*
PRENTICE-HALL OF JAPAN, INC., *Tokyo*
SIMON & SCHUSTER ASIA PTE. LTD., *Singapore*
EDITORA PRENTICE-HALL DO BRASIL, LTDA., *Rio de Janeiro*

To my wife, Susan,
and my parents, Richard and Anna

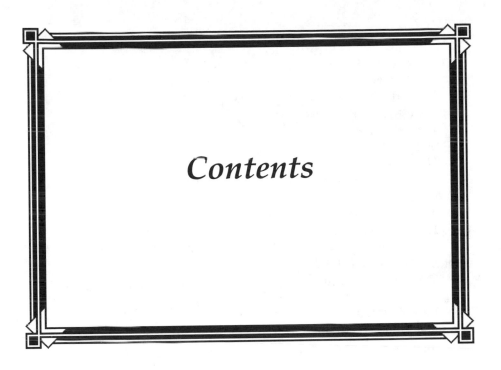

Contents

Chapter 3   Information Technology and Anti-Competitive Practices   47

Chapter 7   Ethical Issues and Information Security   185

Annotated Bibliography   213

Index   220

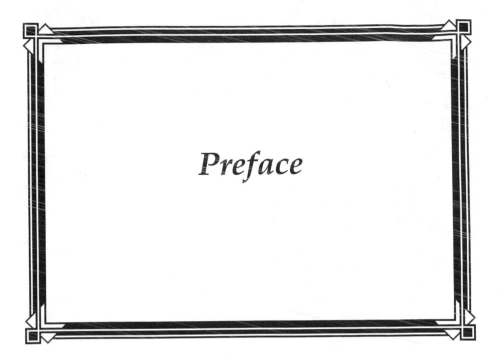

Preface

Every decade seems to produce some well-publicized, acute ethical problems which pose a formidable challenge to society. In the 1970s the issues revolved around degradation of the environment and payoffs to foreign officials. Our chief ethical concerns in the 1980s shifted to hostile takeovers, leveraged buyouts, and insider trading. Now, just as business ethics textbooks have begun to incorporate cases on these forms of unethical behavior, a new set of issues has begun to emerge.

One does not have to be a great seer to realize that the ethical dimension of computer technology will likely be one of the dominant issues for the 1990s and beyond. Given the ubiquity of information technology and its extraordinary impact on professional and personal lives, this area will present significant new tests for a manager's integrity and professional behavior.

Indeed there is a general perception in many circles that social and ethical considerations are having a hard time keeping up with revolutionary and rapid developments in technology. As America embraces the information age, it does not always pay attention to the risks and the social costs of technological advancements. In short, technology often moves much faster than ethics, and the lag poses some serious perils for all of us. This book is an effort to close this gap by provoking managers and students to reflect upon the social and ethical ramifications of managing information.

It would be a mistake, however, to consider the ethics of computer technology as unique, separate from general business and social ethics. The premise of this text is that these "revolutionary" problems can be confronted with the same analytical tools and ethical categories used for more traditional concerns. It will be illuminating, then, to regard these new dilemmas from the perspective of rights or duties or maximization of consequences. Our ethical tradition is rich enough to provide ample background for the thoughtful and comprehensive treatment of these new problem areas. To be sure, it may be necessary to revise our definition of certain rights such as privacy in light of the new realities created by the phenomenon of "digital disclosure." Although we might need to reinterpret what the right to privacy means on the frontiers of cyberspace, it is important to underline that the notion of a right to privacy, a right to control information about oneself, has not lost its intelligibility.

Also the use of traditional ethical categories does not imply that these perplexing issues can be easily resolved. Many of the problems raised in this book represent tough ethical quandaries fraught with moral ambiguity. No moral artifice can simply reconcile the difficult tradeoffs often required by these complex issues. Hard analytical work, serious dialogue, and often considerable compromise will constitute the only path toward the normative guidelines demanded by these problems. It is my hope that the discussion and case studies in this book will provide an opportunity to move this important process forward and prepare us for the future.

Before concluding this Preface, let me add a few words about the scope and unique features of this book. It is written primarily for ethics courses that focus on computer science or information management. There are many fine textbooks for these courses but few that integrate a large number of case studies based on actual incidents with a discussion of normative ethical principles and background material on technical issues. Chapter 1 gives an overview of the technologies that can engender ethical problems. Chapter 2 provides some background on various ethical frameworks that can facilitate the analysis of the case studies. Chapters 3 through 7 explore the following ethical issues that are the by-product of enhanced information technology capabilities: anti-competitive practices, vendor/client relations, privacy, intellectual property rights, and security. Several of these issues, such as vendor-client relations and information technology's role in anti-competitive practices, have not received much attention in books on computer ethics. But all of these issues represent major managerial challenges to both suppliers and users of information technology.

It should also be pointed out that this book will focus exclusively on the challenges of information technology that surface in a corporate environment. As a result, the case studies present dilemmas that are typically encountered by information technology vendors and by corporate managers responsible for developing, implementing, and using information technology systems for competitive advantage. We will eschew, therefore, some commonly discussed social issues such as the problem of universal access, the military use of computers, information technology and the Third World, and the phenomenon of "hackers." Furthermore, we will not explicitly consider social problems that will inevitably accompany the evolution of technology such as impersonalization of communication. These are all interesting and important areas but they are beyond the scope of this book.

Finally, I owe a great debt of gratitude to several individuals who helped make this book possible. I would especially like to single out my wife, Susan T. Brinton, for her efforts in typing, editing, and proofreading this manuscript. Thanks go to the following reviewers: Wilfried Sieg, Carnegie Mellon University; Lee C. Rice, Marquette University; Heinz C. Luegenbiehl, Rose-Hulman Institute of Technology; and Russell E. Willis, Iowa Wesleyan College. I am grateful to Father William Neenan, S.J., Academic Vice President of Boston College, for his generous support of this project. Let me also take this opportunity to acknowledge my other colleagues at Boston College, particularly those at Bourneuf House, who have helped to create an atmosphere that is conducive to this sort of reflection and research.

Richard A. Spinello

1

An Overview
of Information Technology
and Ethical Issues

Any technology tends to create a new human environment.[1]
Marshall McLuhan

INFORMATION TECHNOLOGY AND THE CORPORATION

Information is one of our most valuable commercial resources. Organizations that can collect, analyze, synthesize, and evaluate information before their rivals do are likely to have a competitive advantage. Because of this critical importance of information, contemporary professionals are often referred to as "knowledge workers" and "information specialists." They work to cultivate from many different sources the information needed for sound decision making. The lack of timely, accurate information is a serious obstacle for anyone making the sort of complex decisions necessary in today's corporate environment. According to Arno Penzias:

> ....a healthy flow of information separates winning organizations from losers. 'Deciding' means acting on information. Barring blind luck, the quality of a decision can't be better than the quality of the information behind it.[2]

[1]Marshall McLuhan, *Understanding Media: The Extensions of Man* (New York: Mentor Books, 1964), p. iv.
[2]Arno Penzias, *Ideas and Information* (New York: W. W. Norton & Company, 1989), p. 22.

But information should not be confused with data. Overwhelming amounts of data are now available in electronic media. One basic goal of information technology (IT) systems is to transform this copious amount of data into information and usable knowledge as expeditiously as possible. The evolution and diffusion of these systems during the last twenty years have helped this goal to be realized effectively and consistently.

Because of the compelling need to generate and control information, IT systems have become a major resource in today's corporate environment. Almost every major corporation relies heavily on information technology in order to manage its various resources, increase productivity, and thereby compete effectively. Moreover, a well designed IT system is a prerequisite for informed decision-making. As one observer has noted, "effectively managing information technology can mean the difference between a successful, growing organization and one that slowly stagnates as its environment and business change."[3]

To be sure, there have been significant advances in the sophisticated technologies of computer hardware, software, and networking, which have greatly enhanced the capacity for delivering vital information to decision makers. The core technology that is rapidly reshaping corporate structures and our whole society is undoubtedly the networked computer. Thanks to this technology, organizations can exchange vast amounts of information simply and cheaply. Computers are now easily connected to a global information infrastructure that is expanding the possibilities for transforming the way business is done. Thanks to networks, engineers and designers can collaborate on research projects even though they are thousands of miles apart. Similarly, companies can electronically order goods or services from their suppliers. For example, the DuPont Company no longer receives invoices from its vendors; instead, it simply pays off its bills electronically. The company has even eliminated the use of purchase orders with some of its major suppliers; according to *Business Week*, "When the suppliers see that DuPont is running short on an item, they simply deliver replacement goods."[4]

But these technologies have also been costly for many corporations eager to adapt state-of-the-art information systems. They have added staff and departments and invested billions of dollars to take full advantage of emerging technologies in order to develop systems that will produce substantial leverage over their competitors. Examples of such IT systems are not as common as one might think, since they have not always been achieved so easily, but some effective systems are American Airlines' well-

---

[3]John Simon and Thomas Davenport, "Managing Information Technology: Organization and Leadership" (Cambridge, MA: Harvard Business School Publications, 1989), p.1.
[4]Howard Gleckman et al., "The Technology Payoff" *Business Week*, June 14, 1993, p. 59.

known *Sabre Reservation System*, Baxter Healthcare's *ASAP Express* system for ordering hospital supplies, and Otis Elevator's *Otisline* information system.

Let us consider one of these systems. *Otisline* has given the Otis Elevator corporation a competitive advantage by increasing its capacity to coordinate its activities. Thanks to *Otisline*, Otis's customers can call in elevator maintenance problems, which are recorded in the central database and then electronically transmitted to a repair person who follows up on the request for service. This system has notably improved the management of the company's repair activities. In addition, *Otisline* has made it easier for senior managers to detect chronic maintenance problems and deal with them preemptively, thereby enhancing customer satisfaction. It has been estimated that the *Otisline* system has reduced maintenance calls by almost 20 percent.[5]

However, some argue that, as technology becomes more pervasive, any advantage accrued from a strategic computer system will be short-lived, since competitors will rush to imitate that system. As barriers to imitation become more difficult to establish or sustain, most companies will find themselves implementing such systems for competitive parity rather than to distinguish themselves from their competitors.

Still, many IT systems are having a significant beneficial impact on corporate America. For one thing, there is considerable evidence that computer systems are improving productivity, particularly in the service industries such as banking, where the same amount of work can now be accomplished with fewer people. For example, in some banks computers handle a large proportion of customer service calls, so fewer customer service representatives are needed. Sophisticated information technology systems not only are increasing efficiency, productivity, and coordination, but are also having a profound effect on organizational structure and employee work patterns. Peter Drucker describes this organizational transformation as "the shift from the command-and-control organization, the organization of departments and divisions, to the information-based organization, the organization of knowledge specialists."[6] This organization will be flatter and simpler than its predecessors, with a heavy reliance on task force teams and smaller self-governing units. Thus, information technology encourages collaboration while also accelerating responsiveness. This has been one result of the *Otisline* system, which permits information to bypass middle managers and go directly to senior-level managers. Companies using such systems have the potential to eliminate layers of middle management and flatten the organizational structure.

[5]For more background on this case study see Donna Stoddard, "OTISLINE (A)," in James I. Cash et al., *Corporate Information Systems Management: Text and Cases*, 3rd ed. (Homewood, IL: Irwin, 1992), pp. 205–17.
[6]Peter F. Drucker, "The Coming of the New Organization," *Harvard Business Review*, January–February 1988, p. 53.

For most corporations that are caught up in this transition the primary challenge is managing information and dealing with the relentless migration of paper-based information to an electronic format. Recent advances in networking, database management systems, and hardware are leading the way to larger-scale and more comprehensive information management systems. Such advances include the integration of images, voice, and text into database management systems; more powerful microcomputers; higher-density storage devices such as CD-ROM as well as optical disk technology; and faster, more efficient networks. These and other trends are giving rise to a new and dynamic generation of information management. Accompanying these developments is the profound transformation of the telephone and related telecommunications technologies, which have produced products such as cellular phones, pagers, and traveling office devices that integrate the cellular phone, fax, and electronic mail.

These converging technologies, however, create exceptionally challenging difficulties for organizations and society, and some of the most controversial and intractable challenges are ethical ones. Hence the broad question that this book addresses: What are the implications of these converging technologies for corporate responsibility and public policy? In order to deal with this question, it would be instructive to consider first a general overview of the ethical and social issues being raised. They range from concerns about privacy and intellectual property rights to new forms of competition made possible by advanced systems.

Perhaps the primary question to consider is whether traditional standards of behavior should be applied in the face of these powerful technologies, or whether we need new norms and even new definitions of concepts such as privacy and intellectual property? Also, in the absence of regulations or other guidelines, how can we rely on managers to behave responsibly in these areas? All too often such decisions are made by ill-informed and unobjective managers who are pressured to implement IT systems as quickly and expediently as possible. In this environment there is little incentive for considering larger social implications.

But managers ignore these social ramifications at their peril. Unless explicit attention is paid to these issues, managers may find themselves in a quagmire or confronting a public relations disaster. How, then, do managers and IT professionals take into account the social impact of various IT systems? Our premise here, as was stated in the Preface, is that traditional norms and ethical insights can provide a valuable framework for analyzing this new breed of moral problems. Thus, Chapter 2 reviews these frameworks, and we will rely on them in our further discussions. The principles of fairness, equity, and natural rights are still applicable and can help illuminate the "right" or most proper course of action. But before we treat these ethical frameworks in depth we will consider several key technological developments and illustrate how they provoke some difficult moral problems on the exciting electronic frontier of "cyberspace."

TECHNOLOGICAL CAPABILITIES

Let us look at several interrelated technologies to evince how they generate ethical dilemmas and public policy issues that defy facile solutions. These technologies are computer software for information management, expanded hardware capabilities, and, above all, computer networks. These three basic technologies are the main components of the infrastructure that helps form the essential web of an organization's information technology.

As we examine these technologies, we will consider how they provoke certain critical and controversial ethical concerns. Of course, most of these ethical issues arise from the *interaction* of these technologies, but it is enlightening to consider such issues at least initially in relation to a specific technological development. In the context of this discussion we will also briefly treat the special problems generated by expert systems.

Computer Software

Computer software encompasses a wide range of tools from operating system software to popular applications such as spreadsheets, databases, and word-processing packages. The database in particular has had a profound impact on information management. A database is simply a collection of information organized according to a logical structure. For example, a firm's employee database would include an employee's address, phone number, department, employment history, and so forth.

Since the early 1970s there has been a dramatic increase in the capacity of computers to store this sort of information and, as a result, a tremendous proliferation of sophisticated software for information management. The most prominent form of this software is undoubtedly the database management system or DBMS. Hierarchical and network database management systems have been utilized since the 1960s. These systems, designed for utilization on large mainframe computers such as the IBM, arrange data in a top-down or hierarchical fashion with pointers between records for exceptionally quick access. They have been replaced, however, by the relational database developed by Edgar F. Codd of IBM in 1970. This database gained immense popularity in the 1980s because of its extraordinary flexibility and simplicity. In the relational model each record is conceived as a row in a two-dimensional table and each field or category of information becomes a column in the table. Records are retrieved through queries (e.g., "find me the record with the social security number 128-30-0000"), and thanks to query optimizers and other techniques, retrieval is very fast even on large, unordered files.[7] All of these database models allow for the efficient storage, retrieval, and correlation of vast amounts of data.

A related technology that makes efficient data management possible is sophisticated storage devices. Indeed, the moving force behind the expanded use of information technology systems has been low-cost, efficient storage. For example, personal computer disk drives can now store almost a gigabyte of data. In addition, magnetic disk storage mechanisms are rapidly being replaced by optical disk technology, which has the advantage of greater density and enhanced durability. A 12-inch optical disk, for instance, can store 2.5 million pages of textual data! Moreover, optical disk drives also offer superior retrieval capability, locating information much more rapidly than conventional disk drives. This technology, then, makes possible ever larger and more efficient DBMS applications. Furthermore, the optical disk system is in an embryonic stage of development, so more dramatic advances are likely.

These databases and storage devices facilitate the collection, manipulation, retrieval, and dissemination of information, thus making it possible for information to be treated as a commodity that can be packaged and sold efficiently. This capacity for handling copious amounts of data gives rise to social and ethical questions about privacy, ownership of information, data security, and so forth. The credit bureau industry, for example, has exploited database technology and low-cost storage devices to build an information system that tracks valuable credit and financial information on approximately 80 million American households. These data have been collected from credit card companies, banks, and many other sources. Some credit bureau companies sell selected data to vendors who use the information for a targeted direct mail campaign.

Other companies routinely collect data about their customers and use the data for secondary purposes. For example, most large retail companies such as Sears Roebuck, J. L. Hudson, and Kmart collect data from customers who make a purchase using a credit card; these data are then stored in a database and used for various promotional and marketing purposes.

But this standard procedure of collecting, storing and distributing information about consumers raises some obvious ethical problems. To begin with, do these companies really "own" this information and, if so, can they dispose of it as they see fit? For example, can credit bureaus sell these data to other companies for direct mail marketing without the con-

---

[7]For more background on the relational database model consult the case study "The Product Manager" in Chapter 4.

sumer's explicit permission? Or is doing so a violation of personal privacy? In other words, can information provided for one purpose be used for another purpose without permission? In short, how do we reconcile the right to personal privacy with these new technological capabilities? The old rules predicated on the proprietary nature of information no longer seem to apply, but what new policies or ethical norms are taking their place?

Another vexing issue arising from the expanded use of software programs concerns intellectual property rights. For instance, a software program stored on a diskette that is sold to someone for his or her exclusive use can be easily copied by someone else. Unfortunately, this form of stealing has become all too common and must be addressed by proper education and other techniques. But a more problematic issue concerns the use of "reverse engineering," a method used by some companies to clone the software system of a competitor. For example, there have been several legal battles over the allegation that one company's user interface software was based on the "look and feel" of a competitor's interface. There is also the more general question of how we should protect software. Is software like a machine or process and therefore patentable? Or is it more like an esthetic creation, such as a book or poem, which is entitled to copyright protection? Clearly, the legal and moral issues that evolve from the need to protect intellectual property are complex. Other controversial questions raised in this area include the following:

- To what extent can copyright and patent laws protect software? Should this protection extend only to source code? Or should it apply to the command structure and command sequence and perhaps even the "look and feel," that is, the general appearance of a user interface?
- Does the investment of resources in a software program or application development process engender property rights? If so, how do we balance this right with the social good that comes from the free and unencumbered exchange of information?
- Software companies rely on nondisclosure agreements to protect trade secrets. But how far can these agreements go, and how does one draw the line between an employee's general knowledge and a firm's proprietary information?

These and several other controversial issues will be discussed in some depth in the chapter on intellectual property rights.

Networks

A vital component of the information infrastructure is the network which permits computers to communicate with one another. In some respects networking has created some of the most significant possibilities for computing. The ability to exchange information on data networks is crucial for many organizations, since it enables workers to collaborate on projects even from remote locations.

It also makes possible a "virtual corporation" and even a "virtual community." Indeed, through the miracle of networking we can transcend spatial limitations and connect with interested parties all over the world. Thus electronic communication is reshaping the fabric of our society.

Networks range from the LAN (local area network), which permits communication among different computers in the same building, to WANs (wide area networks), which facilitate long-distance communication between computers through high-speed links. LANs can be connected to WANs (through gateways) and they can also be connected to other LANs, thereby intensifying the complexity of the network.

The reach and speed of networks has increased dramatically just during the last several years. Networks can sustain communication rates ranging from several characters per second to a billion bits (gigabits) per second. The critical measurement is bandwith, which is a network's capacity measured in bits per second. Presently there is adequate capacity for an immense volume of electronic communication, thanks to high bandwith fiber optic cables that comprise this country's "data superhighway." As a consequence, computer-based communication is many times faster than the telephone or conventional mail delivery. Workers can send a message literally across the globe within seconds. Thus, companies have been quick to implement sophisticated computer networks because of their speed and enhanced efficiency.

Managing these expanding networks of heterogeneous computer systems that are entangled with other networks clearly poses many formidable challenges for corporations. These problems range from working out high-level strategies to managing the low-level details of the day-to-day operations. One of the more difficult challenges concerns the ethical, legal, and social ramifications of relying so heavily on these national data highways. As Anne Branscomb has perceptively observed, "The electronic environment of computer networks is marked by versatility, complexity, diversity, and extraterritorality. All these characteristics pose challenges to the laws that govern generating, organizing, transmitting and archiving information."[8]

The problem, then, is that networked computing challenges the laws and norms that have traditionally prevailed to control the distribution and ownership of information. The exchange of information or programs in a network at breathtaking speed can sometimes pose critical problems for the information manager. As we shall see in the case study "The Internet

[8]Anne Branscomb,"Common Law for the Electronic Frontier," *Scientific American*, September 1991, p. 154.

Worm" (Chapter 7), it took only a few hours for a "worm" program developed by a Cornell graduate student to disable many computer systems on the worldwide Internet network.

Thus the electronic environment of computer networks is a mixed blessing since it militates against a secure environment. In most of these computer transactions, which amount to electronic impulses in the network, it is imperative to ensure data integrity and preserve confidentiality. Security breaches can have grave and far-reaching adverse consequences, involving the destruction or modification of corporate data, the loss of system availability, or the disclosure of sensitive information to the wrong parties. Obviously, such security breaches can be costly for the victims.

Ethical considerations provoked by this challenge of maintaining security include the following: Where is the locus of responsibility for security in a networked environment and who is liable if there is a security breach? Should those individuals who are most at risk from such breaches have some input into security decisions? How do we balance the need for security and confidentiality with the first amendment and this society's commitment to free communication and protection of civil liberties? More precisely, how do we reconcile electronic civil liberties with cogent network and system security?

To be sure, there are many risks involved in relying so heavily on vast, entangled networked computer systems. Those features that make the network so valuable are the same ones that make it vulnerable to harmful intrusions. In Chapter 7 we will elaborate upon how these ominous security risks can be minimized through the development, implementation, and maintenance of a coherent and comprehensive security policy for the whole organization.

It should also be noted that the ubiquitous computer network exacerbates many of the privacy issues discussed above. Networking introduces another layer of complexity to the problem of preserving personal privacy without denying access to authorized users. For example, how can we distinguish between public information and private information that is shared across a network? And how do we treat computer communications and information sharing in the context of the First Amendment? Finally, how do we control the distribution of personal information, which can be transmitted so quickly and efficiently?

Computer Hardware

We turn our attention now to the actual computer itself, often known as the CPU (central processing unit). As with software and networks, there have been many notable advances in hardware. For example, supercomputers, which manipulate billions of commands per second, are now used for multiple scientific applications such as analyzing complex medical images. Parallel processing machines, which execute even the most complicated commands in ever shorter time frames, are making many text management and scientific applications more feasible. The most notable and significant trend in computer hardware, however, is the rapid proliferation of personal computers (PCs) and workstations. Indeed this trend toward the use of personal computers seems unstoppable. These powerful machines, often connected by means of a local area network, are gradually displacing the mainframe and minicomputers that dominated the MIS environment in the 1970s and 1980s. These systems now have the same powerful processing capabilities and internal memory as their mainframe ancestors.

By now everyone is familiar with the legendary success of PC vendors such as Apple Computer. The first Apple machine was sold in 1976, and by the early 1990s Apple had grown into a multibillion-dollar company. Thanks to vendors such as IBM and Apple, the personal computer has become a commonplace and powerful tool in organizations and households. As a consequence, computers "are no longer the private preserve of government, large businesses, and research institutions; extraordinary power is becoming available to a wide segment of society."[9] But with this power comes the potential for abuse and the need for users to act responsibly.

Some would argue that one of the main areas of abuse is management's use of the personal computer to keep tabs on its employees. This capability, often referred to as electronic monitoring or surveillance, can be accomplished through a network of personal computers and a software package such as CBPM (Computer Based Performance Monitoring). A telemarketing company can monitor its employees, for example, by using personal computers and the phone system to measure work performance, including the length of customer phone calls, the time between phone calls, and the time an individual telemarketer spends away from his or her desk.

This growing reliance on electronic monitoring raises many ethical concerns; paramount among these are employee privacy and fairness in the workplace. When, for example, does monitoring become intrusive and a form of harassment? Is reliance on the quantitative data yielded by these systems the fairest means of evaluating employees? To be sure, personal computer technology has revolutionized the way people work, but is one by-product of this revolution a depersonalized work environment with overly ambitious and onerous performance standards? We will treat these issues in the context of a larger discussion on personal privacy in Chapter 5.

Finally, we must not neglect a more generic issue raised by each of these technologies: the vendor's power over its heavily dependent users.

---

[9]Richard Rosenberg, *The Social Impact of Computers*, (Boston: Harcourt Brace Jovanovich, 1992), p. 68.

According to one analysis, "those who supply the hardware, software, and the technological expertise often possess a significant amount of control over the host organization."[10] This phenomenon raises moral questions about the suppliers' responsibility to maintain, support, and upgrade their software, hardware, and networking systems. For example, how candid should vendors be about future releases, and what is their obligation to provide for some ongoing utility of their products? Also, what is the suppliers' liability for flaws or "bugs" in these systems, especially when they have a negative impact on a customer's business? Perhaps all of these issues can be reduced to this one: Given their investment and stake in information technology, what is the extent and scope of the customers' rights?

Expert Systems

Before we move to a discussion of these substantive issues, we should say a word about the special problems created by expert systems. Many analysts predict that "knowledge bases,", which store expertise and informal reasoning along with more conventional forms of data, will become as common as the ordinary database. Essentially, expert systems seek to incorporate the judgment of experienced professionals into the software in order to facilitate decision making. They usually deal with complex subject matter that requires considerable human expertise and careful judgment.

Expert systems use their "knowledge" to constrain or delimit the search for solutions. The knowledge, which has been gathered by "knowledge engineers" from professionals in the field, is usually encoded by computer programmers in the form of "if–then" rules. These rules are intended to reduce the random search for solutions and guide the program to the most likely and plausible solution for the problem at hand.[11]

Expert systems are still in their infancy but they present exciting opportunities to exploit the knowledge and experience of a corporation's wisest and most capable workers. As one observer notes, "Organizations can contribute years of experience managing the transition of expertise from one human being to another. With ES's [expert systems], we have injected a machine to trap and exhibit human knowledge that was previously in human minds alone."[12] For instance, in the banking industry,

---

[10]Mary Gentile and John Sviokla, "Information Technology in Organizations: Emerging Issues in Ethics and Policy" (Cambridge, MA:Harvard Business School Publications, 1991), p. 5.

[11]A simple "if–then" rule might be as follows: *If* a company has had a positive net worth for the past three years, and it has increased its profits for the past three years, *then* it is creditworthy and deserves a bank loan.

[12]T. Grandon Gill, "A Note on Expert Systems" (Cambridge, MA: Harvard Business School Publications, 1988), p. 16.

expert systems are being used to review preliminary loan applications. Also, credit card companies such as American Express use these systems to analyze the credit status and account activity of their cardholders.

Obviously, the growing use of these expert systems has some serious social and public policy implications. Specifically, who "owns" the knowledge and expertise that is incorporated into expert system programs? Is the real owner the company or the experts who contributed their accumulated knowledge and experience? The answer to this question is critical for establishing fair compensation policies. For example, if this software is licensed and generates large profits, shouldn't the experts be entitled to some of these profits? More important, where is the locus of liability if one of these programs malfunctions and yields bad advice or faulty guidance that results in costly business mistakes or even human injury? Should the burden of liability fall upon the programmer, the expert, the knowledge engineer, or the end user? Finally, if professionals rely too heavily on these systems, will their dependence threaten their autonomy as decision makers? As expert systems increase in popularity, it will be essential to come to terms with these and related issues.

CONCLUSIONS AND A LOOK AHEAD

The point, then, is clear: The remarkable ubiquity and growth of user-friendly software, PC hardware, and networking technologies creates new problems and ethical dilemmas as well as significant opportunities to increase productivity, enhance efficiency, and improve overall decision making. We have raised some of the most salient questions and issues in this cursory overview of these technologies.

Although we cannot address in this book all of the social issues raised by these technologies, we will attempt to treat the most prominent ones. In particular, special attention will be paid to the critical issues of privacy and intellectual property since they have been at the center of highly provocative debates and have also led to some well-publicized lawsuits. Our main purpose is to raise questions, to offer some ethical analysis of selected issues, and to provide some tenable frameworks that will help the reader address these matters along with others that are not covered in this book. Managers who are proactive in this dynamic area and who consider these complex issues carefully will avoid embarrassing ethical quandaries and expensive lawsuits, along with disgruntled employees and customers.

We might conclude this chapter by turning our attention to the opening citation from communications genius Marshall McLuhan: "Any technology tends to create a new human environment." The computer technologies we have examined are unquestionably transforming our environment. We must, however, be circumspect so that this new environment is not hostile to personal rights or the values of fairness and justice. Hence the need to reflect deliberately and carefully on the moral problems that we will be treating in the chapters ahead. Our worst apprehensions about technology may be realized, if, as some warn, it encumbers our basic liberties and becomes an "almost unmitigated curse" beyond our control.[13] In short, technology can be a liberating force or it can be an oppressive one —to some extent this will be determined by how well we address the concerns presented in this book.

---

[13]Edward Mesthene, *Technological Change: Its Impact on Man and Society* (New York: Mentor Books, 1970), p. 22.

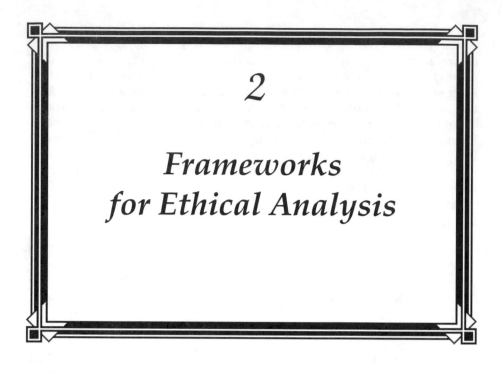

2

Frameworks for Ethical Analysis

THE PRACTICALITY OF ETHICS

It is important to understand at the outset what we are doing when we "do" ethics. Aristotle tells us that ethics is a "practical" endeavor which gives us practical knowledge. But what precisely does this mean? Does Aristotle simply mean that ethics provides us with practical opinions about human actions or behavioral standards which help us choose between right and wrong? According to one distinguished philosopher, Aristotle had much more in mind:

> He meant that one does ethics properly, adequately, reasonably, if and only if one is questioning and reflecting *in order to be able to act* —i.e. in order to conduct one's life rightly, reasonably, in the fullest sense well.[1]

In other words, ethics is practical because living and acting in a certain way is the primary goal of doing ethics. The purpose of ethics is to help us behave honorably and attain those basic goods that make us more

---

[1]John Finnis, *Fundamentals of Ethics* (Washington, D.C.: Georgetown University Press, 1983), p. 1

fully human. Ethics of this type, often called *normative ethics*, is distinct from the discipline of *metaethics*. Metaethics is the study of moral discourse, the meaning of ethical terminology, and the provability of ethical judgments. It deliberately eschews the old Socratic questions that are also asked by Aristotle: "How should life be lived?" or "What is the good life?" Normative ethical inquiry, on the other hand, is a quest for the practical truth of how one's choices and actions will be good and worthwhile. Thus, whereas the goal of metaethics is an appreciation of the structure of moral language, the goal of normative ethics is an identification of the true human good.

Normative ethical inquiry, then, seeks the truth not only for its own sake but also as a basis for choosing proper actions and the right way of life. Unfortunately, as Aristotle also tells us, ethics is not an exact science and therefore we cannot attain the level of objective truth that is possible in the rational sciences or mathematics. Therefore many contemporary philosophers have embraced various forms of relativism or moral skepticism.

But the fact that ethical judgments do not have the same objectivity as scientific ones does not mean that ethics consists merely of emotional expressions and subjective opinions, or is a matter of convention and taste. Moral judgments can and should be based on rational moral principles and sound, carefully reasoned arguments. Normative claims are supported by an appeal to defensible moral principles which become manifest through rational discourse. Also, simply because there is no uniquely correct solution to a moral problem, we must not assume that all solutions are equally valid. We can assess moral positions according to objective criteria—in terms of whether they respect basic human rights, remain open to human fulfillment, maximize the social good, and so forth—and therefore disqualify some solutions to ethical dilemmas in favor of others.

In this chapter we will consider some basic moral principles and theories that will serve as normative guidelines for addressing the moral issues provoked by information technology. We will also consider moral responsibility and the distinction between individual and corporate responsibility. In general, this chapter presents an overview of the tools necessary for serious ethical analysis. We begin by clarifying why and how ethics must be distinguished from the law, since there is sometimes a temptation to equate the two.

LAW AND MORALITY

Beyond any doubt, law and morality do have in common certain key principles and obligations. In some areas, such as intellectual property, law and morality can become seriously entangled. Indeed the interplay of legal and ethical issues in intellectual property cases makes them extremely complex.

However, despite this interrelationship, it is too simplistic to reduce morality to legality or to embrace the suggestion that following the law exhausts an executive's moral responsibility. Individuals and corporations cannot assume that just because the law permits a certain action, that action is morally acceptable. History is replete with examples of so-called "laws" that have been blatantly immoral. We need look no further than the hideously discriminatory laws of Nazi Germany or America's own slavery laws to illustrate this point.

Of course, the law does often embody moral principles along with standards of fairness and procedural justice. However, since this is not always the case, we need to evaluate issues from a moral as well as legal perspective. For example, the Courts may allow a software vendor to copy the "look and feel" of another's product (such as a spreadsheet), but it doesn't necessarily follow that this action is not tantamount to the theft of intellectual property. One must also consider this behavior from a moral point of view, asking questions such as the following: Whose rights have been violated? Whom could the action injure? Clearly, then, law and morality do not always coincide. Legal constraints do not necessarily provide sufficient guidelines for addressing complicated ethical issues in information technology.

Another problem with exclusive reliance on the law as a moral guideline is that the law is essentially reactive. Laws and regulations rarely anticipate problems or possible inequities; rather, they react to problems that have surfaced, and usually in a painstakingly slow manner. For example, in the view of many privacy advocates, the legal system has been too slow to react to the steady erosion of privacy resulting from the technological advancements enumerated in Chapter 1. But if companies resolve to be morally responsible about such issues, they will not wait for new laws or regulations, but rather will regulate their own corporate activities appropriately.

Thus, although it is certainly critical to comprehend the legal dimension of some of the problems that we will be considering, legal issues should not be confused with moral ones. As we shall see, moral issues focus on rights and duties, whether harm has occurred, and similar areas. Our main purpose here is to help individuals think through the "right" thing to do, and this may sometimes go beyond the parameters of the law, especially when the law is ill-defined or has not caught up with the relentless pace of technological change.

INDIVIDUAL AND CORPORATE RESPONSIBILITY

In addition to the distinction between law and morality, we must also appreciate the important distinction between individual and corporate responsibility. An underlying assumption of our analysis throughout this

fiduciary = relating to either a
holding in trust for another.

Frameworks for Ethical Analysis   17

volume is that individuals are responsible for their actions. To some extent, these responsibilities are shaped by our personal value system. In effect, we are all moral agents who have various moral responsibilities in our different roles as citizens, neighbors, parents, professionals, and so forth. Obviously, when someone is hired into a corporation, that person does not abandon his or her moral commitments. However, there are sometimes conflicts between an individual's personal moral values and organizational values. For instance, one may value honesty but find oneself in an organization where lying and deception are taken for granted as a means of doing business. These practices will surely conflict with that manager's personal moral conviction, thereby creating a difficult dilemma: Should the person be loyal to the organization or to his or her own values? Regardless of how one resolves this problem, an individual's responsibility for his or her actions can never be shrugged off. As Karl Llewellyn reminds us, "Choice is your own. You answer for your choice. There are no rules to shoulder *your* responsibility."[2]

To further complicate matters, corporate executives assume yet another set of responsibilities, since they have a fiduciary obligation to act in the best interests of the shareholders. The question now is raised as to whether this fiduciary responsibility in any way constrains their *moral* responsibility? Executives also have obligations to the corporation's other constituencies such as labor unions, customers, suppliers, and government agencies. These obligations can conflict with the fiduciary obligation to stockholders or possibly with a manager's personal moral convictions. Thus corporate managers may experience conflicts between their obligations to shareholders and various other constituencies as well as conflicts between their organizational duties and personal value system.

Finally, the corporation, which is analogous to a person, can be viewed as a moral entity with various rights and obligations of its own. Thus it must be held responsible for its corporate acts. Although this view is not embraced by all contemporary philosophers, it is well grounded in the philosophical and legal tradition.[3] Moreover, it does seem plausible to maintain that a corporation with a climate that fosters moral behavior, either informally or through a formal ethical code, is more responsible than the one that ignores moral issues or even encourages reprehensible behavior in the name of higher profits or other corporate objectives. Of course,

analogous = similar in function but not in structure or evolutionary origin

[2]Karl Llewellyn, *The Bramble Bush: On Our Law and Its Study* (New York: Oceana Publications, 1981), p. 17.

[3]See, for example, the writings of Kenneth Goodpaster such as "The Concept of Corporate Responsibility" in *Just Business: New Introductory Essays in Business Ethics*, ed. Tom Regan (New York: Random House, 1984), pp. 292–322. For a discussion of the legal perspective on this issue consult Christopher D. Stone, *Where the Law Ends* (New York: Harper & Row, 1975), pp. 58–69.

even if corporations are held accountable for immoral activities, this fact does not mitigate the responsibility of executives or others in the company. Thus, for example, under certain conditions we might hold both individuals within the corporation and the corporation itself liable for the theft of intellectual property, especially if the corporate culture was one that implicitly (or even explicitly) tolerated such behavior.

Some of the case studies in this book will primarily focus on corporate responsibility. They will consider, for example, whether or not the corporation has acted with respect for the rights of others, whether it has taken seriously its ethical duties as well as its economic ones.[4] *Revlon vs. Logisticon* in Chapter 4 and *The Credit Bureau Industry* in Chapter 5 are examples of such cases. Other case studies will emphasize individual personal values. For example, *The Product Manager* case in Chapter 4 deals with how an executive's duties to his company conflict with his personal integrity when the availability of a new software product is announced.

BASIC ETHICAL THEORIES

We turn our attention now to the ethical theories and principles that will serve as the guidelines for our analysis and lead us to the normative judgments that will help us to differentiate right from wrong conduct. These theories define what it means to act morally. Thus, if our choices are guided by a particular theory, it can be plausibly demonstrated that the moral principles of the theory demanded that we make this decision. As we shall see, these theories are by no means flawless, nor can they function as formulas that give us simple answers to complex moral dilemmas. Rather, they are "avenues" or approaches to such problems that facilitate analysis and reflection on the issues.

For the most part we will be considering modern ethical theories, and these can be divided into two broad categories: *teleological* and *deontological*, the ethics of ends and the ethics of duty.

The term *teleological* is derived from the Greek word *telos*, which means "end" or "goal". Teleological theories give priority to the good over the right, and they evaluate actions by the goal or consequences that they attain. In other words, the right is adjectival to the good and dependent upon it. Thus, right actions are those that produce the most good or optimize the consequences of one's choices, whereas wrong actions are those that do not contribute to the good. We will consider one example of a teleo-

---

[4]For a more thorough discussion on the nature of corporate responsibility see Kenneth Goodpaster and John B. Matthews, "Can a Corporation Have a Conscience," *Harvard Business Review*, January–February 1982, pp. 132–41.

adjectival = specifies & emphasizes

logical approach to ethics: utilitarianism. Utilitarianism is a form of consequentialism, a theory predicated on the assumption that consequences
determine the rightness or wrongness of moral actions.

Deontological theories, on the other hand, argue for the priority of the
right over the good, or the independence of the right from the good.
Deontological is also derived from a Greek word, *deon*, which means "obligation". According to a deontological framework, actions are intrinsically
right or wrong regardless of the consequences they produce. The ethically
proper action might be deduced from a duty or a basic human right but it
is never contingent on the outcome of an action. Deontological theories
include both duty-based and rights-based approaches to ethical reasoning,
sometimes referred to as *pluralism* and *contractarianism*, respectively. We
will discuss both of these theories after our treatment of utilitarianism.

UTILITARIANISM (1)

The Theory   *UTILITY - Happiness*

Classic utilitarianism was developed by two British philosophers, Jeremy
Bentham (1748–1832) and John Stuart Mill (1806–1873). According to this
theory, the good or the end (*telos*) is happiness or more specifically, "the
greatest happiness for the greatest number." This good can also be
described as "utility," and this principle of utility is the foundation of
morality and the ultimate criterion of right and wrong. According to
Bentham,

> By the principle of utility is meant the principle which approves or disap-
> proves of every action whatsoever, according to the tendency which it
> appears to have to augment or diminish the happiness of the party whose
> interest is in question, or what is the same thing, in other words, to promote
> or oppose that happiness.[5]

Thus, actions are right in proportion to their tendency to bring about
happiness, and wrong to the extent that they bring about pain or less happiness than another alternative.

It should be emphasized that an action is right if it produces the most
happiness not for the person performing that action but for *all* parties
affected by the action. In summary, then, utilitarianism is the moral doctrine that we should act in order to produce the greatest happiness for

---

[5]Jeremy Bentham, *An Introduction to the Principles of Morals and Legislation* (London, 1789),
chap. 1, sec. 2 in *Ethical Theories*, ed. A. I. Meldon (Englewood Cliffs, NJ: Prentice-Hall, 1967),
p. 369.

everyone affected by an action. Like all teleological theories, utilitarianism is committed to the maximization of the good (happiness or utility), that is, it is committed to the optimization of consequences.

Utilitarianism assumes that we can somehow measure the benefits and harms produced by an action and thereby determine a sum of those benefits and harms. According to Velasquez, "the principle assumes that all benefits and costs of an action can be measured on a common numerical scale and then added or subtracted from each other."[6]

In practice, therefore, utilitarianism requires one to develop and execute a sort of moral calculus. This is usually in the form of a cost–benefit analysis that can be utilized in situations where there are several possible courses of action. Once one has determined all of the alternatives, each alternative is evaluated in terms of its costs and benefits (both direct and indirect). On the basis of this analysis, one chooses the alternative that produces the greatest net expectable utility, that is, the one with the greatest net benefits (or the lowest net costs). One might use the grid in Table 2.1 for this analysis.

Table 2.1   Grid for Utilitarian Analysis

Choose the alternative with the greatest net benefit.

	Benefits	*Costs*
Alternative 1		
Alternative 2		
Alternative 3		
etc.		

A key notion in the principle of utility is happiness. But how do utilitarian philosophers define happiness? Bentham simply equates happiness with pleasure; this view implies that the objective of ethical analysis is to maximize pleasure in the world. Mill agrees with Bentham to a certain extent but argues for a hierarchy of pleasures. For example, intellectual pleasures are seen as superior to sensual pleasures. Other philosophers, known as *pluralistic utilitarians*, have maintained that happiness involves many intrinsic values such as friendship, knowledge, courage, and health.

But despite this ambiguity and disagreement about what constitutes happiness, the core idea of utilitarianism that only consequences matter has considerable merit. Even philosophers who categorically reject utilitarian-

---

[6]Manuel Velasquez, *Business Ethics: Concepts and Cases*, 3rd ed. (Englewood Cliffs, NJ: Prentice-Hall, 1992), p. 61.

ism would admit that a basic requirement of ethical reasoning is attention to the probable consequences of one's decision. Also, utilitarianism is appealing to many as a natural, common-sense approach to morality. Many managers and professionals make decisions focusing on consequences and considering the costs and benefits of various alternatives. When these managers assert that they have a moral obligation to do something, they usually justify that obligation in terms of the net benefit an action will have. Another key advantage of utilitarianism is that it requires one to consider as objectively as possible the interests of all parties affected by one's action. This theory is thus superior to ethical egoism, which does not take into account the interests of others.

As an example of utilitarian reasoning in business decisions consider Karl Kotchian, the former president of Lockheed, who was accused in the early 1970s of paying $12 million in bribes to Japanese officials in order to persuade them to buy Lockheed's TriStar plane. Kotchian advanced two arguments to defend these illicit payments: (1) they did not violate any American laws, and (2) in the long run they were beneficial to many constituencies in the United States who reaped big rewards as a result of the purchase of these planes. Stockholders certainly benefited through enhanced profits; at the same time, Lockheed's suppliers, its employees and their communities, and to some degree the entire U.S. economy benefited from this action. Moreover, the Japanese received an excellent airplane at a reasonable price. Of course, there were some costs to Lockheed's competitors and perhaps to the general level of trust in society, but one could reasonably argue that these were most likely outweighed by the tangible benefits received by Lockheed's diverse stakeholders.[7]

The Lockheed example illustrates a key aspect of utilitarianism: What matters first and foremost are the consequences; how these consequences are achieved is only a secondary matter. This aspect points to one of the most serious deficiencies of utilitarianism. It strongly implies that there are no intrinsically evil acts. To be sure, utilitarians would maintain that deceit, murder, theft, and the like are usually morally wrong because of the harmful consequences they bring about, but at the same time, these actions can be ethically justified if they can be proven to produce the greatest good or maximize net expectable utility. Presumably, then, even human or moral rights are not absolute, since a person's or group's rights could be taken away for the sake of maximizing utility. But are there not rights that transcend utilitarian calculations, such as the rights to life and liberty? If we could somehow maximize happiness for a society by enslaving a small segment of that society, would that action be morally justified?

---

[7]See the discussion of Lockheed in John R. Boatright, *Ethics and the Conduct of Business* (Englewood Cliffs, NJ: Prentice-Hall, 1993), pp. 42–43.

Another difficulty with consequentialism or utilitarianism concerns how we define the "good" or "happiness." There seems to be no univocal definition of this sometimes elusive commodity. A failure to agree on the meaning of happiness, the goal of all actions, poses real problems for properly evaluating those actions.

In addition, the utilitarian approach assumes that the goods involved in each alternative can be measured and evaluated according to some common standard. Often this is simply not the case. For example, how do we compare these two options: An automobile manufacturer can install safer back seatbelts in one of its most popular models at a cost of $87 million, or it can refuse to do the installation, endure some bad publicity, but save $87 million. It is estimated that the seatbelts would probably save about ten lives a year. If we attempt a cost–benefit analysis to arrive at a decision, how can we compare lives saved with dollars and cents? Aren't these goods completely incommensurable? Or consider two goods such as justice and theoretical truth. If these goods are at stake in a moral decision, how does the consequentialist choose between them? Thus, according to philosopher Germain Grisez, if a consequentialist admits that two goods are "fundamental and incommensurable, then the consequentialist also admits that the 'greatest net good' is meaningless whenever one must choose between promoting and protecting or impeding and damaging these two goods in some participations."[8]

The final difficulty with this popular theory is a practical and procedural one. Can managers and professionals work through the moral calculus objectively? Can they avoid self-serving assumptions and various prejudices in the process of moral reasoning? Unfortunately, all too often consequentialist reasoning that does not overcome those assumptions ultimately yields mere rationalizations of unethical or selfish behavior.

The task of objectively considering carefully all the diffuse consequences of an action and estimating the costs and benefits can at times be overwhelming and ultimately self-defeating.

Utilitarianism and Information Technology

As we have observed, utilitarian analysis entails identifying the costs and benefits of each alternative and selecting the one that maximizes utility or benefit for all parties affected by the decision. This framework can be useful in resolving certain ethical problems that arise for IT professionals and other managers. These illustrations that follow should also suggest many other possibilities for the application of utilitarianism.

Recall our discussion in Chapter 1 regarding the threats to workplace

[8]Germain Grisez, "Against Consequentialism," *The American Journal of Jurisprudence*, 23 (1978), 39.

privacy posed by new IT capabilities such as electronic monitoring. Corporations that seek to justify the use of this controversial technology could argue that such monitoring maximizes utility. Although there may be some costs for employees in terms of inconvenience and loss of mobility, these costs are far outweighed by appreciable benefits such as increased productivity and efficiency. This tangible result in turn will benefit consumers who will pay lower prices and shareholders who will enjoy a greater return on their investment. Higher productivity and efficiency is also positive for the whole economy, since the resultant monetary savings can be used for other investments. It could also be argued that the employer will benefit not only through increased productivity but also by having more thorough, objective data for evaluating an employee's performance. The result might be fairer employee appraisals, which in turn would benefit the employees themselves. Thus, from a utilitarian perspective, a strong case can be made to legitimize the practice of electronic monitoring. Of course, these arguments are not necessarily decisive, but they do illustrate how this theory can enable one to make a convincing ethical case for the use of monitoring.

We might also consider how the utility principle could be applied to the problem of defining the scope of intellectual property rights. As we will explain in Chapter 6, some countries have much looser protection of property rights than the United States. The Japanese, for example, have patent laws that permit the "laying open" of patents; this practice encourages others to use patent information as a basis for further innovations or commercial applications. Once again a tenable rationale for this approach can be developed by invoking utilitarianism: through loose protection of intellectual property, society benefits through the more rapid diffusion of technology. Thus, a scheme of weak protections will inevitably lead to beneficial social consequences. To be sure, there are utilitarian arguments on the other side of this issue, since stronger protection can be seen as an important incentive to stimulate innovations. But regardless of where one stands on this issue, the point is clear: The utilitarian perspective can play a major role in developing cogent ethical arguments to support one's position.

DUTY-BASED ETHICS

We turn our attention now to deontological ethical theories. We will first consider pluralism or duty-based approaches as expressed in the philosophies of Immanuel Kant (1724–1804) and W. D. Ross (1877–1940).

Immanuel Kant

Kant's ethical theory is indeed a model of the deontological approach to morality, which stresses fidelity to principle and duty. Kant's ethical philosophy, known for its severity and inflexibility, focuses on duty divorced from any concerns about happiness or pleasure. This philosophy is developed in Kant's second critique, *The Critique of Practical Reason*, and in a more concise work, *Fundamental Principles of the Metaphysics of Morals*.

Kant's moral philosophy is firmly opposed to utilitarianism and modern natural rights theories first developed by Hobbes and Locke. In the Preface to *The Critique of Practical Reason* Kant indicates his intention to construct a "pure moral philosophy, perfectly cleared of everything which is only empirical, and which belongs to anthropology."[9] This pure moral philosophy is grounded not in the knowledge of our human nature but in a common idea of duty. This common idea of duty, including imperatives such as "One should not tell a lie," applies not only to all human beings but to all *rational* beings, including God Himself. Thus if duty is applicable to all rational beings and even to God, it cannot be based on human nature. Morality, then, for Kant consists of obligations that are binding on any being that is rational.

But what is this common idea of duty? To begin with, duty embodies the idea that one should do the right thing in the right spirit. According to Kant, "an action done from duty has moral worth, not in the purpose that is attained by it, but in the maxim according to which the action is determined."[10] Thus an action's moral worth is found not in what it tries to accomplish but in the agent's intention and the summoning of one's energies to carry out that intention. Purpose and consequences cannot be taken into account to establish the validity of the moral law or to make exceptions to that law. In direct contrast to utilitarianism, the moral individual, for Kant, must perform actions for the sake of duty *regardless of the consequences*.

But what is the basis for this duty? In Kant's systematic philosophy our moral duty is simple. The moral law, like the laws of science or physics, must be rational. Also, the moral law must be universal, since universality represents the common character of rationality and law. This universal moral law is expressed as the categorical imperative: "I should never act except in such a way that I can also will that my maxim should become a universal law."[11] The imperative is "categorical" because it does not allow for any exceptions.

A "maxim" as referred to by Kant is simply an implied principle underlying a particular action. If, for example, I usually break my promises, then I act according to the private maxim that promise breaking is morally acceptable when it is in my best interests to do so. But can one

[9]Immanuel Kant, *The Critique of Practical Reason* (London: Longmans Green, 1909), p. 3.

[10]Immanuel Kant, *Grounding for the Metaphysics of Morals* (Indianapolis: Hackett Publishing Company, 1981), pp. 12–13.

[11]Ibid., p. 14.

take this individual maxim and transform it into a universal moral law? As a universal law this maxim would be expressed as follows: "It is permissible for everyone to break promises when it is in their best interests to do so." Such a law, however, is invalid since it contains a logical contradiction. Universal promise breaking is logically impossible (like a square circle), since if everyone broke promises, the entire institution of promising would collapse; there would be no such thing as a "promise" because anyone making a promise would lack credibility. This maxim would thus destroy itself as soon as it was transformed into a universal law.

Kant's categorical imperative, then, is his ultimate ethical principle. In the simplest terms, it is a test of whether an action is right or wrong. If an action cannot pass the test of universalization, it is immoral and one has a duty to avoid it. The categorical imperative is a "moral compass" that gives us a way of knowing when we are acting morally.

Although there is only one categorical imperative, it can be expressed in several ways. In some regards Kant's second formulation of this imperative makes his position even clearer: "Act in such a way that you treat humanity, whether in your own person or in the person of another, always at the same time as an end and never simply as a means."[12] This principle of humanity as an end in itself serves as a limiting condition of our freedom of action. We cannot treat other human beings exclusively as a means to our own ends. Quite simply, one's projects or objectives cannot supercede the worth of other human beings. For Kant, this principle can be summed up in the word *respect*: The moral law can be reduced to the absolute principle of respect for other human beings, who deserve respect because of their rationality and freedom, the hallmark of personhood for Kant.

Clearly, Kant's ethical theory has many virtues, but it is also fraught with serious problems because of its rigid absolutism. Do we really have absolute duties to keep promises or tell the truth? What if by lying to a criminal or a madman I can save the life of an innocent person? Am I still obliged to tell the truth under such circumstances? Kant would appear to say that the duty to tell the truth always prevails since lying cannot be universalized. But this stance seems to violate moral common sense, since we all recognize conditions when lying or deception is appropriate behavior. Consider the overwrought but helpful example of telling a lie to save someone from a ruthless murderer. In this case there is a conflict of universal laws: the law to tell the truth and the law to save a life in jeopardy. We must, of course, admit an exception to one of these laws. As A. C. Ewing points out,

> ...in cases where two laws conflict it is hard to see how we can rationally decide between them except by considering the goodness or badness of the

consequences. However important it is to tell the truth and however evil to lie, there are surely cases where much greater evils can still be averted by a lie, and is lying wrong then?[13]

Thus it is difficult to avoid an appeal to consequences when two laws conflict, and this problem is a grave one for Kant.

Also it is worth pointing out that some philosophers, such as G. W. F. Hegel, have criticized Kant's categorical imperative because, being only a formal principle, it is empty and deficient. For Hegel, the moral law presented by Kant requires an empirical content, some genuine substance, and there is no content that can fit with its formal universality. Also, in some cases the universalization of a maxim such as "One should help the poor" is contradictory, since it would result in the elimination of poverty. Hegel argues that for duty to be respected, duty must preserve its opposite; the duty to help the poor, for example, requires the perpetuation of poverty. On this basis, Hegel rejects Kant's conception of duty and his formal approach to ethics.[14]

In some respects, however, this criticism, which has been repeated by other philosophers, is somewhat unfair to Kant. There is a content to Kantian moral philosophy that is implicit in the categorical imperative. Recall that the second formulation of this imperative commands us to treat humanity as an end, never as a means. Thus the dignity of the other as an end is the unconditioned principle and "content" of Kant's moral philosophy.

It is true, of course, that the categorical imperative is a very general moral principle, but this is precisely what Kant intended. It is a guide that provides us with a test for determining our concrete ethical duties. Indeed, it becomes clear that this emphasis on respect for persons endows Kant's ethics with a certain vitality. For Kant, the ethical life is never achieved; rather, we are always striving to close the distance between our real moral situations and the ideal of the categorical imperative.

W. D. Ross

The British philosopher William D. Ross, in his book *The Right and the Good*, developed a duty-based ethical theory that can be viewed as an extension of Kant's focus on a single, absolute duty. Ross claims that through reflection on our ordinary moral beliefs we can intuit the rules of morality. These moral rules or duties are ultimate and irreducible; hence, they are the first principles of moral reasoning. Ross, however, in contrast to Kant, refuses to

---

[13]A. C. Ewing, *Ethics* (New York: Free Press, 1965), p. 58.

[14]Hegel's criticism of Kant is expressed in works such as *Natural Law*, trans. T. M. Knox (Philadelphia: University of Pennsylvania Press, 1975).

accept these duties as absolute or prevailing without exception. Rather, he argues that they are *prima facie* duties, which means that they are moral imperatives that should apply most of the time under normal circumstances, but they are not categorical imperatives which hold regardless of the situation.

In simplest terms, a *prima facie* obligation is a conditional one that can be superceded by a higher obligation, usually under exceptional circumstances. We do, for example, have a *prima facie* duty to be honest and truthful, but if a murderer comes to your home looking for his wife whom you have hidden in the basement, your obligation to tell the truth becomes subordinate to your obligation to protect human life. A moral principle can be sacrificed only for another moral principle. Although these *prima facie* duties must not be dismissed lightly, each of them has exceptions and in extraordinary circumstances can be overridden.

According to Ross, there are seven basic moral duties that are binding on moral agents:

1. One ought to keep promises and tell the truth. (*fidelity*)
2. One ought to right the wrongs that one has inflicted on others. (*reparation*)
3. One ought to distribute goods justly. (*justice*)
4. One ought to improve the lot of others with respect to virtue, intelligence, and happiness. (*beneficence*)
5. One ought to improve oneself with respect to virtue and intelligence. (*self-improvement*)
6. One ought to exhibit gratitude when appropriate. (*gratitude*)
7. One ought to avoid injury to others. (*noninjury*)

Ross does not maintain that this list is exhaustive, but he does believe that these duties are self-evident and indisputable. They are manifest to the mind through simple intuition. As he writes in and *The Right and the Good*:

> I am assuming the correctness of some of our convictions as to *prima facie* duties, or more strictly, am claiming that we *know* them to be true. To me it seems self-evident as anything could be, that to make a promise, for instance, is to create a moral claim on us in someone else. Many readers will say that they do *not* know this to be true. If so, I certainly cannot prove it to them: I can only ask them to reflect again, in the hope that they will ultimately agree that they know it.[15]

As Ross indicates here, he makes no effort to provide substantial arguments that will convince us to accept these duties. Anyone who doesn't see them must be obtuse or morally blind!

[15]W. D. Ross, *The Right and the Good*, quoted in R. Fox and J. CeMarco, *Moral Reasoning* (Fort Worth, TX: Holt Rinehart, 1990), p. 142.

One final issue regarding these *prima facie* duties points to a deficiency in Ross's approach to morality: How do we handle cases in which duties conflict? If two such duties are in conflict, Ross recommends that this basic principle be followed: "That act is one's duty which is in accord with the more stringent *prima facie* obligation." If there are more than two duties in conflict, then we must abide by a different guideline: "That act is one's duty which has the greatest balance of *prima facie* rightness over *prima facie* wrongness."[16]

Both of these principles, however, are somewhat vague and seem to raise more questions rather than help us reach answers. What does Ross mean by "stringent"? What makes one obligation more compelling or stringent than another? Ross's silence on this critical issue represents a serious flaw in his ethical philosophy. Likewise, Ross's second principle is riddled with ambiguity. His statement that we should choose the duty that yields the greatest proportion of "rightness" doesn't offer us much assistance in deliberating over the question of which duty takes precedence.

Despite these shortcomings, however, Ross's theory is not without merit. A focus on one's duty in a particular situation is an excellent starting point for determining the right course of action in an ethical dilemma. Moreover, Ross's approach, unlike that of Kant, provides for considerable flexibility and so is more applicable to complex moral problems. Finally, several other ethical theories, such as natural law, highlight similar obligations, but these duties are derived differently than are Ross's.

Universal Acceptability

A variation of Kant's morality that is worth a brief treatment here is the notion of universal acceptability. This is another way of formulating and interpreting the categorical imperative. It considers an action from the perspective of the victim and other disinterested parties. The criterion for differentiating between right and wrong, then, becomes the following: Do all rational beings accept this action or decision regardless of whether they are the perpetrators or the victims? In other words, would the victim and other neutral parties consider my actions moral and aboveboard? This sort of thinking forces us to step out of our egoistic framework and consider our actions from the perspective of others, especially the potential victim. This approach is consistent with Kant's ethics and what has been traditionally known as the Golden Rule: Do unto others as you would have them do unto you. Thus the key to this ethical viewpoint is to pose the simple question: Is my action universally acceptable even to those who are directly affected by it?

[16]Ibid., p. 144.

Another approach is to consider whether one's actions can pass a "publicity test." Would others accept what I have done if it were to become public knowledge? In her essay "Ethics without the Sermon," Laura Nash phrases the question this way: "Could you disclose without qualm your decision or action to your boss, your CEO, the board of directors, your family, or society as a whole?"[17] If we felt diffident about such disclosure because we thought that this "public" could not accept our actions, then there is probably something seriously wrong.

Pluralism in the Context of Information Technology

Let us now consider the practical value of pluralism or an orientation to ethics based on duty. How do we apply such an ethic to resolving moral issues that arise through information technology? To begin with, from Ross's general list of *prima facie* duties, corporations and IT professionals can elicit some specific secondary obligations. These include the following: Avoid using computers to harm others; respect intellectual property; respect the right of privacy; be honest about product capabilities and availability. In addition to these and other moral obligations, there are duties that managers assume by virtue of their role as economic agents. These include fiduciary obligations to shareholders and other corporate stakeholders such as customers, employees, and others.

Managers, therefore, must take into account all of these various obligations when they make decisions, and doing so can pose many problems. For example, in Chapter 4 we will consider the unique position of IT vendors. These vendors often possess considerable leverage over the future economic success of their customers. They must sometimes make difficult decisions regarding continuing support for software or hardware. The goal of profitability can conflict with the customer's need for a product with ongoing usefulness. The pluralist mode of reasoning would direct such companies to balance their duty to seek profits and maximize returns for its shareholders with ethical duties such as honesty and the avoidance of any ostensible harm to its customers.

More specifically, in making product announcements vendors must seriously consider the ethical duty to avoid fraudulent, deceptive, or misleading claims. This is a fundamental ethical imperative which cannot be easily dismissed for the sake of financial expediency. Of course, how a manager balances this obligation with his or her other duties is a formidable challenge. Moreover, from a Kantian perspective one cannot justify

---

[17]Laura Nash, "Ethics without the Sermon," in Kenneth Andrews, *Ethics in Practice* (Cambridge, MA: Harvard University Press, 1987), p. 252.

misrepresentation about products since, as with lying, the maxim on which such misrepresentation is based could never become a valid universal moral law.

RIGHTS-BASED ETHICS 3

Theoretical Overview

A third distinct approach to ethics focuses on a respect for individual rights. This avenue of ethical thinking, with its focus on moral principle instead of consequences, is another example of a deontological approach to ethics. A right can be most simply defined as an entitlement to something. Thus, thanks to the First Amendment of the U.S. Constitution, all Americans are entitled to freedom of speech. This right is derived from and guaranteed by our legal system so it is a "legal right." There are also moral or human entitlements that all human beings should have by virtue of being human. Such rights are are not confined to a particular legal jurisdiction but are universal, since they are grounded in human nature. In addition, these human rights are equal rights; everyone, for example, equally shares in the right of free expression regardless of nationality or status in society.

Philosophers make an important distinction between negative and positive rights. Negative rights imply freedom from outside interference in certain activities. Examples of negative rights are freedom of expression, the right to liberty, and the right to privacy. Thus, if one has a right to privacy in the workplace, an employer cannot interfere with one's private affairs. The corollary of these rights is one's duty to avoid such interference. A *positive right*, on the other hand, is one that gives a person "whatever he or she needs to freely pursue his or her interests."[18] The rights to health care and education are examples of positive rights. If someone had a right to medical care, there would be a correlative duty on the part of some agent (probably the government) to provide that care in some fashion. In American society there has been far more emphasis on negative rights than on positive rights.

The rights-based viewpoint is synonymous with *contractarianism*, which has its roots in the social philosophy of Hobbes, Locke, Rousseau, and others. According to these philosophers, morality is grounded in the so-called "social contract". This contract is necessitated by the pre-political state of nature which preceded civil society and in which there was absolute freedom and a constant state of war and strife. In order to overcome these intolerable conditions, a civil government is established and all individuals

[18]Velasquez, *Business Ethics*, p. 76.

enter into a tacit, implicit contract with that government to respect each other's desire for life and liberty. In return, civil society agrees to respect and protect the basic rights of its citizens, specifically the rights of life, liberty, property, and so forth. Society owes each individual protection of these rights in exchange for their obedience to the law. These are contractual rights, synonymous with the legal rights guaranteed by the Constitution.

Several contractarians, such as John Locke, have argued for the social contract but also support the notion that our rights are fundamental and not dependent on this contract. Locke maintained that the rights of life, liberty, and property are natural, God-given rights that can never be abrogated by the state. What Hobbes and Locke and other social contract philosophers have in common is their strong emphasis on rights as the fundament of morality. According to this perspective, moral reasoning should be governed by respect for individual rights and a philosophy of fairness. As Ken Goodpaster observes, "fairness is explained as a condition that prevails when all individuals are accorded equal respect as participants in social arrangements."[19] In short, then, contractarianism focuses on the need to respect an individual's legal, moral, and contractual rights as the basis of justice and fairness.

For our purposes, a rights-based analysis of moral problems should consider whether a particular course of action violates an individual's human or legal rights such as the right to privacy, the right to own property, or the right to the fruits of one's labor. As we shall see in subsequent chapters, the primary challenge in this sort of analysis is the difficulty of establishing the parameters of these rights. Like pluralism, this approach to morality is markedly different from utilitarianism, which regards rights as subservient to the general welfare. Those who embrace contractarianism would categorically reject the utilitarian claim that rights can be circumscribed if by doing so one can maximize the common good.

Finally, one can surely observe that an ethical theory based on rights has certain shortcomings. For one thing, in American society there is a tendency to argue for a proliferation of various rights without an accompanying discussion of the limits that must be imposed on those rights. What are the limits of the right to free expression, for example? Also, this avenue of ethical reflection can lead to introversion and a focus on my rights instead of on the correlative duties imposed by another's rights. In addition, philosophers provide little guidance for reconciling conflicting rights, and this failing can make the practical application of this theory somewhat difficult. These shortcomings, however, by no means undermine this avenue

[19]Kenneth Goodpaster, "Some Avenues for Ethical Analysis in General Management," in Kenneth Goodpaster, John Matthews, and Laura Nash, *Policies and Persons*, 1st ed. (New York: McGraw-Hill, 1985), p. 497.

of ethical reasoning, which has many important features including its special focus on basic human values such as equality and freedom.

Rawls's Theory of Justice

John Rawls follows in the tradition of Hobbes and Locke and represents a contemporary approach to a deontological moral framework that emphasizes rights as the basis of morality. Rawls's ethic focuses on justice as fairness and gives priority to the right over the good. The right actions are those that are consistent with his principles of justice, which emphasize an individual's basic rights or liberties.

Rawls's theory of justice establishes conditions that must be established in order for anyone to reach an agreement acceptable to all parties. According to Rawls, the principles of justice are those that equal, rational, self-interested individuals would choose as the terms of a social contract for themselves and their descendants. Rawls postulates a fundamental, pre-political "original position" where this choice would be made. This corresponds to the state of nature in the traditional theory of social contract. It is a hypothetical construct which enables one to formulate principles of justice that would command universal assent. It is assumed that all parties act under the "veil of ignorance," which prohibit the knowledge of any contingencies one could conceivably use to exploit others. Thus, one is not cognizant of his or her own natural abilities, social status, interests, intelligence, and conception of the good life. One is cognizant only of certain general facts such as elements of social and economic theory. This veil of ignorance makes it impossible to design principles to suit one's own circumstances and ensures pure procedural justice, since the results are free from any arbitrary influences.

Although parties in the original position do not know their conception of the good nor any specific needs and desires, they do realize that they desire as much as possible of primary social goods. Among these goods are rights, opportunities, powers, income, wealth, and self-respect. These are goods necessary for one's self-fulfillment and the advancement of one's interests and goals, as well as the overall plan of life.

With this in mind, Rawls argues that those in the original position are virtually compelled to be fair to everyone so that they can be fair to themselves. And given their aversion to risk and the chance that they could be among the disadvantaged of society, Rawls assumes that the rational, safest course of action would be to adopt the perspective of the potentially most disadvantaged group in society. It would be to their advantage to maximize this position in case they themselves were included in this group. This reasoning leads to the following principles:

First Principle: Each person is to have an equal right to the most extensive total system of equal basic liberties compatible with a similar system of equal liberty for all.

Second Principle: Social and economic inequalities are to be arranged so that they are both: (a) to the greatest benefit of the least advantaged, consistent with the just savings principle, and (b) attached to offices and positions open to all under conditions of fair equality of opportunity.[20]

The principles are arranged in lexical order, which means that the second cannot be satisfied at the expense of the first.

In the first principle Rawls is arguing that those in the original position would certainly demand an extensive system of liberties, which are essential if one is to pursue different goals, develop one's personality, and fulfill one's life plan. Included in this list of liberties is the right to vote, freedom of speech, liberty of conscience, and "freedom of the person along with the right to hold personal property."[21] Also, according to Rawls, "These liberties are all required to be equal by the first principle, since citizens of a just society are to have the same basic rights."[22] This important statement merely means that these political liberties must equally apply to everyone. Thus, for example, it is required that the rules for the acquisition and transfer of property will equally apply to all citizens. Each person has an equal right to acquire, own, and dispose of property. However, the statement does not mean that everyone must own the same amount of property.

While the first principle guarantees a system of equal liberty, the second, known as the *difference principle*, deals with the distribution of social goods. According to Rawls, those in the original position would not opt for an egalitarian society wherein all goods are distributed equally. Rather, they would choose the second principle. This means that disparities in the distribution of wealth and other social goods would be tolerated only if they could be shown to benefit the "least advantaged," the lowest on the social scale. Thus a just society is not necessarily an egalitarian one, but one in which inequalities must work to everyone's advantage, especially the most disadvantaged.

It is evident that Rawls is indebted to the contractarian tradition since he relies heavily on the notion of individuals agreeing to a contract outside of an organized social system. Moreover, this contract is the ground of their rights, duties, liberties, and the condition for the distribution of society's goods. Rawls's theory, like that of Locke and other predecessors, emphasizes fundamental rights or liberties which can never be suspended for any utilitarian considerations.

---

[20]John Rawls, *A Theory of Justice* (Cambridge, MA: Harvard University Press, 1971), p. 302.
[21]Ibid., p. 61.
[22]Ibid.

Rawls's ethic and the viewpoint of a rights-based approach to morality has many difficulties. One difficulty with Rawls is that the implementation of the difference principle could prove to be an almost impossible task. To begin with, there is a serious problem in the identification of the "least advantaged" who must be somehow aided by inequalities in society. Are they simply those with the lowest income? Couldn't one make the case with equal persuasion that the least advantaged are prosperous blacks or Hispanics who can't live where they want or well-payed but overtaxed, undervalued, and "alienated" assembly line workers? In short, many different groups in society could qualify in some way as being the "least advantaged," posing problems for translating Rawls's difference principle into concrete terms.

Rights, Justice, and Information Technology

The issue of rights seems especially acute for IT professionals because of the formidable threat that technology could pose to some commonly accepted rights. This threat is probably most pronounced in the area of informational privacy. As a result, it seems essential to formulate the scope of an individual's "information rights," that is, the rights that individuals should possess regarding their personal information that is scattered about in various databases. At a minimum, every person deserves a right to the privacy, accuracy, and security of such information.

Let us briefly elaborate on these rights. To begin with, individuals have a basic right to privacy since privacy is essential for the protection of their freedom and autonomy. Personal information should be regarded as confidential; it should not be distributed to other interested parties without the subject's permission. One could maintain, therefore, that this fundamental right to privacy should serve as a constraint on certain data collection and dissemination activities.

Second, individuals have a right to the accuracy of their personal information. This information should be kept up-to-date, germane, and verified. Thus, banks, credit bureaus, hospitals, and others have an obligation to ensure that its information on a data subject is as accurate and error-free as possible.

Individuals also have a right to the security of their personal information. This means that data collectors and handlers have an obligation to protect computer systems from breaches of confidentiality. In summary, therefore, the data subject has the right to have its data maintained in a way that keeps it confidential, accurate, and secure.

But these information rights for an individual must be juxtaposed against a corporation's "information property rights." Organizations claim with some legitimacy that their information resources are their property and that they have a right to dispose of their property as they see fit. How do we establish which set of rights takes precedence? The problem is that certain rights are like Ross's duties: They are *prima facie* or conditional claims that can conflict with other rights. We will consider these conflicting rights in Chapter 5 and attempt to establish some balance between these competing claims.

Finally, Rawls's rights-based theory dwells on the important issue of justice, which is certainly applicable to many problems that arise in the sphere of information technology. Equal access, for example, is an important justice issue, albeit one that will not be dealt with in this book. Another issue is the potential for information monopolies in some industries. Is absolute control of information in an industry consistent with standards of justice and fair play? Moreover, since IT gives rise to new forms of competition and new industry arrangements between competing firms, there are many issues of justice at stake. We will consider these at some length in Chapter 3, but it is worth noting here that Rawls provides a useful framework for assessing the fairness of these information partnerships.

NORMATIVE PRINCIPLES

In addition to this treatment of ethical frameworks it is also important to introduce several moral principles that are relevant for making ethical decisions in the area of information technology. To a great extent, these principles are based on the moral theories we have just considered. Those theories might not formulate these principles in the same way or give them the same emphasis, but they accept them as part of the moral decision making process. Because of their simplicity and concreteness, these principles can sometimes serve as a more practical and direct way of coming to terms with a moral dilemma. For example, the basic principle of nonmaleficence or "avoid injury to others" is more transparent and intuitively obvious than Kant's categorical imperative.

We will discuss here three key normative principles that have some applicability to computer ethics: autonomy, nonmaleficence, and informed consent. Like the theories, these principles serve only as general and incomplete guides for action. They are not hard and fast rules that can produce easy answers to complex ethical problems. They merely provide a basis for making decisions according to a valid moral principle rather than to capricious feelings or tendentious evaluations.

The Principle of Autonomy

Kant and other philosophers have stressed that a vital element of personhood is the capacity to be self-determining. The Kantian notion of personhood emphasizes the equal worth and universal dignity of all persons, because all rational persons have a dual capacity: <u>the ability to develop</u> a rational plan to pursue their conception of the good life, and also the ability to respect this same capacity of self-determination in others. In other words, for an individual to be truly human, that person must be free to decide what is in his or her best interests. Not only is autonomy a necessary condition of moral responsibility, but also it is through the exercise of autonomy that individuals shape their lives. When someone is deprived of autonomy, that individual is not being treated as a person deserving of respect. Indeed, none of us likes to have our freedom compromised through the actions of others.

But what does all this have to do with information technology? In what ways does the expansion of information technology interfere with autonomy? Or do these technologies actually support the exercise of autonomy? On the one hand, quicker access to information can help an individual to make informed decisions more quickly and efficiently. However, as we shall see in several chapters, computer technology can interfere with autonomy when it is used to encroach upon one's personal privacy. Privacy is a necessary condition for autonomy, since our freedom is inhibited when our actions are being scrutinized by others. In addition, our autonomy is impaired when we lack control over our personal information that is in the hands of others. Hence, unless computer technology is implemented responsibly, it can be hostile to the important value of autonomy.

It is also worth pointing out that if professionals such as doctors use expert systems to help make decisions, they might not question the decisions that emanate from those systems. This phenomenon is known as the ELIZA syndrome—expert systems are endowed with such authority that "users feel compelled to accept whatever they suggest."[23] But when technology takes on this aura, it limits a physician's autonomy, since it could prompt him to abdicate his basic professional responsibility. This is another way in which technology can become a threat to autonomy.

The Principle of Nonmaleficence

The principle of nonmaleficence is best summed up in the simple phrase used in the medical profession, "above all, do no harm." According to this most basic of all moral principles, one ought to avoid needless injury to others whenever possible. Thus, one should not use computers or information technology to inflict harm on other people, either directly or indirectly. For example, if hackers or disgruntled employees infect a mission-critical application with a debilitating virus, they are causing significant injury. When

---

[23]Goran Collste, "Expert Systems in Medicine and Moral Responsibility," *Journal of Systems Software*, 17 (1992), 21.

computer systems are disrupted in this way, the result can cause irreparable damage to a business and considerable inconvenience for its stakeholders

This negative injunction against doing injury to others is sometimes called the *moral minimum*, that is, however one may choose to develop a moral code, this injunction must not be excluded. To be sure, most moral systems will go well beyond the moral minimum, as we have already seen, but at the core of these and other theories is this moral imperative to avoid injury to others. According to one group of authors:

> We know of no societies, from the literature of anthropology or comparative ethics, whose moral codes do not contain some injunction against harming others. The specific notion of *harm* or social *injury* may vary, as well as the mode of correction and restitution but the injunctions are present.[24]

It seems evident that this moral principle can be quite helpful in analyzing moral dilemmas or quandaries that emerge in the field of information technology. A reasonable starting point for the analysis of such quandaries is a consideration of whom, if anyone, has been harmed or injured in each case. In other words, an exploration of the actual or potential damage or injury is a good initial test of the morality of such activities. For example, if one is assessing a breach of security, a key issue must be the extent to which individuals or organizations have been harmed by this breach. Obviously, an incisive analysis will go beyond this question, but it does serve as a logical, albeit sometimes neglected, starting point.

Informed Consent

The final normative principle to be considered is informed consent. "Consent" implies that someone has given agreement freely to something. But for such assent to have significance, it should be "informed," that is, based on accurate information and an understanding about the issue at hand. If someone consents to accept a hazardous assignment, for example, that person must be given as much information as possible about the risks of undertaking such an activity. If this information is deliberately withheld or is incomplete because of carelessness, then the consent is given under false pretenses and is invalid.

The principle of informed consent can play an important role in the evaluation of moral issues relating to informational privacy. A case can surely be made that if personal privacy is to be protected, information acquired for one purpose cannot be used for other purposes without the free and informed consent of the subject. Thus, if a credit card company collects data about my various purchases and buying habits, those data

---

[24]Jon Gunneman, Charles Powers, and John Simon, *The Ethical Investor* (New Haven, CT: Yale University Press, 1972), p. 20.

cannot be sold to other vendors without my informed consent. I should be informed about who will be getting these data and how they will be used, and with this background information I can then choose to give or with-hold my consent. The principle of informed consent, then, serves as a con-straint in the treatment of information as a commodity and the free exchange of personal data across computer networks. How informed con-sent can be realistically implemented and balanced with other concerns is discussed in Chapter 5.

This normative guideline has played an especially critical role in med-ical ethics. An important issue in this discipline concerns individuals who volunteer for medical research projects. According to the principle of informed consent, individuals should decide whether or not to participate in such risky projects only after they have been provided with adequate infor-mation to make a sound decision. Some might insist that the role of informed consent in the area of medical research is far more legitimate than its role in protecting informational privacy, but Carol Gould rightly observes that these uses of this principle are definitely analogous and that the importance of this principle for computer ethics should not be underestimated:

> In the case of personal information, the consent does not seem to concern an action done to one…or the use of a part of one's body or of something that belongs to one exclusively. Rather, it is consent to the obtaining and use of information about oneself. However, in this case too, the consent is required to preserve the right of privacy, not the privacy of one's body but of personal information, which, as in the case of the body, one has a right to control.[25]

Finally, one may also argue that some version of this principle may also serve as a guideline in the area of computer security. For example, when an organization collects and stores sensitive information about many individuals, those individuals have a real stake in that organization's secu-rity system, since they can be adversely affected by security breaches. In these cases it might be suitable for the organization to inform these individ-uals or their representatives of its security measures and to rely on at least their tacit consent regarding the adequacy of the security systems in place. We will consider this issue in more depth in Chapter 7.

A GENERAL FRAMEWORK FOR ETHICAL ANALYSIS

In addition to the normative principles just considered, we have presented here three ethical frameworks and noted the general polarity between tele-ological and deontological approaches to morality. The former is a prag-matic morality of ends while the latter stresses fidelity to principle in the form of rights or duties. Despite these differences, each approach repre-

---

[25]Carol Gould, "Network Ethics: Access, Consent, and the Informed Community," in Carol Gould, ed., *The Information Web: Ethical and Social Implications of Computer Networking* (Boulder, CO: Westview Press, 1989), p. 28.

sents a unique perspective from which one can deliberate over moral issues. All theories seek to elevate the level of moral discourse from preoccupation with "feelings" or gut reaction to a reasoned and thoughtful consideration of the right course of action.

As we attempt to apply these theoretical approaches to the case studies in this book, a good starting point would be the following questions, which enable us to put these various theories into action:

- *Consequentialism* or *goal-based analysis*: A manager must consider which action optimizes the consequences for all parties involved. Doing this often entails a cost–benefit analysis aimed at identifying the action that will yield a better proportion of benefits to costs than any other option.
- *Duty-based ethics*: A manager who follows this avenue should consider the following questions: Can I universalize the course of action I am considering? Does this course of action violate any basic ethical duties? Are there alternatives that better conform to these duties? If each alternative seems to violate one duty or another, which is the stronger duty?
- *Rights-based ethics*: A manager must carefully consider the rights of affected parties: Which action or policy best upholds the human rights of the individuals involved? Do any alternatives under consideration violate their fundamental human rights (liberty, privacy, etc.) or institutional or legal rights (e.g., rights derived from a contract or other institutional arrangement)?

Finally, how do we incorporate these ethical questions into a comprehensive analysis of cases in this book and elsewhere? Perhaps the best way to proceed is to outline a general approach to these case studies along the lines of the structure in Table 2.2. There are, of course, other questions that can be raised and many different methods of analyzing case studies. This broad framework, however, represents a plausible starting point which can certainly be embellished by the reader according to his or her interests and perspectives.

Table 2.2 Steps for Ethical Analysis

1. Identify and formulate the basic ethical issues in each case.

2. Consider your first impressions or reactions to these issues. In other words, what does your moral intuition say about the action or policy under consideration: Is it right or wrong?

3. Are any of the *normative principles* relevant? If so, what impact do they have on resolving the ethical problem(s)?

4. Consider the issues also from the viewpoint of one or more of the ethical theories and pose some of the questions raised above.

5. Do the normative principles and ethical theories point to one decision or course of action or do they bring you to different conclusions? If so, which avenue of reasoning should take precedence?

6. What is your *normative conclusion* about the case, that is, what should be the organization or individual's course of action?

7. Finally, what are the public policy implications of this case and your normative conclusion? Should the recommended behavior be prescribed through legislation or regulations?

STAKEHOLDER ANALYSIS

One final word about theory. In discussing the various ethical themes, we often referred obliquely to the "parties involved." We should be more precise about those affected by a manager's actions and decisions. They are often referred to as "stakeholders." A stakeholder is defined as any group or individual who can affect or is affected by the achievement of the organization's objectives. Some examples of a corporation's stakeholders are its employees, stockholders, customers, suppliers, communities, relevant government agencies, society at large, and even its competitors.[26]

Much has been written about the ethical relationship between management and stakeholders. A full treatment of this topic, however, is beyond the scope of this work. Suffice it to say that stakeholders are more than mere instrumental forces that can help or hinder a corporation as it tries to reach its objectives. Rather, the moral point of view would strongly suggest that each stakeholder group deserves respect in its own right; the corporation and its managers, in other words, have certain moral obligations to their diverse stakeholders that can be defined by the ethical theories outlined in the previous section.

Stakeholder analysis can probably best be accomplished when it is done in conjunction with one or more of these theories. Such analysis entails first identifying the key stakeholders, those who have a real interest or "stake" in the decision at hand. One must also consider the goals of each stakeholder group along with their preferred outcome and their leverage for affecting that outcome. Finally, managers must consider a moral position toward these stakeholders. If they follow consequentialism, they can decide to maximize *stakeholder equity*, that is, choose the alternative that optimizes consequences for all stakeholders. On the other hand, a pluralist or duty-based approach would require managers to consider its duties to stakeholders and, if there are conflicts, to identify the groups (such as stockholders) to whom the manager has the highest obligation. In these and other ways stakeholder analysis can be integrated with ethical analysis to reach some plausible and coherent resolution to intricate moral quandaries. Including this level of analysis will alert managers to the concerns of the many groups affected by their decisions.

---

[26]For more discussion on this see R. Edward Freeman, *Strategic Management: A Stakeholder Approach* (Boston: Pittman Publishing, 1984), pp. 31–49.

SUMMARY

We began this chapter by underlining the practical nature of ethics: We do ethics in order to be able to conduct our lives rightly and honorably. Normative ethics, the focus of this book, is a quest for the practical truth of how one's choices and actions can be good and worthwhile. We also considered important distinctions between law and morality and between individual and corporate responsibility.

There are various avenues of ethical reasoning. Essentially modern ethical theory can be divided into two broad categories: deontological and teleological, the ethics of duty and the ethics of ends (or consequences). The theory of utilitarianism developed by Bentham and Mill, is a teleological theory and a widely used form of consequentialism. The goal of the moral life, in this theory, is to maximize happiness or utility, so actions are right to the extent that they bring this about. A person should act to promote the maximum net expectable utility for all of those affected by that action.

Kant's moral philosophy, on the other hand, is a prime example of a deontological theory, since it emphasizes fidelity to principle and duty. For Kant, our duty is to follow the moral law, which is summed up in the categorical imperative: Act according to a maxim that is at the same time valid as a universal moral law. In other words, our actions must pass the test of universalization. Kant's moral philosophy can also be summed up in the word *respect*: The moral law requires that we respect humanity as an end in itself. We cannot treat our fellow human beings exclusively as a means for achieving our own purposes in life.

Another version of this duty-based approach to ethics is developed in the philosophy of W. D. Ross. He argues on behalf of *prima facie* duties— honesty, beneficence, justice, and so forth—those duties that can be superseded by a higher obligation, usually under exceptional circumstances. This philosophy allows for more flexibility and compromise than Kant's more rigid approach to morality.

Contractarianism, or a rights-based approach to morality, is another type of deontological theory. According to this viewpoint, morality is grounded in the social contract between government and its citizens, and this contract guarantees us certain inalienable moral rights such as the right to life, liberty, and property. Contractarianism emphasizes fairness, which is achieved when the participants in social arrangements have been accorded due respect. John Rawls's theory of justice represents a rights-based, deontological approach to morality which highlights justice as fairness. According to Rawls, parties in the pre-political "original position" behind the veil of ignorance would choose two principles of justice: the first involves an extensive system of liberties while the second deals with an equitable distribution of social goods. According to the second principle or the "difference principle," disparities in the distribution of wealth and other social goods would be tolerated only if they could be shown to benefit the least advantaged on the social scale.

We next turned to a cursory treatment of three important normative principles: autonomy, nonmaleficence, and informed consent. These principles, less abstract than ethical theories, can sometimes serve as a more practical way of reaching normative conclusions. Finally, we presented a general framework for case analysis that includes the following key elements: identify the moral issues, consider your intuitive or instinctual response, evaluate the issues from the vantage point of the normative principles and the ethical theories, determine if the principles and theories would point to one course of action and, if not, consider which principle or theory should take precedence, reach a normative conclusion about the case, and determine its public policy implications.

Finally, we emphasized that in making these moral decisions attention should be paid to the various stakeholders of a corporation or organization. A stakeholder is any group or individual that can affect or is affected by the achievement of the organization's objectives. Stakeholder analysis can best be accomplished when it is done in conjunction with one or more of the ethical theories elaborated upon in the chapter.

CASES FOR DISCUSSION

Introduction

The following case studies will serve as applications of the ethical paradigms or to concrete situations. The first case involves a manager who is concerned about the possible misuse of data that he is supplying to a new client. The key question in this case revolves around this employee's responsibility: Does he have a moral obligation to do something about this matter despite the company's wishes to the contrary? This case underscores the complexity of conflicting responsibilities and the difficulty of deciding which one takes priority.

The second case raises some provocative questions about an employee's rights in potential conflict with an employer's obligation to protect "vital" corporate information. Does an employee have the right not to be discriminated against because of external activities or because he or she is related to people who work at rival firms? This case is especially significant because it highlights the importance of safeguarding information in our society, an underlying theme of this book.

CASE 2.1

"It's Not Your Job to Be a 'Data Cop'!"[27]

Robert Wessell works for a well-established and highly profitable corporation that has carved out a niche as an information broker. Mr. Wessell is currently the manager of the direct mail division in Chicago. This division rents out various mailing lists to direct marketers. Companies and other organizations purchase these data lists usually in order to target a marketing campaign for certain products or services. Most of the company's customers are reputable organizations and use these data conscientiously for legitimate purposes. For example, some of Wessell's best clients are major charities, which rent these lists to raise money for worthy causes.

But Mr. Wessell has just received a substantial request from a new customer, a West Coast mortgage company that specializes in second mortgages. He recognizes the company's name because it recently gained some notoriety for targeting vulnerable segments of the population. It has allegedly "suckered in" some of these customers by obtaining some equity in their property in exchange for granting a second mortgage at exorbitant interest rates, sometimes exceeding 19 percent (the current market interest rate for a 30-year second mortgage is about 9 percent). Despite the negative publicity, the company has steadfastly denied any wrongdoing. Several states have initiated allegations of these accusations, but so far no charges have been filed.

This mortgage company has asked Wessell's division to download a database that lists personal demographics by ZIP code in several major eastern cities. Given the company's history, Wessell is convinced that it will use this database to target low-income areas for its direct mailing and telemarketing campaigns. Mr. Wessell is loath to respond to this request, and he decides to articulate his concerns to his boss, Ms. Jane Manning, who is the Vice President for Information Services. She listens attentively to Wessell's reservations about this request, but for the most part she is unsympathetic. She advises Wessell not to worry about how the company's customers will be using these data and she points out that the mortgage company is a new client and that this could be a lucrative account. "Further," she tells Wessell, "this organization just can't possibly control how data lists will be used. Besides the charge against the mortgage company is only an allegation and perhaps it isn't even true. Also you have no proof that they will be targeting low-income families; your suspicions may be completely unfounded." Wessell offers a mild protest and rebuttal of her arguments, but to no avail. Ms. Manning ends the meeting by exclaiming, "Look, Robert, it's not your job to be a data cop!"

[27]This case study represents a hypothetical situation.

Wessell is still unsatisfied, and he now feels perplexed about the scope of his responsibility. Should he try to get more information about how the mortgage company will be using this list? Or are these concerns really not his responsibility? Maybe his boss is right: He can't possibly be a watchdog for all of his customers. Nevertheless he feels quite uneasy about complying with this client's request and wonders what he should do, especially in light of Ms. Manning's indifference.

Questions

1. Identify and analyze the basic ethical issues in this case.

2. What is Wessell's responsibility if the mortgage company does use this data list in an unscrupulous way?

3. What should Wessell do? Defend your answer by reference to one or more of the ethical theories in this chapter.

CASE 2.2

Vital Information at Complex[28]
Thomas Donaldson

Martha Van Hussen, Regional Director of sales at Complex Corporation, was feeling vaguely uneasy as she sipped her morning coffee and glanced again at the latest memo from corporate headquarters. The memo stressed once more the need to block absolutely any information leaks to competitors both about changes in Complex's rapidly evolving line of computer software products and about its latest marketing strategies. Complex found itself in the middle of one of the hottest and most competitive markets in the world. The software it handled was sold primarily to banks, savings and loans, and brokerage firms, and although in the beginning Complex had been virtually alone in the market, in recent years a number of increasingly aggressive competitors had slowly whittled away at Complex's market share. The difference between a sale and a lost sale was frequently only the difference between being able to boast or not of a minor software innovation. Martha reminded herself as she looked at the memo that great hopes were being attached to the company's new "Data-File" line of products to be publicly announced in three months. Already salespeople in the division had been briefed on the new line in behind-closed doors sessions to prepare them for selling the new products effectively.

---

[28]Copyright © 1982 by Thomas Donaldson. Reprinted with permission.

What worried her was not so much that one of her salespeople would *intentionally* provide information to competitors, as that someone might allow an *unintentional* leak. It was true, she confessed to herself, two mem bers of her twenty-member sales force had been disgruntled over recent salary decisions and had threatened to quit. But she doubted they would actually commit an act of outright sabotage. More problematic was the fact that one of her salespersons, Frank Wright, was married to an employee of one of Complex's major competitors. Because Frank's wife, Hillary, was a software designer, Martha knew she could interpret any relevant informa- tion, even off-hand information offered in casual remarks, decisively. Of course, Martha had no reason to question the conduct of either Frank or Hillary. Both seemed to be good, down-to-earth types, and she had espe- cially enjoyed chatting with them at a recent dinner party. Frank, further- more, had done well during his first three years with the company. To fur- ther complicate the overall problem, two other members of her staff had relatives working for competing firms. In one case the relative was an uncle, and in the other it was a cousin. She also knew that her sales staff met infrequently with other salespersons from rival firms at conferences and exhibits.

Martha reminded herself that she had already called her people together to emphasize the need to protect vital corporate information. She had also sent each employee a copy of a recent memo from corporate head- quarters and had reminded them of the item in the Company's Code of Conduct stipulating that disclosure of vital information was a cause for dis- missal.

The question nagging her now was: Is there something more I should do? Should I take specific actions in specific cases? If so, what? Was it fair to penalize a person simply because he or she had the misfortune to be related to a competitor's employee? As she pondered these issues, one fact stared her in the face with perfect clarity: Any leaks, either now or in the future, could seriously jeopardize the company's well-being; moreover, if any leaks were traced to her division, *she* would be held responsible.

Two days later Martha received a phone call from the vice president in charge of her division, Mr. John Sears. Mr. Sears informed her that evi- dence had emerged indicating that crucial product information had been leaked by a member of her department. Two things were known for cer- tain: (1) Complex information had been obtained by a major competitor, and (2) some of the information leaked had been circulated only to Van Hussen's staff. Mr. Sears was reluctant to divulge more, but he did remark that he was doubtful that more information would be forthcoming to use in tracing the leak to a specific member of Van Hussen's department. He con- cluded the phone call by saying, "I want you to do whatever is necessary to stop this problem."

Questions

1. In your estimation, what is the key ethical problem or dilemma in this case?

2. Analyze this case from the rights-based ethical perspective. Do employees have the right not to be discriminated against in their accessibility to information (in other words, can Ms. Van Hussen declare certain information off limits for an employee like Frank Wright whose wife works for a competitor)?

3. What course of action would you recommend for Ms. Van Hussen?

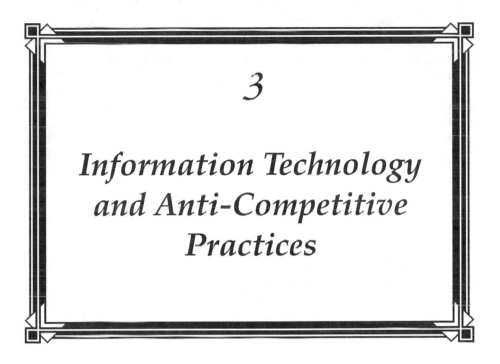

3

Information Technology and Anti-Competitive Practices

The issues of competition and fair play have been seriously neglected subjects in treatises on business ethics. Perhaps the reason for this neglect is the difficulty of determining guidelines for competitive fair play and the belief that there should be few if any constraints in the predatory world of business competition. Moreover, textbooks on corporate strategy and business policy tend to reinforce this viewpoint. The goal of any strategy is to thwart the efforts of the competition and, if possible, drive them out of business. In recent years there has been even greater emphasis on competitive attitudes and practices thanks to the work of scholars such as Michael Porter, whose books, *Competitive Strategy* and *Competitive Advantage*, have been extraordinarily influential.

To be sure, it is essential that a business be competitive and develop practices and policies that will help it prevail against its competitors. But we must admit that there have to be limits to these practices, that there are boundaries within which business competition must be pursued. Some of these boundaries are defined by law but others are poorly defined and therefore rather obscure. Bribery, price fixing, infringement of patent or copyright laws, and the theft of trade secrets are all unfair business practices that are prohibited by law. As one judge pointed out, the necessity for healthy competition in the context of a free market economy "must not force us into accepting the law of the jungle as the standard of morality expected in our commercial relations."[1]

In this chapter we will consider the competitive power of information technology (IT) systems, especially their ability to yield a significant competitive advantage for organizations that develop well-conceived strategic systems. We will also consider the use of IT to improve communication within an industry and thereby facilitate cooperation in determining prices and other factors. As we have been at pains to insist, information technology has the potential to change the way firms compete. Thanks to the power of certain IT systems, we also face the threat of an information monopoly in certain industries, and this could be devastating for companies that cannot access or control the information they need in order to conduct their business.

We must carefully consider, then, how IT can enable firms to achieve competitive advantage and what limits must be imposed to prevent any unfairness. We must also discuss the use of IT to circumvent the competitive norms of the marketplace. The issues in this regard are much trickier, since it is difficult to discern when sophisticated electronic communication might itself become a form of collusion that violates antitrust laws and thereby undermines free and open competition.

IT AND COMPETITIVE ADVANTAGE

As we observed in Chapter 1, the primary goal of information systems is to provide an organization with some sort of sustainable competitive advantage or leverage over its competitors. Some companies that have invested heavily in information technology might contest this claim, since they have not realized any such advantage despite all the promises of hardware and software vendors.

Beyond any doubt, however, there have been some exceptionally successful information systems which have had an appreciable strategic impact in many industries. The legendary applications of companies such as United Airlines, Federal Express, Banc One, Frito-Lay, and American Hospital Supply (now Baxter Healthcare) are still the subjects of much admiration and emulation. Each of these organizations has successfully applied various electronic technologies to build competitive advantage and enhance organizational effectiveness.

---

[1]Judge Goldberg, "*E. I. duPont deMours & Co. v. Christopher*, 431 F. 2nd 1012, 1016 (5th Cir., 1970), cert. denied, 400 USA 1024, quoted in Lynn Sharp Paine "Ideals of Competition and Today's Marketplace," in *Enriching Business Ethics*, ed. Clarence C. Walton (New York: Plenum Press, 1990), p. 93.

A strategic information system (or SIS) supports and shapes a company's corporate strategy through technology. If a system is really "strategic," it will differentiate the company's product or service, permit substantial cost reductions, or allow for the superior management of critical corporate resources (such as inventory). According to Professor F. Warren McFarlan, a strategic information system will create significant leverage for an organization if it accomplishes one or more of the following:

- raise entry barriers for the industry
- build in switching costs
- change the basis of competition
- change the balance of power in supplier relationships[2]

Let us briefly consider each of these key advantages. An IT system can raise entry barriers by offering a new service or feature that is difficult or expensive for potential competitors to imitate. For example, an on-line electronic order entry system might become the normal method of sales and distribution in an industry. If aspiring new competitors do not have the resources and skills to construct such a sophisticated system, they face a major hurdle for gaining a foothold in this industry. Baxter's *ASAP Express* computerized order entry and inventory control system produced entry barriers in the hospital supply industry, as hospitals became accustomed to an automated on-line system for ordering supplies and equipment. Clearly, a new competitor would have to offer a comparable system unless it could participate in a rival's system for a fee.

Switching costs are impediments that prevent buyers from changing to another vendor. A buyer who has made a substantial investment in a product may be reluctant to switch to a new vendor. This investment goes well beyond the price of the product: There is also an investment in learning how the product functions, how it must be maintained, and so forth. Thus, for example, a customer might become so dependent on an easy-to-use and efficient order entry system that has been mastered by its employees that it will be loath to switch to a new supplier. To some extent this was also the case with *ASAP Express*.

Third, under some circumstances a strategic information system has the potential to transform the entire basis of competition. This might occur in industries where there is intense competition based on factors such as product differentiation. If an IT system is developed that can dramatically reduce costs, it could alter the ground rules for competition as companies are then forced to compete on the basis of cost (rather than differentiation or

---

[2]F. Warren McFarlan, "Information Technology Changes the Way You Compete," *Harvard Business Review*, May–June 1984, p. 98.

some other factor). Cost reductions attributable to an IT system could include significant staff reductions, superior inventory control, and the like.

Finally IT has the potential to shift the balance of power in a company's relationships with its suppliers. The most prominent success story in this area is Just-in-Time (JIT) inventory systems, which have permitted companies to control more efficiently the process of ordering from suppliers. The core of JIT is a smooth flow of product through the production system relying on minimal inventories. The result is considerable savings because less money is invested in idle inventory. Some IT systems are linked to multiple suppliers and check automatically for the lowest price each time an order is placed. These and similar systems can give corporations increased leverage over their suppliers.

It is obvious, then, that IT has the potential to change significantly the way companies compete. But what are the characteristics of these SIS applications that provide *enduring* competitive advantage, that is, one that cannot be easily duplicated by competitors? As advances in technology become more pervasive, it is likely that any advantage gained from these proprietary computer systems will be short lived, since competitors will quickly imitate such systems.

One can, however, attempt to create either technical or organizational barriers to inhibit such imitation. Technically sophisticated systems that require substantial customization of software, sophisticated networking, and integration with other systems offer major barriers for potential imitators. This was certainly true of airline reservation systems such as *SABRE* and *APOLLO*, whose technical complexity was a notable deterrent for competitors, especially small players in the industry such as Frontier and Southwest Airlines. Another barrier could emanate from *organizational* changes that result from the system's implementation. If these changes are complex and time-consuming, other organizations may be discouraged from attempting to imitate them. It must be emphasized, however, that as computer functionality becomes more sophisticated and less costly, it is increasingly unlikely that any information system will itself provide a sustainable business advantage.

INTERORGANIZATIONAL SYSTEMS

Some of the systems referred to in the previous section, such as United Airlines' *APOLLO* and Baxter Healthcare's *ASAP Express*, are known as interorganizational systems (IOS). The formal definition of an IOS is an "automated information system shared by two or more companies."[3] It is

---

[3] J. Cash and B. R. Konsynski, "IS Redraws Competitive Boundaries," *Harvard Business Review* March–April 1985, p. 134.

important to understand the nature of an IOS as distinguished from the more typical distributed computing system. Distributed computing systems provide the ability to access data transparently across heterogeneous computers in a network. Users can access data on any node in the network regardless of its location. But while distributed computing systems are *within* an organization and under the control of that organization, an IOS permits information to be shared across organizational boundaries. It may link a corporation with its customers, suppliers, or even its competitors. Thus an IOS often has a more significant impact on an organization's IT strategy than do standard applications. As many companies have discovered, an IOS can be a key tool for achieving a sustainable competitive advantage in a particular industry.

The traditional interorganizational system is also one form of an *information partnership*, which is much broader than a typical IOS. In an information partnership several companies might pool their resources to develop a collaborative information system. These arrangements can take many forms, such as joint marketing partnerships, intra-industry partnerships, and IT vendor-driver partnerships. Consider, for example, an intra-industry partnership such as *IVANS* (Insurance Value Added Network Services), which links many large and small insurance companies to thousands of independent insurance agents. Through *IVANS*, these agents can access policy and price information for a variety of insurance companies. According to authors McFarlan and Konsynski, information partnerships such as *IVANS* have many virtues since they "provide a way to reduce risks in leading edge technology investments."[4]

These systems are gradually becoming more widespread thanks to dramatic advances in computer networking and telecommunications along with standards on protocols and data transmission. For example, the development of fiber optics networks has vastly improved data transmission to even the most remote locations. Also because of speedier computers and less expensive storage media, data can be better archived, retrieved, and delivered to the end user in a customized format.

Obviously, an IOS or information partnership must provide advantages for all involved parties. It must also provide for exceptional data integrity, security, and privacy beyond the norms of standard in-house systems. The most elementary and common IOS's have functionality for "boundary transactions" such as order entry or JIT systems. More complex systems capture, retrieve, and analyze shared information, but so far such systems are still relatively rare.

The most prominent, successful IOS's connect vendors with cus-

[4]B. R. Konsynski and W. F. McFarlan, "Information Partnerships—Shared Data, Shared Scale," *Harvard Business Review*, September–October 1990, p. 115.

tomers. Baxter Healthcare's famous *ASAP Express* system has gone through multiple iterations but remains a model IOS. This much-admired system enables hospitals to order various types of hospital supplies such as gowns, rubber gloves, and syringes on-line from Baxter. The hospitals own their own terminals but lease communications lines. The advantages of such a system to the hospital are manifold: lower inventory levels (and hence lower costs), improved inventory control, less paperwork, and reduced administrative expenses, since there is less likelihood of errors occurring. *ASAP* has also provided a powerful, sustained competitive advantage for Baxter Healthcare by creating a major new stream of revenues along with formidable entry barriers; it has also increased significantly the switching costs of its customers.

In recent years the *ASAP Express* system has expanded to include other suppliers. The Baxter Healthcare Corporation found that in the long run an automated order entry system does not lock in as many customers as it had anticipated. Most customers still prefer some choice of vendors. As a consequence a new and more widely accepted version of *ASAP Express* was born, which offers a package of multivendor services, allowing orders to be placed with different vendors in a standard format using the same hardware equipment. This IOS has attained the dual objective of increasing the market efficiency of the industry while providing many notable advantages to its sponsor.

There are many obvious benefits for a company such as Baxter Healthcare in this multivendor system, but there are many risks as well. One important risk is the sponser's legal liability if the system fails or there are serious security breaches. There is also some potential for abuse on the part of the sponsoring organization. One possible issue here is access to data of other system participants. In the case of Baxter's *ASAP Express*, the system was tightly secured and all activities audited by a third party. Another issue concerns fees. The sponsoring company normally makes all the decisions about who can participate, what the fees should be, and related matters. Here too there is potential for controversy if the participation fees are too high or if there is disparity in fees charged to different participants. Sponsoring companies must be sensitive to these legal risks as well as with the need for an equitable arrangement in these situations.

Professors Michael Vitale and Russell Johnston describe in some detail the benefits of an IOS to the sponsoring company. They maintain that the biggest benefit of an IOS with multiple vendors is an appreciable increase in revenues. Other benefits include the opportunity to attract new customers, the enlarged scope of the system, increased customer awareness, the "halo effect," the ability to exploit these systems for marketing information, and the influence on the very structure of the industry. Several of these factors deserve further comment.

Increased customer awareness of the sponsoring company's product can result from favorable display of that product or service, substitution for a competitor's products, or cross selling. Since the sponsor controls the system, it can determine the basic format of the system including the all-important display of the data. Obviously it is in the sponsor's best interests to display information about its product as prominently as possible.

The halo effect occurs if customers want to deal with the IOS sponsor because of its enhanced image as a technological leader.

Another benefit comes from the increased knowledge of market and competitive conditions, since the sponsoring company could be privy to information about a competitor's products, prices, discounts, and so forth.

Finally, a popular IOS can lead to industry restructuring since it may compel smaller players to exit the market if they cannot afford to link up with the industry-wide system.[5]

Interorganizational systems such as *ASAP Express* along with information partnerships are becoming widely adopted across a broad spectrum of industries. As we have seen, they permit notable opportunities for external coordination which should help make markets more efficient and individual firms more productive. Buyers will easily be able to compare products, prices, and discounts from many different vendors. Moreover, participants will be better able to leverage the resources that they commit to state of the art information technology systems. As a result, the IOS and information partnership will undoubtedly become the norm in many other industry settings.

THE IOS AND ETHICAL CONCERNS

The Issues

The steady growth of interorganizational systems poses several ethical and social problems for sponsoring and participating organizations. Most of these issues revolve around appropriate norms for the organizations that control an IOS or those that have the dominant role within an information partnership.

To begin with, how far can these organizations go to enhance their competitive position at the expense of the other participants? Is it ethical, for example, to utilize biased displays that favor the most powerful sponsoring organization? This controversy became prominent in regard to United Airline's *APOLLO* and American Airline's *SABRE* reservation sys-

---

[5]Russell Johnston and Michael Vitale, "Creating Competitive Advantage with Interorganizational Information Systems," *MIS Quarterly*, June 1988, pp. 153–65.

tems. Smaller competitors that used United's APOLLO alleged that their flights were unfavorably displayed so that it was easier for travel agents to choose United's more clearly displayed flights. American Airlines also programmed its reservation system with a bias toward its own flights. (See the case study *Airline Reservation Systems* at the end of this chapter for more material on this practice).

Another ethical issue concerns the extent to which the dominant organization should exploit IOS systems to gather sensitive information about its competitors. What sort of information should be considered proprietary? Should a company's buying patterns and other information that can be derived from an IOS or partnership be made available to all of the system participants for a reasonable fee?

As we observed in the discussion on Baxter Healthcare's *ASAP Express*, there is also the issue of fair pricing of fees. If participation in an industry-wide IOS becomes essential for competing in that industry, is it fair to engage in aggressive or discriminatory pricing? Such pricing policies will likely have a greater impact on small competitors and may even drive them out of business. How, then, does an organization establish an equitable fee structure?

All of these questions are relevant to some lawsuits still pending against United and American Airlines regarding their treatment of smaller airlines such as Frontier. As was noted above, these two powerful airlines are alleged to have used their computer reservation systems to gain unfair advantage over smaller competitors. The overriding issue is, given the dependence on information in almost every industry, is it permissible for certain firms to use their information systems as a lethal competitive weapon?

This raises a fundamental moral and social problem for the information age: Can society tolerate the presence of an "information monopoly" in certain industries? For example, suppose the dominant firm in an IOS controlled price and product information or other essential industry-wide data. "Control" under these circumstances might imply better access to these data than one's competitors or the ability to determine how these data are communicated to customers. Isn't this power as pernicious and anticompetitive as other forms of monopolies since its ultimate effect could be a diminution of competition? Can the key stakeholders such as government regulators, customers, or other competitors allow one firm to control such vital information resources for an entire industry? Moreover, is this control responsible behavior and within the bounds of fair play? Perhaps this dark side of industry-wide information systems will never be realized on a large scale, but nevertheless these questions cannot be ignored.

In order to formulate some tenable answers to these questions, it is essential that we come to terms with the difficult-to-define boundaries of fair play. When does competition become unfair and unethical? Are firms left morally free to use any tactics to gain market share as long as those tactics are not prohibited by law? The law has been reactive, slow to keep up with technological advances. Also, laws are often unnuanced, allowing companies to exploit loopholes. But if the law fails us, where can we turn for reasonable guidance?

An Ethical Approach

Our purpose here is not to articulate definitive answers to such challenging questions, since doing so would undermine the use of the case studies in this chapter to provoke the reader's own thinking on these complex matters. We can, however, offer some suggested approaches and reflections. Above all, we can demonstrate how some of the ethical insights explained in Chapter 2 might serve as a vehicle for developing some resolution of these issues.

As we noted in that chapter, every corporation has an obligation to consider the best interests of its diverse stakeholders: customers, suppliers, employees, government agencies, society at large, and others. Stakeholder analysis makes the corporation a more attentive and responsible social agent since it cultivates a broad view, focusing attention on the social dimensions of various strategic decisions. Many corporations fail to realize that their competitors are also stakeholders deserving of considerate treatment. This point is especially important given the value of open and free competition in a free market economy. Tad Tuleja, who argues persuasively on behalf of respect for competitor rights, observes that this position is not incompatible with a vigorous, "hardball" approach to competition: "An ethical stance toward the competition does not require that you let them win the game, only that you do not use tactics that you would deplore if they were used against you."[6] This statement is consistent with the ethical viewpoint of *universal acceptability*, which requires that any action be morally acceptable to all interested and disinterested parties.

Thus the sponsoring organization of an IOS or the dominant parties in an information partnership should consider very carefully the interests of all their stakeholders when determining policies and setting participant fees. This is not to suggest that all stakeholders should be treated equally. There are many reasons for giving the highest priority to the shareholders or owners of the corporation, since managers have a fiduciary obligation to those shareholders. However, according to Ken Goodpaster, "this does not mean that [other] stakeholders lack a morally significant relationship to

---

[6]Tad Tuleja, *Beyond the Bottom Line* (New York: Penguin Books, 1985), p. 148.

management." Managers must take the interests of other stakeholders seriously and behave toward them in a manner consistent "with the reasonable ethical expectations of the community."[7]

Clearly, it is not in the best interests of the community for one corporation to exploit its monopoly of information to the detriment of its competitors, since ultimately this situation would have a negative impact throughout the industry and beyond. Essentially, such a monopoly is not different from cornering the market for some other indispensable input or raw material. Information is a precious commodity for any industry and this critical resource must be shared equitably for the general vitality of the industry and the common good. It should not be monopolized and used as a weapon to drive others out of business. At the very least, then, these corporations must balance their natural competitive instincts with a concern for the wider interests of others, specifically their stakeholder constituencies. From a duty-based perspective, they must consider the question of how to balance their obligations to various stakeholders while avoiding policies that will subvert competitors' rights along with the information needs of society.

We can similarly examine the issue of competitive fair play from the viewpoint of the rights of the IOS or information partnership participants. As we observed in the previous chapter, a rights-based approach to morality is expressed in the framework of contractarianism, which acknowledges the rights of individuals, as members of a social arrangement, to be treated with equal respect. The principles determining those rights must be judged by some standard of fairness. A typical standard, according to John Rawls, would be established by a social contract that would be acceptable to all the rationally self-interested parties who are behind the veil of ignorance, that is, ignorant of their own position in society.

Recall that from the vantage point of this "original position," inequities in income or differentials in power are acceptable only when they benefit the least advantaged.

To a limited extent, the contract signed by members of an industry wide IOS creates a similar "social arrangement" and mirrors the more primordial social contract described by Rawls. In other words, we can judge the morality of the contractual arrangement from the vantage point of the original position: In a just social arrangement, significant power or income differentials must redound to the benefits of all the parties to the contract. If this is to be a just and fair contract, the least powerful participant should not be exploited by those who control the system and should receive some genuine benefits from the arrangement.

[7]Kenneth E. Goodpaster, "Business Ethics and Stakeholder Analysis," *Business Ethics Quarterly*, January 1991, pp. 68–69.

From this moral vantage point, justice as fairness would seem to require that the fee charged to all participants be reasonable and consistent with their participation in the IOS system. Moreover, it would not tolerate biases in the presentation of each organization's data. It seems impossible to justify that unequal treatment, such as biased displays, could improve the position of less powerful parties, since they in fact are usually the victims of such bias. Finally, the most advantaged, the dominant organizations, must permit the information to be distributed so that it benefits the least advantaged in some way. This arrangement precludes any monopoly of *essential* industry-wide information or restricted access to such information by direct or indirect means.

In the simplest terms, a Rawlsian moral perspective argues for a level playing field wherever possible, but if the field *is* uneven, a collaborative effort such as an industry-wide IOS should not worsen the lot of the least advantaged participants. Such arrangements should at least hold them harmless or improve their position somewhat in absolute terms. Partners and participants should contribute what they can afford to; moreover, the benefits they receive from these systems should be *proportionate to their contribution*. If an IOS or information partnership is so structured, it will ensure both fairness and profits for all parties involved.

By approaching this issue from the contractarian vantage point, we realize that the more powerful organizations of an IOS or information partnership can realize many benefits from their investment (an increased revenue stream, new customers, an enhanced image due to the halo effect, etc.), but these advantages must be limited by the rights of the participants. The benefits earned by the few cannot be justified if they worsen the lot of others by driving them out of business or causing a serious deterioration in their competitive position. In other words, a just arrangement is one that prohibits the exploitation of its less powerful members but respects their rights for equal and fair treatment.

Another way of approaching the moral dimensions of this issue is discussed in Lynn Paine's work on ethics and competition. She presents an ideal of competition that companies ought to follow. It is comprised of five principles, including the principle of the "level playing field." According to Professor Paine, this principle "is concerned with certain types of inequities among competitors and prevents them from using certain advantages—advantages of size, for example—in their competitive efforts."[8] She argues that this principle is grounded in the ethical notion of equal opportunity. Thus, although there is no requirement that industry players be equal, there must be some constraints placed on methods

[8]Paine, "Ideals of Competition,"p. 103

used to compete in order to ensure "that disparities in abilities and resources are not too great to permit genuine competition."[9] In the case of information technology, it would appear that the disparity in information resources must be controlled for the preservation of each company's opportunity to compete.

We can summarize these various arguments as follows: An industry IOS or information partnership should not be used to exploit less advantaged members; it should not destroy their opportunity to compete; and it should provide them with benefits proportionate to their contribution. Information technology should be used as a competitive *tool* but not as a lethal *weapon* .

This discussion by no means exhausts a treatment of the moral aspects of this complex issue. Many other approaches and different resolutions are certainly possible. It must be realized that it is inherently difficult to cooperate with one's rivals under some circumstances. Hence the boundaries of fair play in intensely competitive corporate environments are difficult to define and justify, since they call for restraint, an almost unnatural reaction when one is constantly seeking to get a leg up on the competition.

There are also compelling pragmatic reasons for treating competitors fairly. Most of us have an intuitive grasp of when the line of fair play has been crossed, and so we tend not to sympathize with the aggressor. A company that spurns or blatantly violates these boundaries invites consumer backlash. In addition, some argue convincingly that market forces will eventually reject biased IOS systems, since unbiased ones are more useful for consumers relying on those systems. As one group of authors observed, "Early developers of single-source of biased sales channels should plan for the transition to unbiased electronic markets. That way, they can continue to derive revenues from market-making activity."[10] In other words, market pressures will force biased systems to give way to unbiased ones offered by other suppliers.

Finally, abuses might also invite government intervention. This could bring about an unwelcome increase in government control of industry wide IT systems or, if power is consistently abused, may even lead to the divestiture of such systems.

Hence there are both ethical and practical reasons for not using information technology as a means of exploitation. The primary reason, however, is that a just society cannot endure unbridled rivalry and inordinate excesses in competition.

---

[9]Ibid.

[10]Robert Benjamin, Thomas Malone, and Jo Anne Yates, "The Logic of Electronic Markets, *Harvard Business Review*, May–June 1989, p. 168.

PRICING: PERFECT AND IMPERFECT COMPETITION

An IOS or commonly owned computer network can also be the source of other abuses, especially if such systems can help some firms to evade the forces of marketplace competition. For example, an IT system might enable an industry to exploit its oligopolistic pricing structure. Before elaborating upon this issue it would be instructive to consider the nature of perfect and imperfect competition such as oligopolies and monopolies and how prices are determined under these economic models.

Clarence Walton defines perfect competition as a "type of price competition with homogeneous products and perfectly free access of all forms to the market."[11] Thus, in order for true perfect competition to exist, products must have no differentiation of any sort, so buyers are indifferent as to which seller they buy from. Moreover, a perfectly competitive market is one in which neither the buyer nor the seller has the power to influence the price of the commodity being sold or exchanged. Rather, the price is set by the market forces of supply and demand. If there is an abundance of supply and little demand, the price will tend to fall; falling prices will prompt sellers to reduce the supply, and this reduction will eventually lead to an increase in the price. According to Manuel Velasquez, "in a perfectly competitive market prices and quantities always move to what is called the equilibrium point."[12] He goes on to explain that "the equilibrium point is the point at which the amount of goods buyers want to buy exactly equals the amount of goods sellers want to sell, and at which the highest price buyers are willing to pay exactly equals the lowest price sellers are willing to take."[13] At this magical equilibrium point every seller finds a buyer and vice versa. The distinguishing characteristic of pure competition, then, is that the quantity produced and the market price are determined by market forces as they respond to changing consumer demands.

Of course, this ideal can never be actualized. There are some sectors of the economy that approximate perfect competition—agriculture, segments of the retailing industry, some service industries—but there has never been a market that maintains perfectly free access to buyers and sellers with homogeneous products. The model of perfect competition is merely a theoretical construct developed by economists, but it nevertheless teaches us the value of competition and functions as a valuable yardstick by which we can measure noncompetitive markets. It provides a picture of how the market conveys consumer demands to producers and how those

---

[11]Clarence Walton, *Conceptual Foundations of Business* (Homewood, IL: Irwin, 1969), p. 345.

[12]Manuel Velasquez, *Business Ethics: Concepts and Cases*, 2nd ed. (Englewood Cliffs, NJ: Prentice-Hall, 1988), p. 182.

[13]Ibid.

producers respond. For many economists, it represents an approximation of the ideal way that the private enterprise system should function.

One type of noncompetitive market is the opposite extreme of perfect competition: *the unregulated monopoly*. A monopoly is a one-firm industry. Since the monopolist is the only seller, the consumer has no choice but to buy from that seller. Also, there are no substitute products and huge barriers to entry. The monopolist has complete control over prices and is able to restrict output and set the industry price to maximize profits. From the consumer's viewpoint, a monopoly leads to an inefficient allocation of society's resources since the price of the product is too high and its output is too low.

Economists have made a useful distinction between a *natural monopoly*, which exists where the market cannot logically have more than one seller (e.g., an electric utility), and a *predatory monopolist*, which has "attained its dominant position by ruthless price cutting practices in order to 'freeze out' the competition."[14] Natural monopolies such as the phone company and public utilities are heavily regulated. Their prices are usually scrutinized and approved by a commission answerable to the public. On the other hand, the anticompetitive behavior that spawns a predatory monopoly is illegal under U.S. antitrust laws. Although these laws have not been strictly enforced since the early 1980s, blatant monopolistic business abuses can be dealt with decisively within our current legal framework.

A more common form of imperfect competition is an *oligopoly*, wherein the industry is dominated by a few sellers. There are many examples of oligopoly industries in the United States, including the automobile, pharmaceutical, and airline industries. One of the major characteristics of an oligopoly is entry barriers which prevent new sellers from breaking into the industry. Formidable barriers to entry include high capital requirements, differentiated products with loyal customers, the costs of switching to a new seller, and dedicated distribution channels.

An important feature of an oligopolistic market structure is mutual *interdependence*. In contrast to the "pure competitor," who is indifferent to the behavior of other sellers, the ologopolist is quite concerned about the behavior of industry rivals—their pricing policies, product strategy, advertising campaigns, and overall strategic direction. On occasion this interdependence goes beyond curiosity and violates legal and moral standards.

How does this happen? In a highly concentrated oligopoly it is relatively easy for a few firms to act in concert. For example, by explicitly or implicitly agreeing to establish prices at a certain level and to restrict their output, an oligopoly can achieve the same effect as a monopoly. According to Velasquez, "this uniting of forces, together with the barriers to entry that

---

[14]Jim Eggert, *Investigating Microeconomics* (Los Altos, CA: William Kaufmann, 1979), p. 106.

are characteristic of oligopoly industries, can result in the same high prices and low supply levels of monopoly markets."[15] As a consequence, oligopolies can generate huge profits but in the process fail to respect basic economic rights.

Explicit agreements to control prices and restrict competition can be accomplished in various ways. The most blatant type of agreement is *price fixing*. Managers of the major firms meet clandestinely and agree to set their prices at a certain level. This practice is illegal but many corporations over the years have violated price-fixing laws. Recent research has demonstrated that price fixing is most likely to occur in mature industries where there are strong cultural pressures to enforce the anticompetitive norms. Managers in an oligopoly can also decide to control supply by causing artificial shortages (thereby raising the price), establish special selling arrangements whereby the buyer agrees to deal with only certain sellers, or charge different prices to different buyers for the same product (price discrimination). Price discrimination is considered a predatory tactic and hence is illegal.

Tacit, implicit agreements are even more common because they are more difficult to detect and prove in a court of law. Economists consider these indirect price setting mechanisms to be forms of tacit collusion. For example, all firms in the industry may follow the price changes of the industry leader, the leader usually being the dominant corporation with the highest market share. This price setting ensures that each firm will return to its original market share and will also achieve higher profits due to increased prices. Even if there is no industry price leader, firms can engage in tacit collusion by raising and lowering their prices whenever any other firm in the industry does so. Tacit collusion abounds among U.S. oligopolies and currently takes place in the automobile industry, the airline industry, and some of the major tobacco companies.

Regardless of whether prices are determined by explicit or implicit agreements, economists maintain that oligopolistic pricing leads to a measurable decline in social utility. Prices are artificially high and are not determined by the forces of supply and demand, as in perfect competition. Also output is restricted, so consumers do not have an adequate supply of the product or service. Finally, these industries will attract fewer resources, such as investment capital, due to the barriers to entry.

In summary, oligopolies are responsible for several adverse consequences and disutilities for society:

- excess profits for the producers
- misallocation of resources
- a price that is higher than the competitive, market price
- reduced output

---

[15]Ibid., p. 197.

Also, both capital and human resources have less freedom and mobility in an oligopoly market structure.

INFORMATION TECHNOLOGY AND NEW OPPORTUNITIES FOR COLLUSION

Information technology and the increasingly pervasive use of industry-wide information systems have made collusion and tacit price control more feasible than ever. Sophisticated computer networks make exchange of data swifter and more facile, especially in certain oligopolistic markets such as the airline industry. Here information sharing per se has apparently become a form of tacit collusion. To be sure, these new forms of collusion pose major challenges for government agencies, since it is now much easier to reach agreements on prices within an oligopoly and at the same time it is more difficult to prove that the agreement was deliberate and hence illicit.

Computerized collusion involves the reliance on industry-wide networks to set prices. This might be accomplished through various forms of subtle signaling. The process is initiated when one company announces a new price on the network. Other companies may follow suit and change their prices accordingly. They may also use a code to indicate their approval or disapproval of the new arrangement. If the rivals indicate disapproval through a code, the initiating corporation changes its price back to the original level. In this way computer networks can be used to facilitate various forms of price fixing. As one observer noted, these networks represent a powerful tool for collusion: "It's easier to reach agreements. It's easier to detect breaches of an agreement."[16]

The airline industry has recently been accused of this practice but has vehemently denied any wrongdoing. It was alleged that the airlines used a commonly owned computer network operated by Airline Tariff Publishing to communicate price changes and price directions to one another. Airline executives have referred to the practice as a form of "electronic negotiation" or "electronic dialogue." But where does one draw the line between such "negotiation" and illicit collusion?

Another practice apparently pursued by the airline industry with the help of its commonly owned database is announcing fare increases in advance. For example, a major airline might give advance notice to travel agents and customers that it intends to raise its fares on a certain route. Through this "preannouncing," an airline can probably ensure that its fare will be matched by competing airlines.

[16]Asra Q. Nomani, "Airlines May Be Using a Price-Data Network to Lessen Competition," *The Wall Street Journal*, June 28, 1990, p. A1. Reprinted by permission of *The Wall Street Journal*, © 1990 Dow Jones & Company, Inc. All rights reserved worldwide.

Thus, computerized industry-wide information systems have essentially redefined the meaning of antitrust and price-fixing activity by offering new methods of communicating data. No longer do managers need to set up covert meetings in dark, smoked-filled hotel rooms. They can easily achieve the same effect across a computer network.

Electronic communication has elevated the art of "signaling" to new, more sophisticated levels. Michael Porter defines a market signal as "any action by a competitor that provides a direct or indirect indication of its intentions, motives, goals, or internal situation."[17] A signal can be a bluff, an admonition, or an honest indication of a company's intended course of action. Signaling is especially common in the context of oligopolistic competition. However, it is worthwhile raising questions about its ethical propriety, particularly when it is used to facilitate price fixing or tacit collusion.

Government regulators have not kept pace with technological advances and so, as of this writing, anti-trust laws have no explicit provisions to deal with these alleged forms of collusion. Hence the airline industry's predictable response that its activities are perfectly legal and permissible. The case studies at the end of this chapter will allow readers to draw their own conclusions about the morality of the airlines' actions along with the public policy implications of such practices.

There are several observations that need to be made, however. First, the ethical and legal rules prohibiting collusion exist for a worthy social purpose: the preservation of competitive markets. When competition is stifled through collusion and price fixing, there is obviously significant social disutility. As we have noted, consumers are charged exorbitant prices, resources are misallocated, and in the long run smaller competitors are driven from the market. The end result is a higher degree of industry concentration, higher entry barriers, and more powerful firms. Economists and ethicians agree that these will lead to a less competitive economy which will have many adverse consequences for both business and consumers in the United States.

Given these adverse consequences, it is necessary to think through reasonable limits to this type of information sharing. To begin with, the use of cryptic codes and electronic signals should perhaps be questioned when their only purpose is to communicate a reaction to another vendor's announcement of a price change. But how far can companies go to signal competitors about the future direction of prices? Also, when we assess these exchanges of information, we must consider the economic relevance and the intent. Is the company increasing its fare for legitimate reasons or is it simply testing the waters? It's obviously one thing to increase fares and

---

[17]Michael Porter, *Competitive Strategy* (New York: The Free Press, 1980), p. 75. (For more background information about market signals see Chapter 4 of this book).

electronically publish the increase on the Airline Publishing Tariff network, but quite different to use this system deliberately to subvert price competition.

It is evident, therefore, that this new managerial capability raises challenging policy questions for managers and government regulators. Are managers obliged to curtail these activities since they are nothing more than a sophisticated form of price fixing? Or does technology, in effect, change the rules? Are new societal norms and a redefinition of price fixing and collusion necessary? The primary function of an IOS is the sharing of information; if some of that information is sensitive data about pricing, can we realistically expect competitors to ignore such information when they determine their own prices? Finally, who is responsible for determining and articulating the new ground rules that seem to be demanded by this new technology? Should we expect managers to take the initiative or should this be the responsibility of larger regulating bodies?

SUMMARY

We have considered how information technology systems, often called *strategic information systems*, can be used by corporations to achieve sustainable advantage over their competitors. One form of a strategic information system is the interorganizational system (IOS) or information partnership whereby several companies pool their resources to develop a collaborative information system. Such systems transcend the boundaries of an organization or even an industry. These systems can yield many tangible benefits for the sponsoring corporation such as increased revenues through participant fees, increased customer awareness, enhanced image from the "halo effect," and the capacity to attain cumulative marketing information. They also, however, create the opportunity for ethical abuses by the sponsoring or dominant organizations, such as charging exorbitant prices to participants and using biased displays that favor their own organization.

However, the rights of participants in an IOS or shared partnership should be fully respected. A Rawlsian perspective would demand that this arrangement not worsen the lot of the least advantaged participants. An IOS, therefore, should not be used to impair a corporation's opportunity to compete. Moreover, there must be some true proportionality between the participant's contribution and the benefits it receives. If the boundaries of fair play are transgressed, there will be consumer backlash along with an increased likelihood of government regulation.

Finally we focused on the use of an IOS and computer networks to engage in collusion and subtle forms of price fixing. Price fixing is a particular problem in ologopolies, that is, firms dominated by a few sellers, where tacit collusion has been a persistent problem. When price fixing does occur, there are negative ramifications for consumers and society, since prices are often too high and output is too low. Collusion through electronic networks is a new phenomenon, and it is difficult to establish that such pricing arrangements are deliberate and illegal. It is alleged that the airline industry uses a commonly owned computer network operated by Airline Tariff Publishing to communicate price changes to one another. When assessing the legality and ethical propriety of such practices, one must consider the intentions of the corporation initiating the price change along with the economic relevance of such a change. It is likely that we will need new guidelines and laws that will redefine the meaning of price fixing and collusion in the information age of networks and information partnerships.

CASES FOR DISCUSSION

Introduction

The axis of discussion in this chapter has been the use of information technology to enhance a corporation's competitive position. The corporations in both of these cases have encountered substantial criticism for their reliance on IT as a competitive tool. The *Airline Reservation Systems* case chronicles the use of a famous IOS to achieve leverage against the competition. To what extent have United and American Airlines behaved irresponsibly in their deployment of these systems? The second case also concerns the airline industry. It describes the way in which electronic dialogue allegedly allowed the airlines to engage in price fixing. This case focuses acutely on the following question: has the information age redefined the meaning of antitrust activity, and, if so, are new ethical norms or laws necessary?

CASE 3.1

Airline Reservation Systems

One of the most successful but controversial industry-wide computer applications has been the reservation systems used by all the major airlines in the United States. The two most prominent computerized reservation systems are American Airlines *SABRE* system and the United Airlines *APOLLO* system. They represent a prime example of how information technology can impact an entire industry, and they also raise important ethical questions about the potential for abuses.

Early History   Automated reservations systems in the airline industry have a long history dating back to the rather primitive in-house systems
of the late 1960s and early 1970s. Initially the data in these systems consisted of passenger names and limited flight information, but the airlines
quickly added new functionality, including pricing data, advance check-in,
and even the ability to generate boarding passes. In 1963, when *SABRE* was
introduced, "it processed data related to 85,000 phone calls, 40,000 con-
firmed reservations, and 20,000 ticket sales."[18]

In the late 1970s several airlines, including American and United,
made these in-house systems widely available to travel agents through
leasing arrangements. They have since become indispensable to these
agents, because they present a clear and comprehensive picture of all flight
information, including schedule and pricing options to any destination.

The practice of disseminating airline reservation systems beyond
company boundaries and into the industry distribution system is known as
retail automation. It began very slowly, initially involving only a few participants. In 1967 American first placed its *SABRE* reservation system in a limited number of agencies and commercial accounts. But the situation
changed when the industry's major players were themselves caught up in
the throes of deregulation.[19]

Deregulation   The Airline Deregulation Act of 1978 represented a
major watershed for the airline industry. Indeed, the reverberations of
deregulation are still being felt throughout this dynamic industry. The primary objective of this act was to help consumers by cutting airline prices
without cutting service. One consequence of deregulation was an intensifi-
cation of aggressive competition—lowered prices, new routes, and so forth.
With the elimination of prescribed rates set by the Civil Aeronautics Board,
airlines began competing with an array of discount fares, and the pricing
structure became exceedingly complex. A route such as Philadelphia to St.
Louis might have multiple fares depending upon how far in advance the
traveler booked the reservation, whether the traveler was staying over on a
Saturday night, and so forth.

All of these changes had a powerful impact on the evolution of airline
reservation systems. These systems now maintained millions of different
fares; according to recent estimates, for example, there are 45 million fares
in the *SABRE* database. Also airlines changed their fares frequently, sometimes daily. As a result, travel agents became even more dependent on

[18]Max D. Hopper, "Rattling SABRE — New Ways to Compete on Information," *Harvard Business Review*, May-June (1990), p. 120.

[19]Duncan G. Copeland and James L. McKenney, "Airline Reservations Systems: Lessons from History," *MIS Quarterly*, September 1988, pp 353–72.

computerized reservation systems to keep track of this volatile data. According to one analysis, "As the nature of passenger inquiries changed from simple seat availability to price shopping, real time access to the carriers' volatile schedules and fares became a necessity for travel agents."[20] In response to these inexorable demands, American and United Airlines added major new functionality to their systems, including improved billing procedures and new accounting features.

As these systems developed in complexity and size, they became much more expensive to create and maintain. Also it became prohibitively expensive for smaller airlines to develop their own systems that would be utilized by travel agents. Thus, airlines such as Frontier, Braniff, Republic, and others were at a serious disadvantage in competing for the attention of travel agents, who booked far more flights than the airlines themselves.

Competitive Advantage By the early 1980s American and United clearly dominated the computerized travel agency markets, with market shares of 41 percent and 39 percent respectively. Other major airlines such as Delta, Eastern, and TWA developed smaller systems, and many airlines could afford no system at all. By establishing a strong foothold in this market, American and United reaped substantial rewards, primarily higher revenues due to increased business. The *APOLLO* and *SABRE* systems did list other flights, but the listings of those flights were usually not prominently displayed, so travel agents who used the system were more apt to book on United or American.

In addition, *SABRE* and *APOLLO* generated fees from other airlines for all flights they booked on these systems. They also received leasing fees from travel agencies and additional fees from airlines that purchased services from these systems. For adopting these systems, travel agencies were paid premiums of up to $500,000 plus extra commission, in addition to free use of the system for three years, free staff training, and other incentives. These extra rewards further solidified the bond between travel agents and the two airlines.

There were other advantages to American and United as well. For example, both had exclusive access to sales data on passengers and bookings. In short, *SABRE* and *APOLLO* were a source of valuable corporate information. According to one observer, "American's marketers used information gleaned from the *SABRE* database to respond rapidly to the strategic moves of rivals, employing such stratagems as bonus incentives, lower fares, or scheduling changes to counter their actions."[21] Further, a rival's

---

[20]D. G. Copeland, "Note on the Airline Reservation Systems, Part II" (Cambridge, MA: Harvard Business School Publications, 1988), p. 8.
[21]Charles Wiseman, *Strategic Information Systems* (Homewood, IL: Irwin, 1988), p. 20.

change had to be entered on *SABRE* in advance, and consequently American had ample time and opportunity to develop its counterattack.

Clearly, then, *SABRE* and *APOLLO* gave their respective carriers notable leverage over their competitors. The main strategic value of these reservation systems was their capacity to give American and United Airlines control over the travel agencies, which are in effect the distribution channels for the industry. Here, then, is a classic example of information technology's impact on the competitive structure and economics of a major industry.

The Cohost Program   Small and moderate-sized airlines that could not afford to develop their own computerized reservation systems had the option of becoming a cohost. For a fee, the flight information of these carriers was given preferential treatment. American Airlines first offered the cohost option in 1978 and signed up five carriers within a year. It is important to note that the "cohost program was a way of extending *SABRE*'s reach to markets served by United, thereby locking in travel agents and slowing the expansion of *APOLLO*."[22]

Obviously, cohosting had advantages for these other carriers. They could, for example, get better access to travel agents and customers through clear, unbiased display of their flight data. They could also purchase reports providing at least some of the competitive information available to the two host carriers.

Moreover, cohost status was a means of thwarting the moves of a competitor in one's territory. Thus, Delta Airlines became a cohost on United's *Apollo* in order to protect its markets in the southeast from the encroachments of American Airlines through the *SABRE* system. This was a market not covered well by United, so travel agents using *Apollo* were inclined to choose Delta's flights since they were given preferential treatment on the reservation system.

Anticompetitive Practices   It has been alleged that both American and United Airlines misused their reservation systems to restrain and inhibit competition among their rivals. Their practices were particularly harmful to minor players in the industry such as Frontier Airlines, a small carrier with a hub in Denver. Frontier flew mainly in the southwest and its routes often competed directly with those of United Airlines, which also had a hub at the Denver Stapleton Airport. Frontier maintained that the *APOLLO* Reservation System was manipulated in such a way that it gave powerful United Airlines an unfair competitive advantage. In testimony before the Civil Aeronautics Board, Frontier officials articulated the following charges against United:

[22]Copeland and McKenney, "Airline Reservation Systems," p. 361.

United Airlines discriminated against some carriers with whom it competed most directly. As a result, for over two years United steadfastly refused to allow Frontier cohost status.

Even after Frontier achieved this coveted cohost status, United's screens were still programmed with bias toward its own flights. For example, a travel agent requesting a list of flights between Denver and Los Angeles would see the United flights as the first and boldest to appear on the screen, even though they might not be the least expensive flights.

APOLLO gave United Airlines access to detailed, sensitive information about competitors' flight data. United generated reports by agency and airline indicating the total number and percentage of passengers booked for a specific time period. This information, which gave United valuable insights into market share, the "performance" of travel agencies, and so forth, was not available to cohosts such as Frontier.[23]

Frontier expressed many other charges against United, its main rival, but these were the most salient and serious. The core of Frontier's complaints was this continuing bias and the exercise of "monopoly power" over critical industry-wide flight information.

The U.S. Justice Department responded to Frontier's complaints by conducting an investigation and by filing antitrust charges against United and American. The Justice Department was most concerned that the *Apollo* and *Sabre* systems had been used to discriminate against smaller airlines. It also criticized American and United for their policy of "noncompetitive pricing" for access to their respective systems. According to the *Wall Street Journal*:

> The Justice Department recommended that the CAB (Civil Aeronautics Board) issue rules cracking down on alleged anticompetitive reservation systems. It urged rules aimed at guaranteeing more competition from other systems offered by non-airlines: equal computer loading, modification and updating of schedule, fare or seat availability information for other airlines programmed into the computer, and nondiscriminatory computer display of flight and fare data for each carrier.[24]

In November 1984 eleven domestic airlines including Frontier filed a lawsuit against American and United, charging that these airlines "possessed a monopoly in electronic booking of airline seats and that they used it to limit competition."[25] The suit alleged that American and United virtually coerced travel agents to give them preference when booking flights.

---

[23]U.S. Civil Aeronautics Board, "Report to Congress on Computer Reservation Systems," Docket 41207, 1983.

[24]Albert Karr and Robert Taylor, "American Air, United accused on Reservations," *The Wall Street Journal*, November 18, 1983, p. B1. Reprinted by permission of *The Wall Street Journal*, © 1983 Dow Jones & Company, Inc. All rights reserved worldwide.

[25]Copeland, "Note on the Airline Reservation Systems," p. 11.

American and United Airlines responded to these allegations by pointing to their substantial investment in *SABRE* and *APOLLO*. Executives from both organizations pointed out that they assumed great risks and financial burden to create these systems, and hence they deserved a reasonable return on their investment as a reward for taking that risk and having the foresight to be pioneers in the computerized reservation business. United Airlines, for example, invested $250 million to achieve this technological edge, while its rivals (such as Frontier Airlines) invested very little and clearly missed the boat by failing to capitalize on the indisputable strategic importance of these systems.

Ethical Issues   Aside from the complex legal issues in this case and the question of whether antitrust laws have been violated, there are difficult moral issues as well. The most salient ones revolve around notions of fairness and equity. United and American appeared to control not merely an efficient reservation system, but an essential facility for effective competition. What is proper behavior in the use of an "essential facility"? Is such control justifiable from an ethical standpoint? Where does one draw the line in competing with one's rivals, particularly in an industry as vigorously competitive as the airline industry? Indeed, in a recent interview Robert Crandall, the chairman of American Airlines, observed that "the industry's unique economics drives us all to engage in the most intense and savage competition found in any business I know of." This fierce rivalry and the nature of the airline business make these questions even more difficult to resolve.[26]

Questions

1. How do you assess the claim that Frontier Airlines "got what it deserved" by its lack of foresight and failure to invest in reservation system technology?
2. Given the intensely competitive environment and the economics of this industry were the practices of United and American aggressive or were they unfair and anticompetitive?
3. Should we accept the position that "anything goes" in the struggle for competitive advantage? If not, what are the boundaries of fair play and the ethical limits of competition?
4. Do you agree with the position that competitors are also stakeholders and deserving of ethical consideration when corporations are making strategic or tactical decisions?

---

[26]Calvin Sims, "Behind Those Bizarre Air Fares," *The New York Times*, June 14, 1992, section 3, p. 13. Copyright © 1992 by The New York Times Company. Reprinted by permission.

CASE 3.2

Computerized Collusion in the Airline Industry

Electronic Price Fixing Allegations of price fixing in the airline industry are certainly nothing new. Major airline carriers have been under intense scrutiny for this offense for some time. In 1982, for example, the Chairman and Chief Executive Officer of American Airlines, Robert L. Crandall, was taped encouraging the president of rival Braniff Airlines to raise its fares by 20 percent. The charges were settled in 1985 through a consent decree in which the company neither admitted nor denied any culpability.

It appears, however, that most of the major airlines have discovered a novel and highly effective way to "set" their prices. At least this is the claim of the U.S. Justice Department. In 1990 the Department's attorneys initiated still another investigation into possible antitrust violations in this volatile and troubled industry. It was prompted by the airlines' use of a commonly owned computer network managed by the Airline Tariff Publishing Company (ATP), in Washington, DC. Through this system, airlines communicate about 170,000 fare changes a day to their extensive network of travel agents. These changes are stored in a central repository, from where they can be copied by airlines into their own reservation systems (such as American Airlines' *SABRE*). ATP's on-line database thus becomes a clearinghouse of fare information and modifications.

According to the Justice Department, the airlines have misused this sophisticated communications network to collude on prices. Obviously, this is accomplished merely by virtue of the fact that the airlines have immediate access to each other's price changes even before these changes reach the public. If Delta Airlines, for example, were to announce a price decrease on its Atlanta to Denver route, Continental and United would know immediately and could therefore act accordingly if they so desired.

Moreover, according to a report in *The Wall Street Journal*, these fare changes sometimes contain codes that are implicit signals to other airlines:

> The most common—and perhaps most questionable—discussion between airlines is played out like this: Carrier A, often a smaller operator such as Midway Airlines or America West, attempts to boost its business by lowering ticket prices. It enters lower fares in the industry's computer system. In response, Carrier B, the dominant carrier at the affected airport, not only matches the new fares but lowers them in other markets that are served by Carrier A.
>
> Carrier B may also attach special codes to its new fares to get its message across. Pricing executives say some carriers have been known to prefix new fares with the letters "FU" to indicate an indelicate imperative. The end result is that Carrier A often cancels its reduction, depriving consumers of a lower fare. This pattern has occurred many times.[27]

---

[27]Asra Nomani, "Airlines May Be Using a Price-Data Network to Lessen Competition," *The Wall Street Journal*, June 28, 1990, pp. A1, A8. Reprinted by permission of *The Wall Street Journal*, © 1990 Dow Jones & Company, Inc. All rights reserved worldwide.

This fictional exchange between the two carriers occurs within the context of a constant dialogue about pricing decisions on the ATP computer system. Some individuals, including many airline executives, regard this type of communication quite benignly; they see it as a subtle form of "electronic negotiation" or innocuous electronic dialogue. Others maintain that these practices are more nefarious since they go beyond the bounds of negotiation and amount to "computerized collusion."

Antitrust Laws   Antitrust legislation makes it illegal for companies to engage in price-setting activities. The laws are especially severe and enforceable for overt and explicit collusion. If the government can prove that executives or their representatives met openly or secretly to discuss and set prices, the U.S. Justice Department would in all likelihood vigorously prosecute such a case on the basis of the Sherman Antitrust Act.

The law is more difficult to enforce, however, when there is tacit collusion or subtle cooperation among company executives who establish prices. For example, if all firms in an oligopoly enter into an unspoken agreement to follow the price leadership of the dominant firm, price fixing or collusion may be difficult to prove in a court of law. To be sure, this use of computer technology to share price information adds to the confusion and ambiguity, since it is not explicitly dealt with in antitrust litigation.

Collusion has been outlawed because it undermines the competitive system in America and has a negative impact on the buyer who usually has to pay higher prices.

Preannouncing Price Increases   Another controversial practice of the airlines is announcing price increases in advance. Most carriers routinely preannounce their fare increases on ATP, sometimes as much as two months in advance. This practice will give the consumer advance notice that the price of a certain fare will rise, but it can also guarantee that the price will be matched by other airlines so that the initiating carrier is not left standing alone with this higher fare. If other carriers signal their displeasure with the increase, there will most likely be a rollback in the price. *The Wall Street Journal* quotes John Timmons, the minority counsel on the U.S. aviation subcommittee, about this practice: "It's an abuse of the system. The information age has redefined antitrust. We don't need Mr. Smith to call Mr. Jones."[28]

Considerable empirical evidence suggests that when such preannouncing is used by a particular airline, its rivals react very quickly to match the proposed fare increase. For example, in August 1989 United proposed a $20 fare increase for most of its Chicago flights. The increases were announced through the ATP system in August but would not become

[28]Ibid.

effective until September. American Airlines, one of United's fiercest competitors especially in the lucrative Chicago market, almost immediately matched the proposed increases with a comparable price hike that would also take effect in September.

It is alleged, therefore, that airlines are using the ATP database as a vehicle to control prices and especially as a means of enticing one's rivals to increase prices. Thus the central issue of this dispute: Is this a legitimate use of this industry-wide database or a clever means of subverting the industry's competitive forces?

The Justice Department Investigation   In March 1992 the Justice Department began the process of deposing the airlines on these alleged price-fixing maneuvers. In December 1992 it filed an antitrust suit "that accused the eight largest American airlines of using a computerized reservation system to fix air fares."[29] Two of the accused airlines, United and USAir, agreed through a consent decree to terminate the practice of electronically communicating future fare increases.

However, the other airlines named in the lawsuit (American, Delta, Northwest, Continental, T.W.A. and Alaska Airlines) consistently insisted that they were not culpable of any wrongdoing. According to an American Airlines spokesperson, "We clearly think this is baseless. We think there is no collusion going on. We think they're going to go through this exercise and find nothing out of the ordinary."[30]

Representatives for the other airlines also maintained that the Justice Department was merely wasting the taxpayers' time and money and should be pursuing real culprits who are truly flouting antitrust laws. They defended the practice of preannouncing by arguing that the airlines announce future air fares for the benefit of consumers and not for their competitors. Further, they were quick to remind Justice Department officials that this industry lost $6 billion in the previous two years. Furthermore, this alleged computerized collusion has not resulted in a higher fare structure in the industry nor in any appreciable improvements in profits.

It remains to be seen, of course, whether computerized collusion will spread to other industries, especially those with volatile pricing activity. Will this practice of the airlines establish a precedent and will electronic dialogue become a pervasive method of price fixing in other oligopolistic industries? If so, it may be necessary to modify antitrust regulations and redefine the meaning of tacit collusion.

---

[29]Martin Tolchin, "U.S. Sues 8 Airlines over Fares," *The New York Times*, December 22, 1992, p. D1. Copyright © 1992 by The New York Times Company. Reprinted by permission.

[30]Asra Nomani, "Airlines Claim Inquiry on Fares Is Unwarranted," *The Wall Street Journal*, March 19, 1992, p. A3. Reprinted by permission of *The Wall Street Journal*, © 1992 Dow Jones & Company, Inc. All rights reserved worldwide.

Questions

1. In your opinion, have the actions of these airlines violated the norms and ideals of fair and open competition?
2. Is signaling customers and competitors about future price changes really unethical? Why or why not?
3. If you accept the conclusion that the airlines have overstepped the boundaries of fair play, how would you establish the parameters of responsible electronic dialogue?

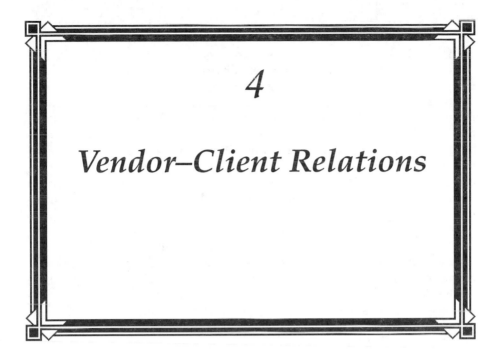

4

Vendor–Client Relations

Whereas the previous chapter focused on anticompetitive practices *within* an industry, this chapter will consider intra-industry conflict, specifically the problems that can arise between hardware, software, and other IT vendors and their various customers. Because of the pervasiveness and indispensability of information technology applications, the computer industry is virtually unique in the powerful leverage that it can exercise over its customers. Clients with sophisticated applications can find themselves at the mercy of these vendors as they wait for fixes to software flaws or product updates. Obviously, untimely delays, defective products, and broken promises about future product releases can cause havoc in a client's operations. Consider, for example, the disastrous effects of accounting software that does not track funds properly.

To some extent the power of these vendors emanates from the complexity of IT products and the incredibly rapid pace of technological change. These factors create the need for considerable post-sales support and product updating along with the need for forthrightness about the future direction and evolution of a vendor's products. When customers invest in a computer system, software, or network products, they are also investing in the vendor's capacity to provide uninterrupted, reliable service and to maintain the product's ongoing usefulness.

To be sure, most businesses confront the array of choices and conflicting standards available today with considerable trepidation. There are numerous hardware platforms, operating systems, software packages, and user interfaces from which to choose. For example, it is difficult for information system managers to determine what machine to use for a given application. Can smaller decentralized PC LAN's be set up or is a central mainframe system required? These and other difficult questions pose a real challenge for managers responsible for making the best use of an organization's hardware resources. In addition, choices among software packages and networks can be especially perplexing since there are still many different standards and few truly "open systems." The wrong choice could be quite costly and may even cause irreparable damage to a company's information strategy (not to mention the manager's own career).

Clients are therefore heavily dependent on software and hardware suppliers for accurate and candid information along with sound, objective advice. This dependence creates special obligations for the vendor to be conscientious about advising its existing clients and its prospective customers. In this chapter we will consider these obligations and attempt to sketch out a general picture of the responsible information technology vendor.

THE CONTRACTUAL THEORY

To appreciate the duty of the information technology vendor to its client base we must first consider the general obligation of any seller in a free market economy. A useful model for expressing this duty is the contractual relationship between the seller and the customer. According to this view, the relationship between a vendor and its customer is based on an implicit or explicit contract, and the vendor's moral obligations are firmly grounded in this contract. It is important to underline that in the absence of an *explicit*, written contract, there is still a certain tacit understanding between the buyer and seller which constitutes an *implicit* contract.

Thus the customer pays a prescribed sum of money and in return receives a product or service with certain features and functions. Through this transaction both parties enter into this contractual relationship. This contract is a "free agreement" that imposes on both parties the duty to comply with its terms. In addition to the explicit terms of the contract there are implicit ones, which impose "secondary moral constraints."[1] It follows that if a contract is really a free agreement, neither party can be coerced. Moreover, a valid contract implies that the consumer has full knowledge of

---

[1]Manuel Velasquez, *Business Ethics: Concepts and Cases*, 2nd ed. (Englewood Cliffs, NJ: Prentice-Hall, 1988), pp. 274–75.

what he or she is getting. This means that there cannot be any misrepresentation about the product features, the warranty, service commitments, and so forth. According to this perspective, then, it is incumbent upon the vendor to honor the explicit terms of the contract along with these secondary constraints which include avoiding concealment or misrepresentation and eschewing any undue influence or coercion.

One can provide many ethical justifications for keeping a promise or contract. Moralists from Kant to Rawls would concur that such agreements cannot be taken lightly. According to Kant's moral framework as described in Chapter 2, one has a duty to abide by a contract under all circumstances since breaking a contract is a practice that cannot be universalized. If contract breaking did become a universal practice, there would obviously be no more contracts!

Rawls too argues for the sanctity of contracts, noting that promises or covenants exist to guarantee the stability of "small scale schemes of cooperation, or a particular pattern of transactions."[2] In these situations one deliberately puts oneself under an obligation to perform a certain task in exchange for the other party's obligation to execute his or her responsibility—a quid pro quo arrangement. Each party to the contract is confident that the other has a sense of justice and will make every effort to live up to the terms of the agreement. According to Rawls:

> Without this mutual confidence nothing is accomplished by uttering words. In a well-ordered society, however, this knowledge is present: when its members give promises there is a reciprocal recognition of their intention to put themselves under an obligation and a shared rational belief that this obligation is honored.[3]

When contracts are violated, then, there are serious moral consequences, since this violation not only harms the victim but also diminishes the level of trust necessary for any individuals to make future contracts and promises. Such behavior violates common standards of justice and fairness and threatens the stability of vitally important cooperative arrangements without which commercial transactions would be virtually impossible.

PRODUCT SUPPORT

We have noted that most IT systems require considerable post-sales support and ongoing product maintenance. This is especially true for software products that are at the center of the information technology web. In exchange for this important service, the customer normally pays an annual maintenance or licensing fee, which usually entitles the customer

---

[2]John Rawls, *A Theory of Justice* (Cambridge, MA: Harvard University Press, 1971), p. 346.
[3]Ibid., p. 347.

to telephone assistance as well as new releases or product updates. These releases or updates will probably include some limited new functionality along with fixes to any defects or "bugs" that have been uncovered. Users count heavily on this support, especially when their hardware systems are upgraded, since the software often will need a corresponding upgrade.

If, however, the vendor is taken over by a competitor, encounters financial difficulties, or goes bankrupt, this ongoing support will likely be threatened or even abruptly terminated. Under such circumstances what are the rights of users and the correlative obligations of vendors? Do the customers who have purchased expensive IT products have a right to the continued usefulness and efficacy of those products? Or is this simply a matter of *caveat emptor* (let the buyer beware)?

Consider, for example, sophisticated software products such as an expensive database management system (DBMS) and 4GL (fourth-generation language) for a mainframe or minicomputer. A client who purchases such a package will also need to make a substantial investment in time and money to learn the intricacies of the system and to build its various applications. The database will ultimately be filled with important data and the system will probably support high-level transaction processing. It will generate reports and undoubtedly provide information that is essential to the company's operations. What happens if the vendor of this software package goes out of business? Now there is no support for this product and no upgrades that would incorporate bug fixes or interfaces to other new technologies.

Serious problems could result from this discontinuation of upgrades. If, for instance, the product runs on version 6 of IBM's MVS operating system and IBM upgrades to version 7, there is no guarantee that the DBMS and 4GL will work with this new operating system without some modifications. With the vendor out of business, the customer now is faced with a painful dilemma: either abandon the software package or don't upgrade the hardware operating system. If the hardware is not upgraded, problems can arise for other software packages run on this system; also, the client could encounter more serious difficulties if IBM eventually refuses to provide support for older versions of the MVS operating system.

Despite the gravity of this issue, it is virtually impossible for vendors to guarantee the ongoing utility of their products, since they do not always have control over their destiny. They can, however, take certain steps to minimize the likelihood that the product will lose its usefulness. These steps might include the following actions or policies:

- In the case of bankruptcy or other grave problems, software vendors should routinely make source code[4] available to their customers. Many companies already follow this policy by putting the source code in an

[4]Source code consists of a computer program's statements written in a high-level programming language such as COBOL, C, or PASCAL.

escrow account with instructions that it be given or sold to customers only if support is totally discontinued. The availability of source code will enable at least some customers to fix bugs, adapt the software to new hardware upgrades, and so forth.

- Vendors must be candid about their future prospects; customers have a right to know about the essentials of the firm's financial condition so that they can assess the probability that the company will be around to support its product in the long run. This information is especially critical for private companies whose financial data are not easily accessible. The requirement of "full disclosure" under the contractual theory would seem to demand that relevant and reasonable financial information be revealed so customers can gauge the potential life span of the product they are purchasing.
- Vendors must make ongoing product support a major issue if they are negotiating as a victim in a takeover or as a partner to a merger. They must zealously protect the rights of their customers for continued support and ongoing product usefulness.
- If it becomes necessary to discontinue maintenance support, IT vendors should provide customers with one to two years' notice of their intention (most contracts stipulate a 30-day notice, but this seems inadequate).

In short, then, honesty and sincere commitment will go a long way to fulfill the vendor's implicit contractual obligations in this difficult area. Clearly, communication that includes prospective information is really the key to ethical and responsible behavior.

THE PROBLEM OF VAPORWARE

A pervasive problem among vendors of high tech computer products has been the tradition of promoting and selling products before they are really ready for the marketplace. Many companies have announced new products long before actual release. In extreme cases, some products exist for years only as press releases. Such mythical products have become known in the industry as *vaporware*. For our purposes, the category of vaporware will also include real products that are brought to market prematurely, often without adequate testing and preparation, including a sufficient infrastructure for supporting the new product; customer support personnel and others in the organization must have adequate training in order to provide a reasonable level of phone support and other assistance to the customer base. Thus, vaporware includes products that are preannounced too far in advance or brought to market prematurely.

There is certainly a plethora of examples of vaporware, but one of the most notorious cases involved Hogan Systems, a producer of mainframe software for the commercial banking industry. When Hogan went public in the early 1980s, it quickly became one of Wall Street's rising stars and, in order to preserve this reputation, the company became obsessed with meeting analysts' expectations for rapid growth. Its entire focus was on the next quarter's profits. In its haste to generate more revenues, Hogan brought to market a program designed to automate the extensive paperwork in documenting a loan. Unfortunately, this program was incomplete and had serious defects due to inadequate testing. Moreover, the company had not yet established a proper support mechanism; hence customers could not get their questions answered and their problems resolved. Yet the company advertised a product of high quality with superior service. It deceived its customers into thinking that they were buying a quality product that had been thoroughly tested and for which an adequate level of service was readily available. As Laura Nash observed about this company, "its failure to achieve quality and take orders anyway was both deceptive and exploiting customers' trust."[5]

Once customers uncovered these problems, they delayed payment to Hogan; consequently its profits plummeted. A new CEO, George McTavish, who came on board shortly after this fiasco, helped overcome Hogan's tarnished image by shipping more reliable products and making the customer support organization an autonomous division within Hogan. McTavish's efforts were not in vain, and after this debacle the company signed a lucrative contract with IBM. Fortunately, the damage Hogan suffered from shipping defective software was not irreparable, but other companies that have engaged in similar practices have not always been so fortunate.

More recently, Apple Computer was sued by a group of shareholders who alleged that several officers of the company made misleading statements about a new disk drive in a company press release. Apple was promoting a new floppy disk drive called "Twiggy," and, according to the press releases, the drive exhibited far better data integrity than other high-density drives. However, according to internal company documents which were released at the trial, Apple executives knew of serious problems with these disk drives at the time of the announcement. They had shown a very high failure rate during a series of quality assurance tests. Apple began to ship the drives with its Lisa computer but later decided to abandon them in favor of smaller disk drives made by Sony. When Apple announced this decision, the company's stock quickly plunged by more than $8 a share.

The problem in this case was that Apple executives knew of the difficulties but never mentioned them in the press releases. They were also aware that the release date for the drives might need to be extended in order to correct the problems. Hence their statements in the press release were deceptive and misleading. A California jury returned a verdict in favor of the shareholders, but as of this writing the case was still under appeal.

---

[5]Laura Nash, *Good Intentions Aside* (Cambridge, MA: Harvard Business School Press, 1990), p. 143.

The Apple case raises several vexing but critical questions about press releases and new product announcements. How certain does the company have to be about the release date or about the product's initial quality when it is making product announcements? Products have the highest failure rate right after they are first released. A profile of the typical product failure rate is presented in Figure 4.1. As one can see, it is shaped like a "bathtub curve" with higher failure rates in the first and third stages. The third stage is irrelevant for software products, which do not wear out. But as the figure illustrates, many products do fail shortly after they are released because they have defects that haven't been worked out or are not uncovered in even the most extensive QA (quality assurance) testing. Thus one might argue that Twiggy did live up to the norms for new products. On the other hand, the company must make a good-faith effort to ensure that the product's initial quality is as high as possible. Apple executives must have suspected that many drives would fail during the warranty period, so their upbeat press releases were misleading to stockholders and consumers. But given the difficulty of determining the quality of many IT products, the question still remains: How much certainty must companies have about a product's quality and viability before that product is announced and brought to the market?

There are countless other examples of vaporware. Indeed, this practice has become almost routine in the software industry, even among some of its major players. For example, Lotus has been heavily criticized for regularly preannouncing its new products. According to a report in *The Wall Street Journal*, "Lotus...was known for announcing products as much as a

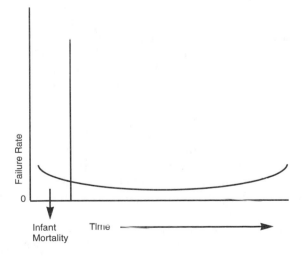

Figure 4.1

year before they were ready for sale, freezing some market segments as customers waited for the promised programs."[6]

Vaporware can take many forms, on a wide spectrum ranging from misleading and exaggerated advertising to the introduction of products that are not ready for the marketplace, but perhaps the most common problem is preannouncing. Products are frequently announced even though design, coding, and testing of the new product have not been completed, often before the products have entered beta testing (i.e., selective customer testing of new products before they are sold to the general public). The reasons are complex, but the primary intention of most companies is to distract a customer's interest in a competitor's products. In order to win over customers, companies will imply the imminence of certain features and functionality. For example, if a vendor begins selling a new software product with many exciting new features, a competitor might announce that its new version of this software has the same features and will be available very soon, even though the product is still in the design stage. In this way they can convince some customers that they shouldn't "jump ship" to a competitor but instead should wait for the new release.

The repercussions of this behavior have been very serious for customers and vendors alike. Among customers this practice has exacerbated the confusion that already plagues this industry. Moreover, it has attenuated trust in vendors' claims and undoubtedly interfered with future transactions. Customers are often not sure which products are real and worth waiting for and which are illusory, perhaps months or even years away from being completed. Also, this practice can be quite harmful and costly to clients. For example, they might be delaying the implementation of important business applications pending an expected new release, which doesn't arrive. Such delays may adversely impact the firm's efficiency, its ability to control costs, and certainly the careers of MIS executives who were responsible for the decision to wait for this new product.

There are, of course, some businesspeople and others who would find no special problem with these practices. In his famous article "Is Business Bluffing Ethical?" Albert Carr argues that bluffing and deception in business are acceptable forms of behavior. He compares the intensely competitive business environment to a poker game, in which bluffing is an essential factor and is expected by the other players. Likewise in business, an executive must be prepared to bluff on certain occasions, and others must have the skill to distinguish a bluff from the truth. According to Carr, "...from time to time every businessman, like every poker player, is offered a choice between certain loss or bluffing within the legal rules of the game.

---

[6]John R. Wilke, "Software Firms Unite to Form Policing Group," *The Wall Street Journal*, October 10, 1990, p. B1. Reprinted by permission of *The Wall Street Journal*, © 1990 Dow Jones & Company, Inc. All rights reserved worldwide.

If he is not resigned to losing, if he wants to rise in his company and indus-try, then in such a crisis he will bluff and bluff hard."[7]

One could certainly argue that preannouncing IT products, using false release dates, and exaggerating a product's capability are all forms of bluff-ing, a necessary aspect of doing business in this aggressive, volatile industry. If we accept Carr's poker game analogy, vaporware is similar to a shrewd move in a poker game. But are Carr's arguments really tenable and does this analogy make sense? Can bluffing be rationalized as Carr suggests?

For many reasons the analogy of business to a poker game seems at best problematic. To begin with, in a poker game every participant knows that anyone at the poker table can and will bluff at any time, but this understanding does not exist in business. Businesspeople, under normal circumstances, expect the truth from their suppliers, customers, and col-leagues. Otherwise, normal business transactions would be virtually impossible. Moreover, whereas deception and bluffing clearly enhance the game of poker and make it more exciting for the participants, they serve to diminish trust in the corporate environment and hence inhibit the effective functioning of organizations.

Thus, vaporware in all its guises must be considered a form of decep-tion which cannot be justified as an acceptable way of doing business. Vaporware is quite harmful to its hapless victims since it can be seriously disruptive to the normal functioning of a business operation. Also, it erodes the level of trust which is the basis for all individual and corporate transactions.

Finally, it seems evident that the deception involved in vaporware is a violation of the implicit contract between vendor and customer. Recall that this contract calls for reasonable full disclosure so that the buyer can enter into the transaction with the right degree of freedom and knowledge. Full disclosure would unquestionably require that a company be conscien-tious about the information it reveals about its products, that it be honest in announcing release dates and in discussing the status of a new product. The information might also need to include the company's estimation of the product's initial quality. The company should also avoid the hyperbole that often obfuscates the facts about a product and ends up bemusing the customer. As one high-tech vendor pointed out, "The oldest marketing technique in the world is to create confusion if you're losing."[8] By leading the marketplace with new product announcements and proposals, compa-nies that have fallen behind in technology seek to buy more time. But often such practices violate the basic contract between seller and buyer and, in the long run, damage a vendor's integrity, credibility, and reputation.

[7]Albert Carr, "Is Business Bluffing Ethical?" *Harvard Business Review*, January–February 1968, p. 153.
[8]"Computer Confusion," *Business Week*, June 10, 1991, p. 75.

How, then, can companies be more responsible in this sphere of activity? First, a clear distinction should be made between a *product announcement* and a *statement of future direction*. Directional information might include a company's long-range strategic, R&D plans for future products and enhancements, but it should be made very explicit that these are general planning statements only. Such information can give consumers valuable insights into a vendor's long-range strategy and facilitate their own long-term planning.

But IT vendors should clearly differentiate such statements of direction from a product announcement. In addition, there should be firm guidelines for making official product announcements that include the release date. *Technological viability* would be an appropriate guideline. For example, a software product would be considered "viable" if it has been successfully designed, coded, and thoroughly tested and is ready for shipment to selected customers for beta testing. Similar criteria could be used for hardware products. Only when the product has passed through these development stages should the company be allowed to announce a release date and initiate its sales and marketing campaigns. The point is that formal product announcements should be made as late in the product development cycle as possible, since the earlier they are made, the greater the chances of slippage in the schedule and the more likely the release date will have to be revised. As we have indicated, the inception of beta site testing seems to be a reasonable benchmark for such announcements.

Obviously, this state of technological viability is somewhat subjective and difficult to determine. Nevertheless, responsible vendors and industry trade groups should seek to work out more precise definitions, taking into account special factors that might apply to a particular industry or product.

If information technology vendors sincerely seek to differentiate their statements about future direction from product announcements, their customers will no longer have to wonder which products or capabilities are real and which are years from realization. The result will be a well-informed customer base and an improved relationship between vendors and clients.

PRODUCT RELIABILITY

A problem related to vaporware is the general reliability of IT products. Reliability is defined as the capacity of a product or system to perform its intended function under normal operating conditions. The ethical question in this area concerns the moral and legal liability of IT vendors for errors and malfunctions that prove to be costly or disruptive.

Since this is such a broad area, we will confine our remarks to the software industry, where the problem of reliability is especially acute because of the peculiar and precarious nature of the programs. Software is radically different from other products. Computer programs are extremely intricate creations with many parts or modules inseparably interconnected. Often a modification to one segment of a program will have repercussions in another segment. A software program, then, is like a complex machine with millions of interacting parts, and so, bugs and anomalies are common and unavoidable. As a result, software companies must devote a disproportionate amount of time and resources to product testing and "debugging." Sometimes, however, even the best efforts of a company are inadequate to ensure a reliable product.

In addition, some software and application developers cut back on quality assurance testing, especially when they are confronting an approaching deadline. The risks of inadequate testing are obviously substantial. Flawed software can impair a mission-critical application or cause other types of damage. Also, as some have pointed out, programmers are reluctant to engage in testing because it uncovers their own errors. According to Dorothy Graham, "testing is the black sheep of software engineering because we are looking for something we really don't want to find, namely, errors."[9]

Thus, for a variety of reasons flaws in software programs happen with great frequency. They also provoke some interesting ethical questions. Are software companies and programmers always *liable* for errors in the software they sell? What if the defects endanger public safety or inadvertently cause serious injury or even loss of life? Also, what if the customer sustains serious financial losses due to a fatal "bug" in the software? Does the user have any recourse?

Before analyzing this problem, we must first distinguish between moral culpability and legal liability. Responsibility is not a univocal concept. For our purposes it means "to be held accountable for." Thus, "to ascribe responsibility is for some person to identify another person as the cause of a harmful or untoward event."[10] One who is the direct or proximate cause of the harmful event is liable for that event. To be sure, there are certain conditions that mitigate or even eliminate responsibility. According to Aristotle's careful analysis in the *Nichomachean Ethics*, these conditions pertain when an action is involuntary. Actions are involuntary when they are done under compulsion or performed in a state of ignorance. I should not be held accountable for some action if I am coerced by external forces into performing that action. Further I should not be held accountable for a harmful action if I am truly ignorant of its injurious consequences. Aristotle rightly distinguishes between excusable ignorance (i.e., ignorance through no fault of one's own) and inexcusable ignorance.

[9]Quoted in Mitch Betts, "Software Testing Hits Bottom of 'To Do' List," *Computerworld*, July 26, 1993, p. 63. Copyright 1993 by Computerworld, Inc., Framingham, MA 01701—Reprinted from Computerworld.

[10]Peter A. French, *The Spectrum of Responsibility* (New York: St Martin's Press, 1991), p. 3

Inexcusable ignorance can take two forms: it can result from carelessness or lack of prudence, or it can be deliberately willed. Obviously, inexcusable ignorance is not exculpatory.[11]

The pertinent moral question in this context is the following: To what extent are software vendors and perhaps even their employees accountable for flaws in software programs? Are they liable for the adverse consequences of those errors? To be sure, since all software has flaws, it would appear to be unreasonable and impractical to hold vendors accountable under all circumstances, particularly when errors are especially difficult to detect or truly unforeseeable. But under just what circumstances should they be held accountable, morally and legally?

Before attempting to answer this question, we must consider the legal sense of liability. There are three basic categories for dealing with claims that defective products have caused physical or economic harm: strict liability in tort, negligence, and breach of warranty. Let us begin with *strict liability in tort*. The phrase "in tort" simply means it is independent of the obligations imposed by a contract. Strict liability in tort, then, means that the vendor is responsible for any injury regardless of whether it was at fault. Thus, the seller is liable for any product defects that cause physical harm to a person or property. It should be pointed out that appeal to the standard of strict liability is usually not a recourse if the damages are purely economic. Also, strict liability in tort applies only to products and not to services.

To avoid *negligence*, the second liability category, the vendor must always exercise "due care" in its conduct to others. In other words, any vendor or manufacturer must exercise reasonable conduct and prudence at all times in the design and development of a product. Unlike strict liability in tort, negligence requires the offended party to demonstrate that the vendor was careless or at fault in some way. Thus anyone who sues for negligence must prove that reasonable care could have prevented the injury or damage.

For software products this definition would imply that the products must be carefully designed, coded, and tested before being released to the public. A company that rushed its product to market without adequate testing might very well be guilty of negligence. Similarly, selling unfinished products could also lead to accusations of negligence unless the vendor makes it clear that the software is not totally finished and explains honestly what the buyer can expect. One problem area here is in determining and agreeing upon standards of testing in each field. It can be difficult to assess the adequacy of testing and whether or not industry standards have been met. Nevertheless, as Deborah Johnson observes, "negligence is a

---

[11]Aristotle, *Nichomachean Ethics*, trans. J. Thompson (New York: Penguin Books, 1966), Book III: 1–5.

morally acceptable legal mechanism for dealing with malfunctions and errors in programs as long as the standards that are set are reasonable."[12] Thus, negligence is an important legal and moral concept that will help us to make some judgments about responsibility and culpability.

The third category of liability is *breach of warranty.* A warranty is simply a promise made by the seller and is considered part of the contractual agreement between the seller and buyer. There are two types of warranties: *express* and *implied. Express warranties* are explicit agreements expressed in writing to the buyer. Such warranties are also created by the seller's statements about the product such as a description of its features or background about performance. These statements could be made in the context of advertising or a sales presentation. It should be observed that most software contracts include some sort of explicit, formal warranty. A warranty often includes a statement such as the following:

> ...the vendor warrants that the software, if installed as specified, will operate substantially in compliance with the specifications; verified software errors will be corrected if they can be recreated on the vendor's system with customer data, or if not corrected, the customer's sole remedy is to receive a refund for the software containing the error.[13]

Such a clause offers some reasonable protection for the customers, who can also choose to augment that protection through contract negotiations with the vendor.

Implied warranty means that when a product is sold the legal system recognizes an implicit guarantee which encompasses two conditions: the product must be fit for its "intended purpose" and it must be merchantable. If a vendor sells software that is inappropriate for the customer's application, there is clearly a violation of the first condition. Merchantability, on the other hand, means that the product is of fair and average quality for goods of that category. Thus, if a system fails repeatedly or cannot perform up to normally accepted standards, it may be judged as not merchantable, that is, as unfit for use. As one might assume, however, there is some ambiguity in the definition of a "merchantable product." If a user's application uncovers an exotic software bug that corrupts data, can the user sue the manufacturer for damages and claim that the product was not merchantable? So far, such lawsuits have not found a sympathetic ear in the courts.

There is some controversy over whether software should be considered as a product or service, since the standards of strict liability, implied warranty, and negligence apply only to products. It is generally recog-

[12]Deborah Johnson, *Computer Ethics* (Englewood Cliffs, NJ: Prentice-Hall, 1985), p. 54.

[13]Joe Auer and Mark Demboski, "Software Contracts," *Computerworld*, November 8, 1993, p. 101. Copyright 1993 by Computerworld, Inc., Framingham, MA 01701. Reprinted from Computerworld.

nized, however, that prepackaged programs (e.g., a spreadsheet such as *Lotus 1-2-3* or a database package such as *Oracle*) are products whereas custom-made programs or applications are a service. According to Jim Prince, the way in which a software product is distributed controls the decision to impose strict liability and other legal standards. Prince explains that "software that is sold 'ready to use', i.e., canned software, represents a method of distribution analogous to the mass distribution of any product … If the program is defective, the supplier is creating a risk of harm by placing the program in the stream of commerce."[14] As with any product, then, the supplier must control the risks and bear the costs of that defective product. On the other hand, when heavily customized software is distributed to a single user, these standards do not apply.

But there are some problems with this general distinction. What if a heavily customized package is sold to a small group of users? Should such software be considered as a service or a product? This is a complicated topic which is too large for a comprehensive treatment in this chapter, but suffice it to say that in these cases the courts would attempt to discern the locus of the defect. In other words, does the defect occur in the generic software or in the modifications or enhancements made to that software.[15]

Most software vendors rely on disclaimers to curtail their liability. These statements are normally part of the licensing agreement in which the vendor indicates that it will not be held liable for any lost profits, revenues, or other direct or indirect damages that result from the use of its product. In this way virtually all the risks of using a particular software package are shifted to the buyer. Courts have recognized these disclaimers provided they were explicit and conspicuously evident to the customer, and unless they are unreasonable or the circumstances are extreme.

From this brief overview of the legal notion of liability we can discern and summarize the main elements of a software vendor's legal responsibility:

- Live up to the terms of its explicit and implicit warranties.
- Exercise due care in testing its products in accordance with generally accepted industry standards.
- Avoid unreasonable disclaimers.

At a minimum, then, vendors must stay within these legal parameters. The law embodies important moral principles that must be respected. It also embodies common standards of fairness and protects the rights of consumers. For these and other pragmatic reasons, vendors should be diligent in living up to their legal responsibility.

---

[14]Jim Prince, "Negligence: Liability for Defective Software," in *Ethical Issues in the Use of Computers*, ed. Deborah Johnson and J. Snapper (Belmont, CA: Wadsworth Publishing, 1985), p. 93.
[15]Ibid., p. 94.

In addition to legal liability we must also consider the extent of the vendor's moral liability for malfunctioning software. To do so we must return to the implicit contract between the buyer and seller. As we have been at pains to insist, this contract requires that the buyer should not be coerced and should receive "full disclosure" regarding the features of the product. It seems legitimate to require the vendor not to misrepresent a product in any way or knowingly to sell a defective product. And if the vendor later learns that the product has certain defects, something that often happens with software, it should warn its customers about those problems. Unfortunately, this has not been standard industry practice. Many software companies are reticent about bugs that in their opinion are relatively minor or will not impact many customers. But some of these bugs can still cause serious problems for users and waste resources as users attempt to find "workarounds." The bottom line, then, is that software customers have a right to be informed of flaws, even if they seem inconsequential to the vendor. This can be accomplished by means of a simple warning notice.

In addition, grave software bugs that destroy data or cause similar disruptive problems should be fixed immediately. Under these conditions companies should feel obliged to fix the bug and issue another release of the product as quickly as possible. A product can hardly be considered viable or merchantable if it corrupts data or otherwise disrupts a user's application. Despite the gravity of these problems, however, it is by no means clear that companies have a legal responsibility to fix these devastating bugs if the damage they cause to a business is only financial. Companies usually avoid legal liability in these cases by stipulating that the product is warranted on an "as is" basis. But as we have repeatedly insisted, companies have a moral duty to provide their customers with a viable and usable product that fulfills the explicit and implicit contract between the buyer and seller.

Customers also ought to be given as much information as possible about product incompatibilities. Sometimes, for example, operating system software is incompatible with application software. Obviously, this could be a disturbing inconvenience for customers. Here there is considerably more ambiguity about responsibility. It's not clear that the vendor has an obligation to ensure compatibility with the vast array of software products available particularly in the PC environment. For the sake of their customers, however, it seems reasonable to demand that companies do significant testing for compatibility and that they be forthright about any incompatibility information they have acquired.

Finally, customers have a right to be informed of a product's quality assurance (QA) status. Before a product is shipped, industry standards dictate that it should go through extensive internal QA testing and then be sent off to "beta sites" for several months. These sites are existing or new customers who volunteer to develop sophisticated applications with the new product and report all problems in a timely manner to the vendor. There are many incentives to volunteering to be a beta site, ranging from the opportunity to work with a new technology to a deep discount on the finished product. The beta sites test the product under real-world conditions and often uncover performance problems, strange bugs, and other defects. This production cycle of design, coding, QA testing, and external beta site testing is utilized by virtually all software vendors and is important to ensure that the final product is of high quality.

Sometimes in their rush to bring a product to market software vendors shirk their responsibility for adequate testing. They might abbreviate the time frame, lower standards, or even bypass beta site testing altogether. If this is indeed the case, customers should be so informed so they can decide whether they want to assume the risks involved in buying such a product. When beta test sites are bypassed, the initial customers unknowingly become beta sites. There is a gross unfairness if they believe they are getting a product that has gone through the normal testing cycles when in fact the company is implicitly using them as guinea pigs. Finally, vendors should not supply beta sites and other customers with *unfinished* products (for example, a product with missing utilities or other vital functionality). They sometimes do this by advertising that a "beta release" or "early available" product is for sale. What if these products are never completed and never really ready for sale? Perhaps this questionable practice can be condoned if the vendor explicitly warns the customer that the product is not finished and candidly explains what is missing and what type of problems to expect.

Thus it seems plausible to argue that software vendors have several obligations: to fix serious software bugs, to inform its customers of product defects along with incompatibility information, to be up front about the extent to which the product has been tested, and to avoid selling unfinished products even to beta sites without full and proper disclosure. Above all, prompt attention to product defects will enable the customer to have greater confidence in the ongoing utility and reliability of the product. More open disclosure policies also will allow customers to make an "informed" decision, which is vital to a fair and open contractual arrangement. Any kind of misrepresentation is a violation of the basic contract between seller and buyer.

A summary of a software vendor's additional moral obligations in the area of product reliability would include at least the following:

- Avoid any misrepresentation.
- Fix defects that corrupt data, and issue a new product release to all users.
- Provide full, prompt disclosure of product defects and incompatibility information.

- Provide accurate representation of a product's quality and testing status.
- Avoid shipping unfinished products (unless there is proper disclosure).

One last word on this critical issue. What if a company fulfills all of these obligations and has been diligent in every phase of its product development but nevertheless a customer encounters a defect that causes serious damage to his or her business. Under the exacting standard of strict liability a vendor might be held liable for this flaw if it led to physical damage to person or property. But is a vendor morally responsible for such an error? This issue of moral culpability is rather ambiguous. It is the nature of software programs to have errors, an inevitable by-product of dependence on many hundreds of lines of interrelated programming code. If a company has thoroughly tested its product in accordance with industry standards, it seems unreasonable to hold it liable for such errors. Also, if we follow Aristotle's analysis, this ignorance could certainly be classified as excusable since it is neither deliberate nor the result of carelessness. It seems excessive, then, to hold software firms morally or legally accountable for *all* its errors if it has exercised due care during the quality assurance testing process. To hold otherwise seems to go beyond the bounds of moral common sense.

We have now treated in some depth the legal and moral liability of software developers for defective programs. Before concluding this discussion on liability, it would be instructive to consider the liability of purveyors of electronic information. What if that information is erroneous and leads to some injury? Do the same rules of liability apply?

If we regard a software program as a source of electronic information, then from a legal perspective the software is functioning like a book rather than a machine or a product. The courts have been loath to hold authors or publishers liable for errors or false information contained in books or other written media. To do so would stifle creativity, inhibit authors, and bring about some devastating consequences for the publishing industry.

An example of software acting like a book might be an automated information system containing medical information. If a user consulted this system for information about a drug to take for a certain malady and that user suffered physical damage due to inaccurate data, does the user have any recourse to sue for damages? And should the vendor be held strictly liable for this misinformation?

Pamela Samuelson has pointed out that the usual categories of liability have not been applied to books. In the case of *Cardozo* v. *True* (1977) the judge ruled that implied warranty did not apply. The plaintiff, Mrs. Cardozo, became ill from a plant while preparing a recipe from a cookbook written by Mr. True. But, as Ms. Samuelson observes, "the Cardozo opinion is one of many in which judges have stated that publishers and booksellers cannot reasonably investigate all the information in the books they sell and should therefore not be subject to warranty liability when information in the work is defective."[16] The courts have also consistently rejected strict liability in tort claims against publishers. In the case of *Winter* v. *G. P. Putnam* the judge was quite definitive about the unsuitability of applying strict liability in cases of erroneous published information.

But are electronic information systems analogous to a book? When is it feasible to consider a software program to be like a book or other publication? As Ms. Samuelson points out, electronic information systems bear a greater resemblance to products than to books since they have a more pronounced "technological character." This notion may increase the possibility of liability for defects in electronic information systems. Also the line between regarding information available in electronic format as a book or as a product seems quite tenuous. For example, if a database is sold or leased by the developer to other companies, which then use it as a source of information, should it be regarded as a book or a product? If errors in such a database cause harm should the developer be held liable? In one sense a database used for informational purposes is similar to a book; nonetheless, databases have even more "technological character" than other forms of electronic information and they do resemble products or machines more than they do books. It is clear that this is a gray area in the law and that future cases will help define the limits of liability for defective electronic information. Suffice it to say that from a moral point of view, vendors of these products are obliged to exercise due care to make sure that these products are as reliable and free from error as possible.

EXPERT SYSTEMS

Expert systems and artificial intelligence (AI) software raise some unusual and provocative ethical questions. The goal of AI is to embody human intelligence in hardware and software so that IT systems can make more intelligent decisions. This goal has been approached in two ways. The first approach involves the creation of computer systems that imitate human thought processes in order to solve a problem, play a game, and so forth. Chess-playing software is one example. The second method is the construction of expert systems which incorporate the "thinking" of experts within systems designed to resolve special problems. Expert systems are currently used in financial planning, stock portfolio management, medical diagnosis, and other areas. According to Peter Keen, "the expert's knowledge is coded as 'rules' which typically take the form of 'if...then...else' statements (for example: if condition A applies, then make inference B, also move on to

[16]Pamela Samuelson, "Liability for Defective Information," *Communications of the ACM*, January 1993, p. 23.

C)."[17] Such systems that simulate human intelligence and make decisions will invariably generate a new species of ethical and legal problems.

Before examining the issue of liability, we must first briefly discuss the people who are behind the development of expert systems (ES). The *knowledge engineer* (usually a computer programmer) is responsible for developing (designing, coding, etc.) the expert system. A *domain expert* has expertise in the area of knowledge that pertains to the system. For example, an economist would be the domain expert for an expert system in monetary or fiscal policy. These are the key parties involved in ES development. One can envision many potential problems, especially if there is miscommunication between the knowledge engineer and the domain expert. By misinterpreting the domain expert, for example, the knowledge engineer could inadvertently invalidate the entire system.

The primary legal question is the following: If a decision of an expert system is wrong and leads to damaging losses or causes serious injury, who is liable? The knowledge engineer? The domain expert? The end user of the system? In some cases it may be relatively easy to pinpoint the locus of responsibility. If the knowledge engineer does introduce flaws into the system because he or she has not understood the domain expert, then the knowledge engineer is clearly liable for problems. In some situations the fault may lie with the end user, who might ask the wrong questions, draw the wrong inferences, or reach the wrong conclusions based on the output of the inquiries. The user must have some expertise in the domain of knowledge of the expert system in question.

On the other hand, situations will abound where responsibility will be hard to determine. For example, experts often disagree about many complicated issues in their domain of expertise. Economists, lawyers, engineers, and medical doctors frequently have conflicting viewpoints. What if the expert's opinion is simply wrong when seen from an alternate perspective? Is he or she still liable or is this a case of *caveat emptor*? What if several experts provide their divergent opinions for a system. The knowledge engineer may then face the daunting task of reconciling conflicting opinions within the structure of the software. If the ES yields faulty or dubious results, do we blame the experts, the knowledge engineer, or both?

In any of these cases the vendor must assume at least some responsibility if the experts or knowledge engineers are proved to be wrong. They are immune from culpability only if the user is clearly negligent, careless, or a neophyte who should not have been using the system in the first place. There have so far been very few legal challenges in the sphere of expert systems, but this situation will undoubtedly change as these systems prolif-

---

[17]Peter G. W. Keen, *Every Manager's Guide to Information Technology* (Cambridge, MA: Harvard Business School Press, 1991), p. 35.

erate. The law, therefore, does not yet offer much guidance in this highly nebulous area. It is not clear, for example, whether strict product liability applies to ES or whether vendors (and maybe experts) can be sued for negligence. As was noted earlier, strict liability is usually not a recourse for economic damage. Personal injury issues are a different matter. For instance, what about expert systems used by physicians? A cursory examination of these systems may help us sort through some of these thorny liability issues.

Indeed, the most intriguing liability questions emerge in the domain of medicine. There is a growing reliance on such expert systems to produce diagnoses and recommend therapy based on a description of the symptoms. *The Internist-1* is an example of such a system.[18] The medical profession's increasing reliance on these systems raises at least two important ethical concerns.

The first issue is the difficulty of incorporating normative elements into the decision-making process. In other words, medical decisions cannot be reduced to deductions based purely on factual data. Sometimes these decisions involve ethical principles; for example, some therapies may entail the termination of a late-stage pregnancy or the withholding of treatment to an infant with major birth defects. Obviously, in these types of situations there are moral issues at stake, and since ethics is prescriptive and there are many conflicting ethical systems, it would be exceedingly difficult to construct a comprehensive medical expert system that could incorporate the normative dimension of recommending a therapy. As Goran Collste points out, "the concept of a complete medical expert system that includes rules for drawing conclusions is built on an illusion; however, such a system could be helpful in reminding the decision maker of the ethical aspects of a problem and thus initiate his or her reflection on moral issues."[19]

A second issue concerns the impact of medical expert systems on the doctor's autonomy. Recall that to act autonomously is to make one's decisions freely and unencumbered by outside influences. As we noted in Chapter 2, autonomy is a necessary condition of moral responsibility. But some observers worry about a physician relying on an expert system. Physicians cannot abdicate their autonomy and responsibility by delegating therapeutic and diagnostic decisions to an expert system, no matter how effective it may be. The expert system can help inform a decision, but there is no substitute for the physician's own judgment and diagnosis. Thus, physicians and other professionals must be more than passive users

---

[18]For a more detailed description of this software consult R. A. Miller, "The INTERNIST-1 Quick Medical Reference Project—Status Report," *Western Journal of Medicine*, 145 (1986), 816–22.

[19]Goran Collste, "Expert Systems in Medicine and Moral Responsibility," *Journal of Systems Software*, January 1992, p. 20.

of an ES. Also, ultimate responsibility for all decisions along with liability for the consequences must reside with the human decision maker, never deflected to a computer system.

It should be remarked that the law would also hold physicians ultimately accountable for their judgments. A doctor who is sued for malpractice cannot pass on the blame for a poor diagnosis to a faulty ES. Of course, as Steven Frank observes, "if the source of the physician's error were indeed traceable to the expert system, the physician might sue the software developer to recover the money that must be paid to the injured patient."[20] But such a suit would have to be based on negligence, since economic loss does not fall under the auspices of strict liability. And if the software developer has exercised due care in designing, programming, and testing the system, it will be difficult to prove such a charge of negligence.

Where, then, does this leave the ES vendors? What can we conclude about their ethical obligations in this difficult area? How can they minimize liability for design flaws or bad decisions? The conscientious vendor should consider taking extra precautions, given the special risks of utilizing this unconventional software. Such precautions might include the following:

- Communicate realistic product expectations; avoid hyperbole about the product's decision-making capability and promptly correct any misperceptions.
- Provide a clear, thorough statement of the risks involved in using this product; include discussion of the product's limitations and potential shortfalls.
- Provide extensive ongoing end-user training to avoid product misuse.
- Communicate the presence of bugs or flaws promptly, and correct them as quickly as possible.
- If major conceptual problems arise such as consistently "bad" decisions or poor recommendations, the product should undergo more substantial modifications and revisions.
- If necessary, remove defective products from the market and provide reasonable compensation to those with legitimate claims.
- When possible, correct the product's misuse by unsophisticated end users.[21]

Following these practices may not guarantee that a vendor of ES products will avoid costly litigation, but it will go a long way to fulfilling the terms of the contract between buyer and seller in a way that is open and honest. Moreover, a vendor's good faith and resoluteness in handling problems will be viewed favorably if legal problems should emerge.

[20]Steven J. Frank, "What AI Practitioners Should Know about the Law," in, *Ethical Issues in Information Systems*, ed. Roy Dejoie, George Fowler, and David Paradice (Boston: Boyd & Fraser Publishing Company, 1991), p. 254.

[21]I am indebted to Kathleen Mykyntn and Peter Slinkman, who suggest some of these ideas in their article on expert systems, "Expert Systems: A Question of Liability," *MIS Quarterly*, March, 1990, pp. 29–37.

SUMMARY

In this chapter we have considered the moral and legal responsibilities of information technology vendors to both existing and prospective customers. To a great extent this responsibility is rooted in the contractual relationship between the buyer and the seller. According to this perspective, the seller is bound by "secondary moral constraints" as well as by the terms of the contract. These require that the seller avoid any undue influence and misrepresentation about the product features, the warranty, service commitments, and so forth.

Most IT products require considerable post-sales support because of their complexity. Serious problems can arise, however, if the vendor goes bankrupt or becomes a takeover target, since such an event can jeopardize the ongoing utility of its products. To avoid such a threat, companies should make their source code available in the case of bankruptcy and be candid about their financial condition so that users can make an informed choice.

We also discussed the special problem of vaporware, defined as the formal announcement of a product that does not yet exist and will not be ready for sale for a long time. Products that are brought to market prematurely can also be considered a form of vaporware. To some extent vaporware is a form of bluffing, which some businesspeople claim is necessary for success in a competitive business world. But as we observed, deception and bluffing diminish trust and hence inhibit the effective functioning of corporations. In addition, the deception involved in vaporware is a violation of the implicit contract between vendor and customer, since the contract calls for reasonable full disclosure. Companies, to be more responsible, must make a clear distinction between a product announcement and a statement of direction. One possible rule of thumb: Product announcements should be made only when a product has reached the stage of *technological viability*, and this is normally when it has been fully tested and is ready for shipment to customer beta sites. The earlier in the product cycle that the product is announced, the greater the chance that the product will not be ready on schedule.

A problem related to vaporware is product reliability. To what extent are vendors accountable for software flaws? In answering this question it is necessary to distinguish between legal and moral liability. There are three relevant categories of legal liability: strict liability in tort, negligence, and breach of warranty. From a legal point of view companies are obliged to test their products fully to avoid the charge of negligence and to live up to the terms of the express and implied warranty. The implied warranty requires companies to sell products that are fit for their intended purpose and merchantable (i.e., of fair and average quality). Moreover, companies have a moral responsibility to avoid any misrepresentation, to fix serious bugs that might corrupt data, to disclose fully and promptly any product defects and incompatibility information, to represent accurately a product's quality and the extent to which it has been tested and prepared for the marketplace, and to refrain from selling unfinished products.

In regard to the liability involved in disseminating defective electronic information, the pivotal issue is whether such software is functioning as a book rather than as a machine or a product. If so, then such systems will avoid legal liability for misinformation; strict liability in tort and implied warranty have not been applied to books. However, because of their technological character, it is by no means clear that electronic information products are analogous to books, and if the legal system opines that they are more similar to machines, there will be a greater likelihood of liability.

Finally, we considered the unique problems posed by expert systems due to the difficulty of pinpointing the locus of responsibility for any problems. It is difficult to establish whether the knowledge engineer or the domain experts or even the user have made the mistakes. In addition, physicians and other professionals must be vigilant that their reliance on an expert system does not adversely affect their autonomy and responsibility. Finally, the primary ethical duty of expert system vendors is to communicate realistic product expectations and to provide extensive user training along with a clear and thorough statement of the risks involved in using the product.

CASES FOR DISCUSSION

Introduction

Both of these cases consider ethical dilemmas in the software industry. *The Product Manager* provides a compelling description of a company apparently engaged in promoting vaporware to its customer base. However, ambiguity about announcing future release dates adds some complexity to this case and poses a true quandary for the company's product manager who must decide what to say at future user group gatherings. In *Revlon vs. Logisticon* we are presented with dramatic evidence of the power that software vendors can exercise over their clients. Has the vendor in this case gone too far and abused that power?

CASE 4.1

The Product Manager[22]

A Meeting in Boston It was late Friday afternoon and Richard Martin was rushing to Boston's Logan Airport to catch the last flight back to San Francisco. As the cab traversed through the busy, confusing streets of

---

[22]The events described in this case study are reported exclusively from Richard Martin's perspective. The names of all individuals, companies, products, and locations have been disguised.

downtown Boston, Richard gazed at the surrounding urban landscape. He felt truly elated over the speech he had just given. He had come to Boston for Jupiter Software's East Coast user group meeting. Martin was the product manager for the company's popular relational database product, *INFORM-2*. In his speech he unequivocally announced that the long-awaited *INFORM-3* would be available on May 1, 1989. In this speech and in private meetings with Jupiter's major clients he exhorted the nervous customer base to wait for this timely new release and not jump ship to more advanced competitive products. Thanks to the work of Jupiter's talented engineering staff, he was able to present a demo of this new product despite the fact that some pieces were still not even coded or designed. The demo was a great success and added significant credibility to Martin's claim that the product would be ready for distribution by May 1.

But as Martin settled into his first-class plane seat and peered at the changing scenery below, his mood began to change dramatically. His trip to Boston was assuredly a great success on one level, but he began to wonder about the ethical propriety of announcing a release date in such unequivocal terms, especially when no one at the company was really confident about this date. His confident and dogmatic style at the meeting masked feelings of concern about the May 1 target, feelings that pervaded the entire company. Unfortunately, this was the first of many such user group meetings; Richard was scheduled to make the same speech and exude the same confidence in several other cities across the United States, Canada, and Europe. But as the plane reached its cruising altitude, he wondered about his future at Jupiter and whether he was the right man to continue this tour of user group meetings.

The Company   Jupiter Software was founded in the late 1970s by three California entrepreneurs. One of them, Larry Connors, was an engineer with undergraduate and graduate degrees from Stanford. After completing his studies, Larry went to work in the data processing department of one of California's largest banks. Shortly after his arrival, he developed a sophisticated input screen which allowed bank clerks to enter data more quickly into the firm's hierarchical IBM database. This tool was quite successful and Larry was sure that he could sell it to other companies with similar data input requirements. He promptly resigned from the bank and formed his own company, Jupiter Software. Larry needed additional capital to get this company off the ground so he invited two friends to invest $25,000 each in return for a major stake in Jupiter. These individuals were silent partners who were not involved in the day-to-day operations of Jupiter. The company earned a small profit on first-year revenues of about $100,000.

During this time much was being written about the potential of relational database technology. Both hierarchical and network databases had prevailed among large commercial users, but these were often criticized for their complexity and inflexibility. Both of these database models arrange records in a hierarchical manner with a master record and its subordinates. But despite their speed and efficiency, these databases did not adapt well to a company's changing information requirements.

The relational model, developed by Edgar F. Codd of IBM in 1970,[23] showed great promise because of its simplicity and flexibility. According to this model, each record in the file is conceived as a row in a two-dimensional table and each field becomes a column in that table. New fields can be added and tables can be joined together if they have an item in common, through a simple "join" or "relate" command (see Exhibit 1). The relational database management system (or RDMBS) was organized for maximum flexibility, ease of use, and quick retrieval of information. The only drawback was its slow performance compared with that of the network and hierarchical models.

Exhibit 1

Sample Database

Customer File:	Cust-No, Cust-Name, Cust-Addr
Order File:	Cust-No, Order-No, Order-Date,etc.

Larry Connors astutely realized that the benefits of relational technology far outweighed its liabilities. He hired a small group of engineers to expand his simple data input form into a full-scale relational database. By 1981 *INFORM-1* was born. It was initially designed for the IBM mainframe but as the product grew in popularity it was ported to DEC, Hewlett Packard, and Data General minicomputers. Sales quickly took off on all of these platforms as relational technology found great favor with many companies looking for an alternative to the more primitive database technologies of the 1960s and 1970s.

By 1984 revenues had reached $12 million and the company was growing rapidly. Larry moved the company from a small building in San Mateo and leased the second and third floors of a major office building in Burlingame, a city close to San Francisco and just on the periphery of the famous Silicon Valley. The engineering staff had expanded to 25, and new sales offices were opened in Boston, the District of Columbia, Atlanta, Dallas, and Toronto. The company also signed on distributors to sell *INFORM* throughout Europe. In 1985 Jupiter's sales almost doubled to $21 million as the company released a new version of the product, *INFORM-2*. This new release included more sophisticated functionality than the first

[23]Edgar F. Codd, "A Relational Model for Data for Large Shared Data Banks," *Communications of the ACM*, 13 (1970): 377–87.

release, such as a better report writer, additional security features, and an input screen or data entry form that provided more substantial validation of data as it was being entered into the database by end users.

Jupiter's niche in the database marketplace was the departmental DBMS, which normally resided on a departmental processor such as a minicomputer. Departmental computing systems were considered a high-growth segment of the market. International Data Corporation, a leading consulting firm, estimated that shipments of departmental DBMS software would increase at a compound annual growth rate of 31 percent through 1991.[24] IDC also projected that the installed base of departmental DBMS's would increase from 139,000 in 1986 to 531,000 in 1991.[25] Surveys of current customers and prospective buyers revealed the salient minimum requirements of an acceptable departmental DBMS:

SQL compatibility (The Structured Query Language was the standard method of querying the database to retrieve the appropriate records.)

Performance-oriented systems

Distributed processing capability

Multivendor interfaces (i.e., to IBM mainframes and various PC platforms)

Transaction processing

Easy-to-use end user interface

As the RDBMS market evolved, commercial systems without these important features would be at a serious competitive disadvantage.

Jupiter's Management Team   As the company continued to expand, Larry Connors realized the need to make the sometimes difficult transition from an entrepreneurial to a management environment. Hence from 1983 to 1984 he brought to Jupiter a skilled team of professional managers. Jeff Bennet became the Vice President of Marketing, lured away from a competitor with a hefty salary and stock options. During this time Richard Martin was promoted to a newly created job, Associate Product Manager for *INFORM-1*. Richard had joined Jupiter in 1983 after receiving his MBA from a prominent East Coast university. His good friend from college, Joe Casey, had joined Jupiter a year earlier as Manager of the Marketing Services Department, and persuaded Richard that this was an opportunity he shouldn't pass up. Richard moved to California after being hired by Jupiter as a consultant and marketing support specialist. He provided training to *INFORM-1*'s new customers in addition to consulting services on how to design and utilize this system efficiently. Richard was highly effective in this role as he quickly mastered the intricacies and nuances of

---

[24]"Departmental Database Management Systems: A Statistical Reference, 1984–1991" (Framingham, MA: International Data Corporation, 1986).
[25]Ibid.

this sophisticated software. Thus, when Mary Hastings, *INFORM-1's* young Product Manager, sought an associate, Richard was her first choice.

The Product Manager reported to the Vice President of Marketing and was responsible for shepherding new releases of the product through various stages from coding to beta testing, and therefore occupied a critical position in Jupiter's management hierarchy. This individual was the key interface person between Jupiter's marketing departments and its engineering staff. Perhaps more than anyone else, the Product Manager had to make sure that a new product or release was what the customer considered important. To be successful at this difficult job, the Product Manager had to have both technical skills and marketing acumen. Both Mary and Richard fit the bill and worked very well together for over a year.

The management team was rounded out by Sales Manager Dennis Johnson and the Vice President of Product Development, Jeffrey Coleman. Coleman had an engineering degree from Stanford and was responsible for managing Jupiter's engineering staff, the QA (quality assurance) teams, and the documentation workers. Finally, during these growth years the company was pressured to elevate its phone support for its rapidly expanding customer base and therefore established a separate Customer Support Department, headed initially by Louise Cassidy from the Marketing Services Department. With this management team securely in place, Larry Connors hoped to take Jupiter to new heights.

1986–1988 Sales for Jupiter's *INFORM-2* product peaked in 1986 at $26 million. By now there were sales offices all over the United States as well as in London, Paris, and Singapore. But as competition among relational database vendors intensified and the market began to mature, it became increasingly difficult for Jupiter's seasoned sales staff to close new business. Although revenues had increased by about 15 percent in 1986, Jupiter had actually lost some of its market share during the previous year as other companies grew at an even faster rate. Its overall market share fell from a high of 9.2 percent in 1984 to about 8.5 percent in 1986. As a result, despite the revenue growth and continued profitability, there was cause for concern among Jupiter's executives.

The reasons for Jupiter's emerging problems were manifold, but for the most part they could be attributed to its failure to keep up with technology. The latest release, *INFORM-2*, was revised in the early 1980s to include some minor enhancements to the data entry screens and the report writer along with some query optimizers to speed up the retrieval process. But *INFORM-2* was being eclipsed by competitive products in both performance and functionality. For example, *INFORM-2* did not provide for on-line transaction processing (OLTP), which was becoming a required feature of relational database systems. OLTP allowed multiple users to work on the same data file by locking a record that was retrieved by a particular user until that user completed his or her update. In addition, INFORM-2 used a proprietary query language instead of the industry standard language, SQL. Finally, the product sorely lacked a robust report writer, and its performance deteriorated significantly when the number of records in the database exceeded 100,000.

Competitors such as Oracle and Ingress became highly adept at exploiting these vulnerabilities and prevailed repeatedly in head-to-head competition with Jupiter. The word in the marketplace was that *INFORM-2* was a fine tool for small to medium size applications but was not well suited for large-scale departmental applications where over 100,000 records and transaction processing were the norm. For these applications, products like Oracle and Ingress were seen as far superior.

The company's managers worked hard to counter this negative image but to no avail. As a result, for the first time in Jupiter's history sales dropped precipitously in 1987 to about $19.5 million and the company posted its first loss of $2.1 million. To get its costs under control, Larry Connors laid off 10 percent of the staff at the Burlingame headquarters and closed three of the company's eight sales offices.

Connors knew all too well that the company's dim prospects could not be reversed unless *INFORM-2* could be revised to include considerable new functionality. A team of engineers had been working feverishly on this project throughout the past year but made little progress. Much of the blame for this lack of progress could be laid at the feet of Coleman, the VP of Product Development. Unfortunately, he was not an effective leader; for example, he had difficulty resolving disputes among his engineers regarding many design issues for *INFORM-3*. In early 1988 Larry Connors, still perturbed by the company's first unprofitable year, met with his board to discuss the fate of Mr. Coleman. It was decided that Coleman had to go; no one had confidence in his ability to accelerate the progress of *INFORM-3's* development. On February 11, 1988, Coleman was asked to resign, and several days later Connors announced that his replacement would be Warren Clemens, a 33-year-old engineering graduate of MIT. Clemens had worked briefly for Coleman, but the two men rarely saw eye to eye, so Clemens had gone to another database company in Silicon valley.

Shortly before Coleman and several loyalists among the engineering staff were fired, Connors arranged a clandestine meeting with Clemens to discuss his possible future at Jupiter. Connors wanted a virtual guarantee from Clemens that he would "get the new product out the door in a big hurry." As a result of this meeting and the prospect of a substantial bonus, Clemens publicly committed to getting this product to the marketplace within 14 months.

On February 21, a company meeting was called in Burlingame and Connors enthusiastically announced the appointment of Clemens as the new Director of Engineering. With Clemens by his side, he also announced the release date for the revitalized *INFORM-3* database: May 1, 1989. Connors exhorted all Jupiter employees to support this effort wholehcartedly, and he encouraged skeptics to seek employment elsewhere: "Jupiter will succeed in getting *INFORM-3* to market by next May. Our whole future depends on this. But we need 110 percent effort from everyone in the company. If you're not committed to this or you think this is impossible, maybe you shouldn't be here!"

Although most of Jupiter's employees were still skeptical, they decided that remaining at Jupiter was probably worth the risk. Many had substantial stock options, so Jupiter's success could pay off handsomely for them. Also, shortly after the meeting Connors distributed more stock options as an additional incentive. But the task ahead was truly herculean. Clemens believed that all of Coleman's work was virtually worthless, so he decided to start from "ground zero." Also, because of the radical nature of the changes, it would be necessary to design and code the product from scratch. According to Clemens, it would not be expedient to modify the "spaghetti-like code" written by some of his inept predecessors. Clemens added six new engineers to the existing staff, bringing the total to 24. Most of them were competent and had had experience with other companies in the Valley. Nonetheless, experts estimated that to construct a viable relational database product for the minicomputer environment it would require at least three years and 35 to 40 engineers. Could Jupiter beat these impossible odds and construct *INFORM-3* in 15 months with only 24 engineers? Connors was convinced that it could and that this project would become legendary in the software industry.

As sales plummeted further in 1988, there was even greater urgency in getting this new product to market. Jupiter's main source of revenue at this point was from the existing customer base. In 1988 there were approximately 2,800 installations of *INFORM-2*. As is customary in the software industry, each site was required to pay an annual maintenance fee, which entitled the customer to product upgrades, bug fixes, compatibility adjustments, and customer support. The fee ranged from $1,200 to $4,100 depending upon the size and memory capacity of the hardware; since the average fee was about $2,600, these fees generated about $7.3 million in revenues for Jupiter.

The customer base, however, was becoming increasingly disenchanted with Jupiter. Many clients had purchased the product in its infancy in the early 1980s and their needs had outgrown *INFORM-2*'s limited capabilities. They had been promised a major upgrade for several years but nothing happened. The company and its managers were often ridiculed at user group meetings for failing to deliver. Some customers purchased a new RDBMS. As one disgruntled user said: "I'm tired of Larry Connors' empty promises. I can't wait any longer for this mythical *INFORM-3*."

By the summer of 1988 there was tremendous discontent among the user base; many customers were skeptical that they would ever see *INFORM-3* after Coleman's abrupt termination. The company was rife with rumors that many clients would not renew their maintenance agreement when annual billing was issued in the fall. Connors knew that decisive action was essential to rescue his floundering company.

A New Product Manager   In the summer of 1988 the development effort for *INFORM-3* was in high gear. Tensions began to mount in the company, however, especially over Warren Clemens's dogmatic and uncooperative management style. As Product Manager, Mary Hasting was responsible for ensuring that *INFORM-3* addressed the needs of the market. But Warren often did not involve her in the design of key modules. When she confronted him about this matter, he would complain: "I just don't have the time to be consulting *you* about this stuff! You'll just have to trust my instincts."

A marketing team was assembled in June and met every week with the lead engineers so that key departments would be informed about the new product and could begin to prepare training manuals, brochures, and other promotional material. It was essential that the marketing and engineering personnel work together to balance market requirements with technical feasibility, but the meetings between them were usually volatile and unproductive. Warren and Mary argued vociferously at times. She continued to demand more involvement in the design of *INFORM-3* but Warren steadfastly resisted. Larry Connors tried to mediate this hostile dispute but usually ended up siding with Warren. On one occasion he excoriated Mary for not being a "team player." By mid-July Mary was completely frustrated, and she handed in her resignation.

Richard Martin was the logical choice to succeed Mary as Product Manager. He had performed admirably as Associate Product Manager, and he was intimately involved in the development effort of *INFORM-3*. He was often more conciliatory to Warren and frequently made valiant efforts to bridge the widening gap between the engineering and marketing groups. Hence on July 15, 1988, he was promoted to Product Manager. At the same time Larry put pressure on Warren "to get Richard more involved." Warren responded by inviting Richard to the Monday morning meetings of the engineering and quality assurance staff under his control, where the lead engineers discussed their progress on the modules.

After Richard attended several of these meetings, it became increasingly clear to him that the May 1 release date was highly improbable. He estimated that the design and coding of a functional system could be completed by May 1 but only under extremely optimal conditions, if all the engineers kept to their demanding schedule and if there were no resignations or long spells of absenteeism. But even under these conditions the product would most likely be ready for quality assurance testing sometime in late March or April. This date would allow only about one month for the QA process—not adequate time to test the product thoroughly and fix all its bugs. Also there would be no time to ship the product to beta sites for testing with real life applications. Beyond any doubt, May 1 was a very optimistic date. In Richard's estimation, the odds were strongly against the product being available then. As the summer turned to fall, several other managers at Jupiter were equally troubled about this ambitious release date.

Fall User Group Meetings   One of the rituals at Jupiter was its fall series of regional user group meetings, usually spread out over October and November. The regional groups were divided into West Coast, Midwest, East Coast, Washington, D.C. (this group catered to Jupiter's many government clients), Canada, and Europe, so there were six key regional meetings in addition to the international meeting held in the spring, and it was customary for the Product Manager and other middle managers to speak at these gatherings. This year the focus of the entire user group was on the soon-to-be-released *INFORM-3*. Attendance would be high since the users had many pressing questions about this new product. Besides technical concerns two questions were uppermost in their minds: Was the development team on schedule, and would they get their copies on May 1 or shortly thereafter?

Despite assurances from Larry Connors, Jeff Bennet, and others, some of the company's most loyal customers joked openly about the May 1 date ("We'll be fooled again by Jupiter!"); many others were skeptical about *INFORM-3*. Larry knew that these meetings were pivotal for Jupiter's survival. In addition to the company's losing revenues by any more customer defections to other products, its reputation would be further damaged. *INFORM-2*'s sales were now almost nonexistent except for an occasional sale in Europe or the Far East. The fall maintenance fees would give Jupiter enough resources to hang on until May, when the sales staff could begin selling the state-of-the-art *INFORM-3*. Therefore it was critically important to instill confidence in the users regarding the May 1 release date.

In September, as Jupiter prepared for the user group meetings, Larry called a meeting of the management committee, including Jeff Bennet, Warren Clemens, Joe Casey, Richard Martin, and Louise Cassidy. He told them it would be vital to assure Jupiter's customers that May 1 was *INFORM-3*'s release date and that there had been no slippage in the schedule. He emphasized the importance of being definitive and exuding confidence. The future of Jupiter depended on their ability to convince customers that they could have a new product in their hands by May 1989. If they could convince most customers to hold on, Jupiter could count on a high maintenance renewal rate.

The meeting grew tense as Richard and others protested Larry's injunction. Richard said: "Well, Larry, I realize how important it is to keep our customers but we don't have a lot of confidence in the release date. At the Monday meeting yesterday I learned of delays and serious setbacks with two key modules. Also the input screens haven't even been designed yet. It's already mid-September—how can we possibly have a salable product by May 1?" Louise concurred: "I'm hesitant about sounding so confident. My group has very little knowledge about *INFORM-3*. Even if we shipped in May, could we support 2,500 customers with a new product? I just don't think so!" Jeff Bennet, Jupiter's Marketing VP, voiced a mild protest but wasn't nearly as strident as the others. Jeff had a reputation for being politically savvy and resisted what he regarded as a challenge to Larry Connors's authority.

Larry listened soberly to his managers but then responded: "We have no choice There are no other sources of cash besides this maintenance revenue. If we lose a big piece of it, we're finished as a company. I know there are some problems with *INFORM-3*, but we can fix them even if I have to do it by myself! We'll get that product out the door by May! This is no time to lose faith. We all just have to work harder to make it happen. Warren and the other engineers are committed to making it happen, and I need your commitment too. As a company we have to be in lock step on this issue and sing from the same hymnal: *INFORM-3* will be available May 1! If you don't think so, maybe I should look for some new managers who have the commitment we need to get the job done."

Richard and his colleagues, chastened by Larry's speech, reluctantly agreed to do everything in their power to convince the user group community that May 1 was a realistic release date. Later that evening at the local bar they talked about what they would be doing. "Maybe INFORM-3 will be ready, " said Joe. "It's a long shot, but it's not impossible." "Well," said Richard, "I would say there's about a 10 percent chance that it will be finished. Those aren't very good odds." "Look," injected Louise, "other software companies around here do this all the time. You guys have heard of vaporware, haven't you? Companies are always announcing products even when they're unsure about the release date. We're no better or worse than they are." "Yeah," said Richard, "if the product is a few months late, who will be hurt? I don't see the harm. On the other hand, if we're ambivalent and lose customers, there might be no Jupiter Software next May. Then the customers will really be hurt—no bug fixes, no new product releases, no customer support." "None of us like it," said Joe, "but what choice do we have? If we don't go along with this, our jobs will certainly be at stake."

The Dilemma   As Richard flew back to Burlingame, he recalled that conversation. He took from his briefcase and reread Larry's recent memo to the whole company exhorting everyone to cooperate for the common good (see Exhibit 2). On the surface, things were beginning to improve. As Larry's memo indicated, the product was beginning to shape up, and there was a tentative plan to get a beta release by March 15. Nonetheless, despite the positive tone of Larry's memo, Richard still thought that this was a real long shot. He had concealed his doubts, however, and won over many "doubting Thomases" among the East Coast users. Richard's speech and the product demo were quite convincing. To prepare the slick demo, several of Jupiter's engineers had simulated pieces of the product that had not even been coded yet, and interspersed them with modules that were completed, so the new product came across to the audience as a seamless whole. It undoubtedly left the impression that the product was on the brink of completion.

Richard also went out of his way to talk with all the major customers at the meeting to assure them that they would have the new product in May. He had known many of these clients for years since he had been to many of the key sites on the East Coast as a trainer and consultant. Most customers liked Richard and felt he was a man of his word who always delivered on his promises. As Richard meandered through the meeting, greeting and encouraging Jupiter's customers, he relied heavily on his credibility to dispel any doubts about *INFORM-3* and Jupiter's future. Judging from the reactions to his speech and the product demonstration, Richard felt quite sure that he succeeded. As he left the meeting, he got a pat on the back from Jeff Bennet, who told him that "Larry would be very pleased."

But now as Richard's plane approached the San Francisco airport, he considered the meetings coming up in the next few weeks. Was he willing to give the same speech and the phony product demonstration to these other groups? Was he prepared to put his credibility on the line once again? Shouldn't he at least qualify the statements about the May 1 release date, let unsuspecting clients know that it's possible but not a sure thing? Richard realized, however, that any sort of ambivalence would be interpreted by Larry as treason and that his job would surely be at risk. He wondered too about the ethical questions. There *was* a slim chance Jupiter would make the May 1 release date, so technically his statements were not lies. But did he have a moral obligation to reveal the whole truth? Software developers were always wrong when they announced release dates, so most customers would be understanding even if the product was late. Wasn't vaporware standard industry practice? Why should Jupiter set new ethical standards?

As Richard's plane prepared to land, he gazed at the bright lights of the San Francisco airport. He could find no easy answers to these perplexing questions. Nor was he sure what he should do at the Canadian user group meeting the week after next. If he gave the same speech, which was such a hit in Boston, it would be another long flight home.

Exhibit 2

Jupiter Software
Office of the President

<u>**Memorandum**</u>

To: Jupiter Employees
From: Larry Connors
Subject: *INFORM-3* status
Date: September 30, 1988

I spent the day yesterday reviewing Product Development's progress on *INFORM-3* with Warren and Richard. We reviewed the symbol table handler, the standard file interface, the screen handler, the data dictionary, the data file editor, the report writer, the output screens, and the commands. The progress to date is really outstanding, and the whole engineering staff deserves a great deal of credit. We also discussed upcoming efforts on the transaction processing facility and the data input screens along with the conversion utility. We reached tentative agreement on a schedule to bring us to the March 15 beta release date.

As each of you is aware, you are now being called on to overcome and rise above your personal limitations. In the next six months, with limited staff, we have to continue to operate our daily business and maintain our current products while at the same time producing all of the elements required for a successful launch of what is substantially a new product. We can do this only with an all-out effort on the part of each individual and 100% team work. We have a great opportunity to turn things around and make this work, but success will require everyone's total commitment and dedication.

Questions

1. Identify and analyze the primary ethical issues in this case.
2. Can the actions of Jupiter's executives be justified by an appeal to Carr's arguments that it's sometimes necessary to "bluff" in business?
3. What would you do if you were Richard Martin? (Before answering this question, consider Mr. Martin's options; your answer should also incorporate some sort of ethical justification.)

CASE 4.2

Revlon v. Logisticon

Logisticon, Inc., is a small software company established in 1974 and located in Santa Clara, California. It supplies its clients with sophisticated inventory management software for mainframes and minicomputers. One of Logisticon's most important customers was Revlon, Inc., which produces and markets a wide range of cosmetic products, perfumes, and toiletries. Its most successful products are Flex Shampoo and the Revlon product line, which includes its popular nail polish and lipstick. Its primary rivals in this competitive market are Procter & Gamble and Maybelline. In 1990 Revlon had a 22.5 percent market share and revenues of about $450 million.

Revlon purchased Logisticon's inventory management product in order to manage and control its wide array of products. According to Revlon officials, Revlon was to pay Logisticon a one-time licensing fee of $360,000 for continuous use of this product. Most sophisticated mainframe software products are "sold" or licensed in this way. Revlon paid $180,000 when the system was delivered, but on October 9, 1990, it indicated that it was refusing to pay its second installment of $180,000. It was Revlon's contention that the system was not performing up to its expectations. According to Revlon's managers, the software had serious bugs that consistently interfered with program development. Revlon continued to use the Logisticon product despite the flaws, however, and it turned a deaf ear to Logisticon's demands for payment.

About one week later, on October 16, 1990, the frustrated vendor connected to Revlon's mainframe computer at about 2:30 A.M. and swiftly executed a series of commands that disabled the software it had supplied. The result was sheer chaos for Revlon, which could not access any of its critical inventory and shipping data. According to a report in *The New York Times*, "the computer disruption closed two main distribution centers in Phoenix and in Edison, N.J., for three days, halting as much as $20 million in product deliveries and idling hundreds of workers...."[26] Revlon immediately filed a lawsuit claiming that Logisticon's precipitous and iniquitous action was a form of extortion and "commercial terrorism."

For its part, Logisticon justified this covert and unorthodox action as a form of repossession. After all, Revlon had steadfastly failed to pay its bills; why, then, should it have continued use of the product? When a customer stops making automobile payments, the bank will often repossess the vehi-

---

[26]Andrew Pollack, "Revlon Sues Supplier over Software Disabling," *The New York Times*, October 24, 1990, p. D1. Copyright © 1990 by The New York Times Company. Reprinted by permission.

cle. Why not use the same tactic with expensive software products? This was Logisticon's only leverage with this recalcitrant customer. It should be noted that Logisticon did not dispute the presence of bugs but it maintained that such defects were to be expected in sophisticated software packages.

Although Logisticon's disabling of this software was dramatic and perhaps unprecedented, other software vendors have used similar tactics to deal with deadbeats. The most common such technique is to plant a "bomb" in the software which automatically disables it on a certain date if payment is not received. Of course, the user is usually made aware of this condition. Once the "bomb" is activated, the customer can no longer gain access to the software. If the payment is made, the customer can usually receives a code or "patch" that will once again provide access to the data or programs. What distinguishes this unusual case is Logisticon's electronic trespassing and clandestine entry into Revlon's computer system to disable the software.

Questions

1. This incident graphically illustrates the potential power of even small, obscure suppliers over more powerful customers. But does it represent an abuse of that power? Did Logisticon act irresponsibly by disabling Revlon's system?

2. Did it matter that this was a licensing agreement instead of an outright purchase? Also, does the fact that Revlon added its labor to this software package engender any sort of property rights?

5

Privacy in the Information Age

THE IMPORTANCE OF PRIVACY

One of the most explosive issues to emerge in this information age is the protection of personal privacy. The converging technologies discussed in Chapter 1 have increased the capability of information technology systems to collect, retrieve, process, recombine, and disseminate all sorts of information. Consequently, corporations and government agencies no longer regard traditional forms of information as confidential. Rather, information has become a commodity to be bought and sold for a reasonable fee.

As a result, the coexistence of information technology and personal privacy is becoming increasingly tenuous. As the boundary between public and private information continues to shift, the debate about how to classify information intensifies. Although some changes to expand the availability of information are warranted and economically feasible, many have occurred in a moral vacuum with little attention to the possible erosion of privacy.

This chapter will focus on two dimensions of this problem: consumer privacy and employee privacy. The former deals with issues such as the information compiled by data collectors, the use of credit information collected by credit bureaus, and the general rights of consumers to control information about themselves and their commercial transactions. The magnitude of this issue is suggested by the results of a 1992 Harris-Equifax Consumer Privacy Survey, in which 89 percent of those polled agreed with the following statement: "Computers have made it much easier for someone to obtain confidential personal information about individuals."[1] Thus many consumers are worried that easy access to their personal information will intrude upon their right to privacy.

The use of consumer information to improve the efficiency of a marketing campaign has become known as *database marketing* or DBM. In some respects these programs have revolutionized the field of marketing. A well-designed DBM campaign can allow companies "to tailor marketing messages and products more specifically to customer groups," and it also improves "the targeting of current and potential buyers."[2] Despite the enormous success of these programs, they have produced some backlash because of their negative effects on the right to privacy, and this will be a major topic in this chapter.

The discussion on employee privacy will deal primarily with the growing reliance on electronic monitoring and other mechanisms to scrutinize work habits and measure employee productivity. This problem is particularly acute as employees are increasingly being subjected to "dataveillance," the systematic use of personal data systems to keep track of their actions or communications.[3] In this context we will also discuss the privacy issues posed by electronic mail and will consider whether the employer has a right to intercept or monitor these messages.

In each of these areas we will seek to articulate minimum standards of responsibility and discuss legitimate parameters of behavior. As a propaedeutic to this discussion, however, we must first consider the legal and moral foundation of the right to privacy. What is the scope of this right and what is its meaning in this particular context?

THE RIGHT TO PRIVACY

Legal Protection

An individual's right to privacy is protected by law, but it is sometimes difficult to assess the nature and extent of this protection. Current privacy law has its roots in the U.S. Constitution. According to various Supreme Court rulings, the Constitution bestows on individuals a right of privacy in accordance with the First, Fourth, Ninth, and Fourteenth Amendments. It is

[1]Mitch Betts, "Computerized Records: An Open Book?" *Computerworld*, August 9, 1993, p.1. Copyright 1994 by Computerworld, Inc., Framingham, MA 01701—Reprinted from *Computerworld*.

[2]Frank Cespedes and H. Jeff Smith, "Database Marketing: New Rules for Policy and Practice," *Sloan Management Review*, Summer 1993, p. 7.

[3]Roger Clarke, "Information Technology and Dataveillance," *Communications of the ACM*, May 1988, pp. 498–512.

important to note, however, that only the Fourteenth Amendment provides a basis for protecting a person's "informational privacy," since this amendment has been frequently invoked to protect citizens against unwarranted wiretapping or other forms of covert surveillance.[4]

Congress also has enacted numerous laws designed to protect the right to privacy. These include the Fair Credit Reporting Act of 1971, the Family Educational Rights and Privacy Act (1974), the Right to Financial Privacy Act of 1978, and the landmark 1974 Privacy Act, which deals with the protection of privacy in the use or distribution of government records. There is a patchwork of legislation but unfortunately no comprehensive set of laws or regulations that clearly states the parameters of one's privacy rights. It should also be mentioned that many states have their own laws about informational privacy, and these may cover restrictions on the use of DBMs and related matters.

One of the most relevant federal regulations for our purposes is the Fair Credit Reporting Act (FCRA), which sets standards for the legitimate use of credit reports and delineates a consumer's rights in disputing those reports. The responsibility of enforcing this act belongs to the Federal Trade Commission (FTC). In general, according to this act, a consumer's credit report should be released to a third party only under the following conditions:

> In response to a court order
> In response to a written request from the consumer who is the subject of the report
> In response to responsible third parties who intend to use the information "in connection with a credit transaction involving the consumer," for employment purposes, to underwrite insurance, or to determine "the consumer's eligibility for a license or other benefit granted by a governmental instrumentality"[5]

Finally, credit information can also be given to those third parties who have a "legitimate business need" for the information. This condition will be discussed further below.

Moreover, according to the FCRA, the consumer has specific rights regarding the dissemination of these reports. The consumer has the right to be given all of the information in his or her credit file (for a fee). Consumers also have the right to be informed of the recipients of their reports if the report was supplied for employment purposes within the previous two years or for any other purpose within the previous six months.

---

[4]Carol Gould, "Network Ethics: Access, Consent and the Informed Community," in *The Information Web: Ethical and Social Implications of Computers*, ed. Carol Gould (Boulder, CO: Westview Press, 1989), p. 22.

[5] "Fair Credit Reporting Act," *United States Annotated Code, Title 15, Commerce and Trade* (St. Paul, MN: West Publishing Co., 1982), Sec. 15.1681.

But despite these types of laws as well as constitutional protection, there are conspicuous deficiencies in the government's protection of privacy. As we have pointed out, the law is not comprehensive and does not create a firmly based right to privacy for all citizens. For example, the purpose of the Fair Credit Reporting Act is to limit access to credit reports, but exceptions are granted for "legitimate business need." This phrase is quite ambiguous, however; just what constitutes legitimate business need? Credit bureaus have interpreted this condition loosely and hence they have considered it permissible to sell selective credit information to a host of different businesses for direct mail or other solicitations.

Given this ambiguity and the gaps in the present laws, many have argued for a constitutional amendment that would protect individuals from having their private information shared or distributed without their approval. Others contend that reform of the FCRA and a buttressing of other regulations that protect personal privacy is essential. One wonders, however, whether we can really entrust another intractable problem to government bureaucracy. It may be necessary for consumer groups and corporations to look for creative solutions instead of more government intervention.

Privacy as a Natural Right

A more important issue for our purposes concerns the natural right to privacy which is the foundation of the legal right. The philosophical literature on the right to privacy is extensive. Some philosophers have argued that privacy is a fundamental, irreducible right, while others have regarded the right to privacy as a necessary condition for other important rights such as the exercise of our freedom or personal autonomy.

A complete treatment of the philosophy of privacy is well beyond the scope of this book, but in order to appreciate the importance of privacy it would be instructive to dwell briefly on the intimate connection between privacy and freedom. Several philosophers have convincingly argued that a shield of privacy is absolutely essential for the exercise of one's personal liberty and autonomy. Freedom, of course, is a vital component of personhood. Kant has argued that freedom and rationality distinguish human beings from all other beings, that our capacity for normative self-determination is a supreme value of our personhood. In other words, I deserve respect from others because I can freely determine my future and destiny. Also, I am obliged to respect this same capacity for self-determination in others.

Hence, according to this Kantian perspective, to respect someone as a person, one must clearly respect his or her freedom, and doing so means taking into account the way this person's projects are affected by our own actions and policies. We have no right to interfere with others' free pursuit of their goals, but this is precisely what we do when we violate their personal privacy. If I openly watch someone's actions, then I am altering the context of those actions and perhaps the person's behavior. If a person knows that I am watching him or monitoring her conversations, the person is apt to be more self-conscious and perhaps inhibited, concerned about whether his or her statements or actions meet my approval.

Furthermore, according to the contemporary philosopher S. I. Benn, even covert watching, which may not cause any direct injury to the unsuspecting victim, is disrespectful and wrong. According to Professor Benn, "covert observation—spying—is objectionable because it deliberately deceives a person about his world, thwarting, for reasons that *cannot* be his reasons, his attempts to make a rational choice."[6] In other words, we manifest no respect for another's project or enterprise if we alter the context or conditions of action and conceal this altering from the victim. A person's enterprise takes on a new significance because it is observed by someone else, even if the person has no knowledge of the scrutiny.

Thus there is a close relationship between privacy and respect for persons as autonomous, free, rational beings. The fact that a person is worthy of respect as a rational autonomous being implies that one must also respect his or her privacy, which is a necessary condition of that autonomy. Intrusions such as surveillance can disrupt a person's activities and thereby interfere with freedom, so they cannot be justified.

This duty to respect another's privacy is a *prima facie* duty; that is, it is not an absolute duty that does not allow for exceptions. For example, the police, under certain conditions have every right to violate the privacy of criminals by spying on them because there is a higher duty to protect the property and lives of the citizens. Under normal circumstances, however, privacy must be respected as an important shield protecting our freedom and self-determination. Thus, as we observed in Chapter 2, when information technology is used to invade privacy in certain ways, there is a potential threat to our dignity as human beings.

CONSUMER PRIVACY

As we consider the moral and legal aspects of the right to privacy, it becomes evident that a key element of the moral basis for privacy is the right to control information about oneself. It is precisely this right that is most threatened by new computer technologies. Advances in these technologies have appreciably increased the volume of information that is collected, stored, and distributed, and also the efficiency with which that

---

[6] S.I. Benn, "Privacy, Freedom, and Respect for Persons," in *Philosophical Dimensions of Privacy: An Anthology,* ed. Ferdinand Schoeman (New York: Cambridge University Press, 1984), p. 223.

information is compiled and disseminated. As one prescient observer wrote, "The foundation is being laid for a dossier society, in which computers could be used to infer individuals' life-styles, habits, whereabouts, and associations from data collected in ordinary customer transactions."[7]

Among the plethora of recent challenges to consumer privacy, two stand out as especially noteworthy. In a highly publicized case in late 1990, Lotus Development Corporation abruptly cancelled the release of a product called *Marketplace: Households* because of unexpected and intense public pressure (see the case study at the end of this chapter). This product, which was developed in conjunction with Equifax, a large credit reporting company, was designed to provide a targeted mailing list drawn from a mammoth database of 120 million names. The purchaser of this list would have permanent use of these names. The lists would be generated on the basis of specific demographic questions about age, income level, marital status, and so forth. Thus, for example, a retailer in Newton, Massachusetts, could buy a list, on a CD-ROM, of all the residents of Newton who are unmarried and over 65 years old with an annual income exceeding $50,000.

Marketplace did not receive a warm reception among consumer groups or right-to-privacy advocates. According to these critics, this product raised serious questions about the use of Equifax's detailed credit information for marketing purposes. They were also alarmed because, unlike the case with the other methods, which permitted only one-time use of mailing lists, the information on the CD-ROM was permanently owned by the user. Despite certain safeguards, there would be little control over how the owners used this information and how they redistributed it to others.

More recently, AT&T has stirred controversy over its project to distribute 800-number directories targeted to carefully selected prospects. For example, one directory might be devoted to travel, and would contain the toll-free 800-numbers of travel agencies, hotels, airlines and so forth. The consumer group for this directory would be those who call such numbers with some frequency. Thus, if a household has made several phone calls within the previous year or two to travel agencies, hotels, or airlines, it would be considered a likely prospect for future travel and hence would receive a copy of this specialized directory. This procedure may sound innocuous, but it presents a problem. The compilation of this directory would require that AT&T search through its electronic phone records to ferret out individuals who have recently called these 800-numbers (this is possible since phone companies record the numbers you have dialed along with how long you were connected). This possibility raises the ethical question of whether such records should be considered private and off limits for marketing and other nonessential purposes. As technological advances

[7]David Chaum, "Security without Identification: Transaction Systems to Make Big Brother Obsolete," *Communications of the ACM*, 21 (1985), p. 1030.

make phone records more accessible, where and how does one draw the line in their use? Will the phone companies continue to examine customer dialing records to determine new kinds of information services that could be marketed to the consumer?

Both of these cases highlight the trend to expand the domain of public information. In the Lotus case, information supplied for credit purposes was to be transformed into pseudo-public marketing data that could be sold for a small fee. In the second example, the strong industry tradition of protecting phone numbers appears to be disintegrating. They both make manifest the porosity of our environment in the "information age" and the apparent need for restrictions and carefully crafted guidelines.

The fundamental problem illustrated by these two cases is that society's assumptions about the proprietary nature of information are undergoing a radical transformation and often without the participation of those who are directly affected. Most of us have assumed that when we provide information about ourselves for a specific purpose, such information is reasonably confidential. For example, when I apply for a car loan, I expect the transaction to be a private affair between me and the bank. In the past, vendors and others saw no value in this information beyond the immediate transaction. However, as such information can more efficiently be collected, stored, retrieved, and disseminated, it now assumes some value, especially as a marketing tool. As a result, collectors of information, both in the corporate and government sectors, now consider much of the information they gather to be suitable for widespread dissemination in the public domain. For many organizations, information has become a commodity that can be collected and redistributed with very little overhead.

Indeed, even state government agencies routinely sell information they have collected about their residents. For example, the Department of Motor Vehicles, in the process of issuing a driver's license, obtains a person's name, height, weight, date of birth, use of corrective lenses, and so forth. Many states now sell this information to credit agencies such as TRW and Trans Union and to direct mail companies such as R. L. Polk, who in turn use these data to draw up targeted marketing lists for resale. Also, in his controversial book *Privacy for Sale*, Jeffrey Rothfeder reveals that agencies of the federal government have about 2,000 data banks on millions of citizens. Many of these agencies "share" this information rather freely or use it to target people suspected of some wrongdoing such as failure to pay taxes.[8]

The upshot of all these unsettling developments is that the boundary separating confidential and public information has shifted dramatically in favor of the public. However, corporations, state agencies, and even the federal government have made this transformation with little or no input

---

[8]Jeffrey Rothfeder, *Privacy for Sale* (New York: Simon & Schuster, 1992), pp. 124–52.

from major stakeholders such as citizens and consumers. They have often acted unilaterally to change the status of information so that very little of what is provided to them is now regarded as confidential and unavailable for other uses. Moreover, they have seemingly ignored the idea that by turning information into a low-cost commodity, they have infringed upon the important rights of individual citizens.

Indeed, this subtle but relentless shift in assumptions about confidential information raises many ethical issues. The primary question is whether privacy rights are being violated by the various practices described here. To begin with, what is proprietary information and when should information remain confidential? For example, if I supply information on a loan application, do I have the right to dictate how that information will be used or do I surrender control over such information? Can information disclosed for one purpose be used for another, *secondary* purpose without the individual's consent? Or does this practice constitute an invasion of privacy? And, if it does, how can an individual retain control over such information?

For corporations, such questions also raise a key management issue: What are the legal and moral ramifications if managers do not take these questions seriously and consider more explicitly the problem of protecting privacy?

Corporations and certain government agencies that buy and sell these lists have maintained that the consumer's right to privacy is not compromised. The argument that such practices allow them to target customers efficiently certainly has some merit. Indeed, a well-targeted direct mail effort through a DBM campaign or some other mechanism is vital for the success of many companies, especially those with limited financial resources. In addition, some of these target prospects will welcome the promotional material, while others will simply ignore it. If the only adverse consequence is more unwanted mail for some people, where is the real harm? The benefits of these mailings would certainly appear to outweigh the costs. Also, nonprofit groups and political organizations rely on direct mail campaigns for financial or volunteer support.

Moreover, those who buy and sell this type of information justify their actions by appealing to the argument of commercial property rights. They contend that they "own" this information and hence have an unambiguous right to dispose of it as they see fit. It is by no means clear, however, that providing someone with information confers this sort of property right. When a consumer provides personal information, he or she does not assign to that vendor a right to use that information for other purposes. Unless there were such an explicit agreement, the "property rights" argument does not seem persuasive.

Defenders of the direct mail industry and the treatment of information as a commodity also tend to oversimplify the repercussions of these practices. For one thing, consumers legitimately worry that despite safeguards this information will fall into the wrong hands. This is possible since it is virtually impossible to keep track of data once they are sold to another organization. In addition, although many legitimate businesses use direct mail campaigns to sell their products, information could easily be sold to unscrupulous direct mail companies that engage in fraudulent marketing campaigns or other scams. Such fraudulent solicitations have bilked consumers out of millions of dollars.

Another difficulty concerns the integrity of the data collectors. Can they always be trusted to use the data appropriately and provide safeguards against potential abuses. For instance, it is now fairly common practice for physicians and pharmacists to sell computerized patient records to specialized data collectors, who in turn sell them to pharmaceutical companies interested in tracking how well their products are selling. These data collectors dial into the PC's of physicians and pharmacists and extract information from confidential records. They contend that the use of these records does not violate privacy since patient names are supposedly deleted. However, physicians and pharmacists who entrust their data to these firms have no way of knowing exactly what information is being extracted. Presently there is significant potential for abuse. There are serious questions as to whether the safeguards protecting privacy are adequate. In this embryonic and unregulated data collection industry what is to stop an unscrupulous firm from extracting and using patient names along with the other data? Moreover, once these companies have collected these data there is no control over their subsequent use. Therefore should the custodians of medical records containing such sensitive information sell them to companies even though they are not certain what information is being extracted or how it will be used? The potential for breaches of confidentiality and considerable harm befalling some patients seems to demand tighter controls and closer scrutiny of how such records can be protected.

Still another problem emanates from the power of *data recombination*, which is the correlation of information from different sources to create *new information*. For example, a data collector can purchase data from a credit agency such as TRW or Equifax and combine those data with files purchased from a state agency such as a motor vehicle bureau. The end result might be a revealing profile of an individual's personal and financial background.

The final problem concerns the accuracy of the data that are being transmitted, resold, or recombined with other data. It is well-known that data files contain outdated and inaccurate information. In addition, the larger the database the more likely there will be mistakes and anomalies.

Furthermore, as these data are shared, the inaccurate information can be propagated in many different files, until it is virtually impossible to correct. In short, then, errors could take on a life of their own and cause innumerable problems for the subject of those errors.

We can summarize as follows the most salient problems with shuffling data around as if they were just a commodity:

- Potential for data to be sold to unscrupulous vendors
- Problems with ensuring the trustworthiness and care of the data collectors
- Potential for data recombination to create detailed, composite profiles of individuals
- The difficulty of correcting inaccurate information once it has been propagated into many different files

It is fair to conclude, then, that the negative consequences of information sharing are more extensive and serious than industry participants are willing to admit. As these data collectors, credit unions, and direct mailers continue to cast their nets wider, consumers will lose more and more control over the information about themselves that was once thought to be confidential. At the same time the harm caused by inaccurate information will be accentuated through this free flow of data. Thus there is real danger that our personal privacy will gradually become more illusion than reality.

Given our previous discussion on the intimate connection between privacy and freedom, it would be instructive to consider how the erosion of privacy through redistributing data adversely affects our autonomy. How is our freedom impaired if our name, address, and other personal information are sold and resold and then end up on junk mailing lists?

One problem in this regard is that under these circumstances almost every transaction assumes greater significance. In our information-sharing society the consumer not only applies for a car loan at the local bank but in the process divulges important information about his or her driving habits and financial history. A consumer making a phone call to a hotel or travel agency is recording an interest in travel for the potential benefit of marketers eager for such information. A serious consequence of these practices, therefore, is that people will think more carefully before engaging in such transactions and leaving behind a permanent record of important personal data. As Richard Wasserstrom observed when privacy is so circumscribed, "life would to this degree become less spontaneous and more measured."[9] As people come to realize that information they provide will be used for other purposes, it is likely that to some extent they will be inhibited from providing that information.

[9]Richard Wasserstrom, "Privacy: Some Arguments and Assumptions," in *Philosophical Dimensions of Privacy: An Anthology*, ed. Ferdinand Schoeman (New York: Cambridge University Press, 1984), p. 328.

Consider, for example, consumers who apply to banks or finance agencies for credit. They may become loath to make the application when they learn that all the information they provide will be listed on Equifax's Credit Seekers Hotline and subsequently sold to various vendors. Also, they may develop a reluctance to pay with a credit card when they learn that those who use Visa and Mastercard with some frequency will be put on Trans Union's "Bankcard Hotline." They may even hesitate to make certain phone calls if calling records are peddled to different proprietors.

To be sure, as isolated events these may not appear to be so serious, but the cumulative effect is likely to be a powerful constraint on the consumer's hitherto unlimited freedom in this sphere of activity. Clearly, then, the indiscriminate sharing of information and the lack of privacy and confidentiality can impair one's commercial relationships and interfere with important business transactions. Without protection in both their commercial and personal relationships, there will be real limits to their autonomy. The consumer should be free to conduct his or her affairs without the burden of an unwanted observer who tracks purchases, buying habits, phone calls, and other activities.

In summary, there are serious adverse consequences for the consumer when his or her privacy is compromised in commercial transactions. Perhaps the most serious consequence is the diminution of freedom in this area. We have been at pains to insist here that privacy is a fundamental natural right because it is an essential condition for the exercise of our self-determination. The extensive sharing of personal data is a clear example of how the erosion of privacy leads to the diminution of that freedom. Once the shield of privacy has been penetrated, the capacity of individuals to control their destiny in small and large affairs is in grave peril.

THE PRINCIPLE OF INFORMED CONSENT AND PRIVACY

If we take the right of privacy seriously, it seems evident that some of the policies and practices delineated here must be terminated or at least modified. It may ultimately be necessary to develop new laws and regulations to prevent the steady erosion of this basic right, but the absence of such laws should not inhibit organizations from becoming more socially responsible in this area. They should strive to be proactive in fulfilling their moral obligation to respect the privacy of others.

How, then, can organizations fulfill their obligation to respect the right of privacy? Can we discern a practical principle to guide their activities in this controversial area?

A good starting point is the assumption that the consumer prefers personal information to be regarded as confidential and not available to be traded as a commodity. To some extent the truth of this assumption depends on the nature of the information. Most people are sensitive about medical, credit, or financial information; however, some may be a bit more lenient when it comes to less significant information such as their purchasing habits. Nevertheless, a vast majority of individuals do desire to control all types of information about themselves by having some say in how that information will be shared with others. This desire imposes on the corporation the burden of seeking the consumer's permission to use that information for other purposes. But what is an appropriate method for seeking such permission?

Before answering this question, we cannot overlook the other side of this equation, that is, the need for various types of information. Targeted mailing lists, marketing surveys, and other types of data about customer prospects are the lifeblood of many organizations, especially smaller organizations and startup firms with limited resources. As was noted earlier, the DBM is an efficient marketing tool that benefits both marketers and consumers. Hence there are substantial economic benefits to the activities of data collection and sharing. In addition, as Deborah Johnson has perceptively observed, "the case for information gathering and exchange of information is made. . .on the grounds that they lead to better decision making."[10] Hence reforms that would unduly restrict the access of information could have grave negative consequences for many corporations and their stakeholders. To be sure, it would be a logistical nightmare to require marketers and DBM users to obtain explicit written permission each time they wanted to use personal data or add someone's name to a mailing list that is to be sold to other proprietors. This extreme a reform would make the use of direct mail campaigns prohibitively expensive. In short, the requirement of *affirmative consent* or explicit permission would practically destroy the direct mail and data collection industries.

However, an alternative to affirmative consent is the principle of *implicit informed consent*, which still safeguards privacy and is more economically viable. This is a slight variation of the principle of informed consent which was introduced in Chapter 1. According to Carol Gould, in the context of privacy issues this principle "imposes upon the institution or agency that has or wants information the burden of seeking the consent of the subject and of informing him or her; thus the information remains under the control ab initio of the person whom it is about."[11] The normative justification for this principle is clearly based on the right to privacy and the derived right to participate in decisions affecting one's personal life and one's exercise of free choice.

[10]Deborah Johnson, *Computer Ethics* (Englewood Cliffs, NJ: Prentice-Hall, 1985), p. 62.
[11]Gould, "Network Ethics," p. 27.

According to this principle, companies that have collected data about customers must diligently inform them about the primary and secondary uses of those data. Consumers must be given an opportunity to consent to these uses or withhold their consent; but the burden is on the consumer to respond, and a lack of response implies consent. Moreover, companies must provide these customers with the opportunity to grant consent for any *subsequent* uses of these data. For example, they must give customers the option to delete their names from mailing lists designed to be sold to other organizations. Those whose names are on such lists must be notified of this fact and be given the opportunity to have their names removed by sending in a response within a certain time frame. If no response is forthcoming, it is assumed that they do not object to having their name and personal data used in this way.

We can summarize this principle of *implicit informed consent* as follows: Corporations must inform consumers about all the various uses of their personal data and refrain from using these data in ways for which consent is withheld; it is understood that no response to a request for the use of information is equivalent the consumer's implicit consent.

It is worth noting that many conscientious publishers already engage in a similar practice out of respect for the privacy of their subscribers. For example, *The Economist* frequently rents its subscriber list to organizations seeking qualified prospects for its products or services, but it sends a booklet to all its subscribers notifying them that they have the right to have their name deleted.

Clearly, the principle of implicit informed consent is far less burdensome than the requirement of affirmative consent, since marketers will not have to wait for explicit permission. This principle is a moral minimum for those who take privacy rights seriously. It seeks to balance the need for information and the protection of informational privacy, as it offers a tenable mechanism for allowing individuals to gain control over how personal information is being used. To be sure, it is a pragmatic approach to the problem and is not without some deficiencies. It will be somewhat costly and raises several practical problems. One concerns the scope of permission granted by the consumer. Should the corporation seek unrestricted permission for the use of someone's name or do so on an ad hoc basis? The latter approach would certainly pose some logistical difficulties. Companies must also be diligent about contacting customers and providing them with a convenient way to respond. Despite these potential problems, however, this approach offers many benefits. It puts the burden on the consumer and yet gives that consumer a measure of control over personal information.

It is also worth noting that the European Economic Community is planning to adopt a wide array of rules to protect the privacy of its citizens, and a key provision entails strict restrictions on the use and exchange of computerized information. According to the European proposals, known as the Privacy Directive, "corporations using personal data must tell subjects of their use; a magazine publisher that wanted to sell its circulation list to advertisers, for example, would have to notify subscribers of its plans."[12] It has not yet been determined whether the subject must grant explicit permission or simply be notified with an option for deletion. European companies would also be required to register all commercial databases with each country in the European Community. These and other proposals incorporate principles of data protection that are seen as critical for safeguarding privacy.

PRIVACY WITHIN THE CORPORATION

Consumers, of course, are not the only group that has a basic right to privacy. Most philosophers and ethicians would insist that the right of personal privacy and other civil liberties also extend to the workplace. Patricia Werhane, for example, includes privacy in her comprehensive list of employee rights. She maintains that the right to privacy in the workplace includes but is not restricted to the following spheres of activity:

- The employee has the right to control or limit access to the personal information that he or she provides to an employer.
- An employee has a right "to activities of his or her choice outside the workplace."
- An employee has the right to privacy of thought[13]

In addition, as we argued earlier, the right to privacy is important because it safeguards another basic right that exists in the workplace: the right to autonomy and free expression.

How is workplace privacy threatened by advances in computer technology? One such threat involves the growing use of network management programs that allow system administrators of a PC network to read the files and documents in users' directories. More advanced programs will even allow these administrators to monitor what is being typed on an employee's computer screen. In addition, communications among different offices and even remote locations are now vulnerable to interception and scrutiny. Obviously this capacity will make it increasingly difficult for

[12]John Markoff, "Europe's Plans to Protect Privacy Worry Business," *The New York Times*, April 11, 1991, p. A1. Copyright © 1991 by The New York Times Company. Reprinted by permission.
[13]Patricia Werhane, *Persons, Rights, and Corporations* (Englewood Cliffs, NJ: Prentice-Hall, 1985), p. 119.

someone to send confidential memos or develop confidential files of electronic information, a constraint that could lead to serious abuses of an employee's civil liberties.

One of the most controversial issues regarding employee privacy involves the status of electronic mail (e-mail) software, which is a popular form of communication in many organizations. Through electronic mail, users can communicate with their colleagues throughout the organization as long as their computers are networked in some fashion. E-mail permits a user to send a single message simultaneously to hundreds of other users, and so it can increase efficiency by reducing paperwork and phone calls.

But as one might surmise, e-mail raises some critical concerns about privacy. For one thing, most e-mail systems generate archives of messages that can be inspected by anyone with the authority or technical acumen to do so. Should these messages be regarded as private, off limits for perusals by supervisors? Or is any form of communication over a network the property of the corporation that owns that system? In other words, do e-mail messages deserve the same privacy protection as regular mail? Are they public, private, or somewhere in between? This is a difficult question to resolve; there are cogent arguments on all sides of the debate. Also there are several lawsuits pending about this issue, and when they are settled we may have a clearer picture of the legal status of e-mail. For example, former employees of Nissan Motor Corp. U.S.A. filed a suit in 1991 claiming invasion of privacy after they were terminated because of the content of some e-mail messages that were intercepted by Nissan's management.

Most corporations would strongly insist that e-mail communications are public and hence subject to inspection at any time without any notice. They contend that the e-mail facility should be used only for business purposes and that the company has the prerogative to monitor those messages when and if it sees fit. The rationale for this policy is that e-mail is like any other business communication. Furthermore, the employer owns *all* resources in the workplace and has the right to determine how those resources will be deployed.

On the other hand, users and privacy experts contend that reading someone's e-mail is a violation of privacy. What's the difference, they say, between reading someone's handwritten mail or combing through someone's desk to find paper documents and reading the same type of information in a digital format? Hence many unions and independent organizations such as the ACLU contend that companies should not open their employees' electronic mail. In addition, the policy of checking on employees' e-mail creates a "Big Brother" atmosphere which dilutes trust in the organization and ultimately has a corrosive effect on morale. Thus a policy of monitoring e-mail may be costly in the long run and not worth the effort.

Regardless of how employers regard this controversial issue, however, they should have a clearly articulated policy regarding some of these questions. If the corporation considers e-mail messages public information, their employees should be informed that their messages are being monitored. Likewise, corporations should stipulate the legitimate uses of e-mail. A carefully worded policy regarding e-mail will go a long way to correct any false expectations on the part of employees and can help avoid legal problems as well as negative effects on morale. There is also a need for a comprehensive policy regarding the examining of all forms of corporate communications such as paper files, electronic mail, and telephone conversations. The more employees are informed about these matters, the better off they will be and the less likely the employer will confront legal problems for its actions.

An even greater threat to privacy and autonomy in the workplace is the prevalence of broad-based electronic monitoring programs that track a worker's productivity and work habits. This technology is currently most widely utilized in service industries such as banking and insurance as well as major segments of the travel industry. There may be some disagreement about exactly what constitutes electronic monitoring, but the following is a concise and accurate definition:

> Electronic work monitoring is the computerized collection, storage, analysis, and reporting of information about employees' productive activities.[14]

Electronic monitoring is normally combined with work measurement systems that set a standard for how long a task should take, compares that standard with the actual completion time, and then issues reports showing variances for each employee. For example, the system may set a standard of one minute for a data entry clerk in a given application, that is, it should take the clerk one minute to enter a record. At the end of a given time period a report will be generated showing the list of variances for each record entered along with a summary or average variance. Similar applications might be used by a firm using telemarketing personnel. In this case it would monitor the time spent on each customer or prospect by calculating the time taken to make and complete each phone call.

It is evident from these examples that routine jobs are most conducive for electronic monitoring and work measurement. Thus, in addition to data entry clerks, customer service workers, telephone operators, word processors, and similar jobs are most frequently subjected to this computerized evaluation. One of the most popular applications is known as "telephone call accounting." Systems are designed "to measure efficiency as well as

[14]John Chalykoff and Nitin Nohria, "Note on Electronic Monitoring," (Cambridge, MA: *Harvard Business School Publications*, 1990), p. 1.

verify the legitimacy of the call."[15] By checking the time, destination, and duration of telephone calls some organizations hope to eliminate long-distance personal calls and other types of abuses that can be expensive. Some systems allow employers to go even further and listen in on phone calls between employees or between an employee and an outside party.

Beyond any doubt, the primary benefit of electronic monitoring systems is their ability to help increase efficiency and reduce waste in an organization. However, these systems may lead to unrealistic and burdensome work standards, which dehumanize workers, increase turnover, and in the long run may militate against achieving real efficiency. These systems may also go too far in invading personal privacy. It can be argued that telephone accounting is necessary to keep spiraling costs under control. However, if corporations seek to achieve this goal by listening in to employee conversations, a case can surely be made that they are violating the employee's right to privacy. If an organization systematically monitors its workers' conversations, it cannot avoid listening to personal conversations in addition to those that are work related. Sometimes in an emergency such conversations with family members or others are simply unavoidable; in these cases the corporation will be privy to information about an employee's personal life that it has no right to possess.

By monitoring work-related conversations and electronic mail in the workplace, the corporation stifles free expression and creates an Orwellian atmosphere that most employees will find oppressive and stressful. One serious problem, of course, is that the information gleaned from such monitoring can be unfairly used against these employees. If the rights of privacy and free expression are to be respected, such surveillance methods must be restricted.

Thus it is not surprising that union leaders and other labor advocates have expressed strong opposition to computerized monitoring systems. They are concerned about invasions of privacy and an overreliance on quantitative data as the basis of performance evaluations. The problem, they contend, is that many aspects of an employee's work are not conducive to such strict quantitative measures. For example, a travel agent may process many more travel reservations than his or her peers but in the process be abrupt and discourteous and thereby alienate some of the agency's customers. Of course, there are benefits to relying on quantitative data, since their use will reduce subjectivity and biases and in the long run could yield a fairer evaluation system.

There are considerable empirical data about the effects of computerized monitoring systems, but they are rather inconclusive. One study, focusing on a monitoring system at a large insurance company, concluded that the system produced fear and resentment among the employees and

[15]Ibid., p. 3.

significantly elevated their stress level. Another exploratory study of several insurance companies and financial institutions concluded that "the introduction of computerized performance monitoring may result in a workplace that is less satisfying to many employees." The study also concluded that "extensive use of numerical performance feedback seems to create a more competitive environment which may decrease the quality of social relationships between peers and between supervisors and subordinates."[16] But the authors of this study also found that most workers were not opposed in principle to such systems, but only to how they were used by management. Also a government study of electronic monitoring reaches an even more disturbing conclusion. According to Dr. Michael Smith of the Office of Technology Assessment:

> Electronic monitoring may create adverse working conditions such as paced work, lack of involvement, reduced task variety and clarity, reduced peer social support, reduced supervisory support, fear of job loss, routinized work activity, and lack of control over tasks.[17]

Other studies, on the other hand, illustrate more positive effects from these systems, such as an improvement in employee evaluations, especially the timeliness and quality of feedback to individual employees.[18] Thus, in general it seems evident that companies contemplating the introduction of these systems should proceed with caution to avoid some of the undesirable effects noted here. Further, at a minimum, companies should clearly state their monitoring policies.

Finally, it should be pointed out that the notion of employee rights such as privacy and free expression is not universally accepted. Many still cling to the traditional doctrine of Employment at Will (EAW), stating that employers may hire, fire, promote, or demote "at will." According to this viewpoint, which has been supported even in recent court cases, "in freely taking a job, an employee voluntarily commits herself to role responsibilities and company loyalty, both of which are undermined by the intrusion of certain employee rights."[19]Advocates of this position would likely claim that employees do not enjoy the rights of privacy and autonomy in the workplace, especially if that right interferes with the efficiency and productivity of the organization. For those who take this position, the electronic monitoring and work measurement methods described here will probably be less problematic.

[16]R.H. Irving, C. A. Higgins, F. R. Safayeni, "Computerized Performance Monitoring Systems: Use and Abuse," *Communications of the ACM*, August 1986, p. 800.

[17]Quoted in Karen Nussbaum, "Computer Monitoring: A Threat to the Right to Privacy," *Ethical Issues in Information Systems*, ed. Roy Dejoie, George Fowler, and David Paradice (Boston: Boyd & Fraser Publishing, 1991), p. 136.

[18]See the article by Irving, Higgins, and Safayeni for a discussion of these studies.

[19]Werhane, *Persons, Rights, and Corporations*, p. 83.

SUMMARY

One of the primary by-products of the information revolution seems to be the attendant loss of personal privacy. This is a critical issue, since privacy is an important natural right. Although the right to privacy is protected by a patchwork of federal privacy laws and regulations, there is no comprehensive set of such regulations. Hence there are many loopholes and shortcomings in the current laws and regulations that protect privacy. Despite the law's failure to keep up with technology, corporations should seriously consider the importance of respecting the natural right of privacy. Privacy is not only important in itself but also as a condition for the exercise of freedom and self-determination. Without privacy, our lives become more controlled and our dignity as human persons can be impaired.

A key aspect of the moral basis for privacy is the right to control information about oneself. It is this right that is most in jeopardy from advances in digital technology. Information has become a commodity that is collected and stored in huge databases and sold to vendors for direct mail purposes. Sometimes this information is recombined with other information, allowing a vendor to develop a composite profile of individual consumers. All of these activities raise important ethical questions for which there are no easy answers: What exactly constitutes confidential, proprietary information in the age of digital disclosure? Can information disclosed for one purpose be used for secondary purposes without an individual's consent?

Many defenders of the direct mail industry and database marketing are quick to point out that the only harm of these practices is more unwanted mail for some people. We have maintained, however, that there are more serious adverse consequences, including the difficulty of correcting any inaccurate information that has been propagated in files, the dangerous power of data recombination, and the possibility that such data will be sold to unscrupulous vendors for use in direct mail scams. We have also claimed that another serious consequence of these information-sharing practices will be some diminution of the consumer's freedom; many will have reservations about engaging in transactions (such as using credit cards) that leave behind a permanent record of personal data.

However, one must also consider the need for information as a basis for good decision making and the importance of targeted direct mail campaigns, especially for companies with limited resources. Given this situation, perhaps a principle of *implicit informed consent* represents a viable compromise between the needs of business and the privacy of consumers. According to this principle, companies must inform consumers about the primary and secondary uses of their personal information and refrain from using these data if consent is withheld; it is understood that a lack of response to a request for the use of this information is equivalent to the consumer's implicit consent. For instance, companies must give customers the option to delete their names from mailing lists destined to be sold to other organizations. The burden is on the consumer to respond, but this practice will nevertheless enable consumers to regain some control over how their personal information is used.

In future years we may find clever technological solutions to the problem of protecting personal privacy. For instance, some have suggested that a system be devised whereby one's electronic identity is simply a number that is not connected to one's physical self. Account numbers would be attached to encrypted identities, so, for example, data collectors could never determine that Sally Jones was connected with account number 2378125.[20]

Privacy is also an issue for employees, who must now face an array of monitoring devices and other technologies that allow corporations to read their files and monitor their work habits. There is also considerable controversy about employees' use of e-mail and whether these electronic communications are public or private. Many organizations regard these communications as public because they are transmitted across company-owned networks, but privacy advocates maintain that they should be considered as private and confidential communications. As we observed, those corporations that do choose to monitor electronic mail will create a "big brother," Orwellian atmosphere that many employees will find quite demoralizing.

We also discussed other types of electronic monitoring and work measurement systems that track employee work patterns. Such systems are often utilized to set a standard for how long a task should take; they then compare that standard with the actual completion time. Although there are some positive effects of such systems such as better and faster feedback, they can also increase employee stress levels and generate considerable apprehension and loss of morale in the workplace. In addition, electronic monitoring systems may go too far when they lead to the establishment of unrealistic and onerous work standards. Indeed, these systems are designed to enhance efficiency, but they could backfire if they end up dehumanizing workers and increasing employee turnover. At a minimum, corporations should make their monitoring policies as clear and comprehensive as possible.

CASES FOR DISCUSSION

Introduction

This chapter has considered two dimensions of privacy: consumer privacy and privacy in the workplace. The first two cases here deal with consumer privacy issues and address the ethical propriety of using "credit" data for

[20]John Perry Barlow, "Private Life in Cyberspace," *Communications of the ACM*, August 1991, pp. 23–25.

marketing purposes. The first case focuses on various policies and practices of the credit bureau industry, and the second looks at a specific controversial product that makes use of those data.

The other two cases deal with privacy in the workplace. The Topper case examines the use of electronic monitoring at a travel agency and questions its legitimacy. The last case, *Incident at Saratoga International*, considers whether or not the interception of employee e-mail messages constitutes a violation of workplace privacy.

CASE 5.1

The Credit Bureau Industry

The purpose of the credit bureau industry is to provide information to organizations that routinely grant credit to their customers: banks, automobile dealers, credit card companies, retail stores, and so on. The organization can request a credit report on a client or a prospective customer and thereby assess which customers might be credit risks. These reports can also be used for other purposes, such as the screening of a prospective employee. Many companies will reject a job candidate who has a bad credit report, since, in their view, it reflects unfavorably on the individual's character.

Credit reports usually contain data about an individual's credit history, including information about credit cards and other credit accounts. The report reveals salient facts about the individual's payment history and highlights any late payments or other problems. It also includes information about the subject's mortgage amount, terms, balance due, and payment record over the past year. In addition, it usually reveals outstanding property taxes and whether or not there are any liens against the property. The report might also include information from various public sources regarding divorce proceedings, marriage licenses, civil lawsuits, and so forth.

Hence these reports are a comprehensive lens on the creditworthiness of a consumer who is a candidate for a mortgage or some other form of credit. Most organizations that extend credit consider them to be an indispensable tool for making credit decisions.

A Brief History The first local retail credit bureau was founded in 1860 in Brooklyn, New York. The expansion of such organizations was quite slow prior to World War I, primarily because only a relatively small segment of the retail business was conducted on a credit basis at that time. After the war, as credit became more popular, local credit bureaus began to emerge throughout the country. In 1906 the Associated Credit Bureaus of

America (ACBA) was established to improve cooperation and exchange of information between local credit bureaus.

These small community-based credit bureaus became a formidable force in American society since they were the most important sources of consumer credit information. Located in nearly every city with a population in excess of 10,000, they operated on the principle of "give and get." Creditors were charged a fee for the credit bureau's service but were also expected to contribute information to the bureau's files. Information on consumers came from a plethora of sources, including employment records, public records, other credit bureaus in the ACBA network, collection services, and so on. Some bureaus resorted to more unorthodox techniques to acquire information on consumers. As recently as 1971 a Washington, D.C., credit bureau hired hostesses to greet new arrivals to the community. After welcoming the newcomers with pleasant conversation and gifts, they would subtly make inquiries about the family's income and outstanding debts.[21]

The dominance and autonomy of the "friendly" local credit bureau has changed dramatically since the early 1970s as the smaller bureaus consolidated into the larger companies. At the national level the industry has become an oligopoly and is currently dominated by three large and puissant companies: TRW Credit Data, Equifax, and Trans Union Corporation. The largest of the three is Equifax, with revenues of well over $1 billion. Moreover, technological changes have helped to transform this industry. The remaining local credit bureaus are linked electronically to the sophisticated computer networks of the "big three." Creditors subscribe to reports from one or more of the these three national companies; they can get these reports directly or through a local bureau linked to one of the national bureaus. The principle of "give and get" remains in effect, since creditors seeking information must share their files with the bureau.

Issues of Accuracy   It is estimated that each of the three national players in this growth industry has files on approximately 150 million consumers. Also these companies are inundated with fresh credit data on a daily basis and usually make 2 billion updates on individuals' records each month! As consumers rely more heavily on credit, demand for credit reports has grown at a breathtaking pace. According to *The Wall Street Journal*, "the industry sells 1.5 million reports a day, not just to banks and stores but also to employers, insurers, car dealers, and landlords."[22]

---

[21]For background information about credit bureaus see Robert H. Cole and Robert Hancock, *Consumer and Commercial Credit Management* (Homewood, IL: Irwin, 1964), p. 211ff.

[22]Michael Miller, "Credit-Report Firms Face Greater Pressure," *The Wall Street Journal*, September 23, 1991, p. 1. Reprinted by permission of *The Wall Street Journal*, © 1991 Dow Jones & Company, Inc. All rights reserved worldwide.

Given this overwhelming amount of volatile data, it is not surprising that many credit reports are riddled with errors. The system was studied in 1989, when 9 million consumers checked their credit files and about 3 million of them claimed that they found information that was erroneous or outdated! The national bureaus have all disputed this extraordinarily high inaccuracy rate. They admit that there are some errors lurking in their files but contend that many of these stem from careless reporting procedures of the banks and stores that supply these data.

In the past several years the credit reporting industry has faced intense criticism from consumers about these persistent inaccuracies and poor customer relations. In 1990 the industry became the number one source of customer complaints in the United States, according to the Federal Trade Commission, which handled over 9,000 of these complaints. An especially embarrassing incident in 1991 generated considerable adverse publicity for the industry along with pressure for reforms. In the summer of 1991, for no apparent reason, all of the residents of Norwich, Vermont, were reclassified as high credit risks in TRW's database. Several individuals could not use their credit cards, and the town clerk received frantic calls from local area banks. Meanwhile mortgages and loans were denied even for the town's most respectable citizens with unblemished credit records. After numerous complaints to a beleaguered customer service staff at TRW, the mystery was solved. Apparently a part-time employee for a small Georgia company that looks up public records for TRW made a serious mistake. While checking over the records in Norwich, she asked for a list of property tax delinquents but instead was given the list of those who had paid their property taxes in full. The employee inadvertently wrote down the entire list of 1,400 residents. The situation was quickly rectified, and TRW referred to its mistake as an isolated situation. But in October 1991 TRW admitted that similar errors had occurred in Woodstock, Vermont, and several other New England towns.

Consumer groups also maintain that such foul-ups are not so isolated. They contend that the industry keeps inaccurate, shoddy data, has deficient security measures, and makes it difficult for consumers to inspect and correct their credit records. Finally they note that when consumers do get a copy of their credit report, they can't understand it; these reports tend to be so arcane and elliptical because of the codes and abbreviations used that the industry sells guides for deciphering them. Consumer groups are therefore advocating a number of key reforms for the industry, including the following:

Improved accuracy: Credit bureaus should swiftly correct mistakes and inform other credit reporters of errors.

Free credit reports: Consumers should be entitled to a free copy of their credit report once a year upon request; the Fair Credit Reporting Act of 1971 currently allows free access to one's credit report only if credit has been denied. (Free, regular credit reports would allow consumers to monitor their files for accuracy.)

Legal liability: Banks and other organizations should be held legally liable for submitting erroneous data about consumers to credit bureaus.

Better service: Errors should be investigated within 30 days; also credit denial notices should include a list of customers' rights.[23]

In response to this mounting criticism, TRW, Equifax, and Trans Union argue that their procedures are essentially sound and secure. They claim that errors are the result of credit grantors and even consumers themselves. They also point out that new regulations might bog down the credit system. That system enables U.S. consumers to buy 5,000 homes, 40,000 cars, and 300,000 appliances daily. As a result, they argue, tampering with this industry could have a negative impact on the whole economy.

More recently, however, the industry has mollified its defensive posture. In October 1991 TRW agreed to give consumers free copies of their credit reports, for which all three companies had been charging $15. In a press release TRW indicated that it would offer one free report a year upon a customer's request. Equifax and Trans Union have not changed their policy of charging for these reports unless the consumer is denied credit.

Mailing Lists   Another controversial practice of the "big three" and other agencies is to sell names, addresses, and limited financial data to junk mailers or direct mail organizations, who in turn sell them to retail companies and others looking for targeted mailing lists. This is a lucrative sideline for these companies, but it falls under a gray area of the Fair Credit Reporting Act. According to this law, credit data can be used only for "legitimate" business purposes, but the word "legitimate" is ambiguous. According to the interpretation of the major firms in the credit bureau industry, the sale of data to junk mailers is not precluded by the FCRA.

Equifax, in cooperation with credit card operations such as VISA, also sends unsolicited credit card offers to customers who meet a bank's criteria for being credit-worthy. This industry-wide practice has become known as *prescreening*. Another example of promotions to attract direct mailers is Equifax's "credit seekers hotline," a mailing list of up to 2 million names of people who had asked for a loan or credit card over the previous month, provided at a charge of 5 cents a name.

It should be remarked that Equifax's mailing list business constitutes only a small proportion of its total revenues. For example, it generated revenues of $11 million in 1990, a year when the company had net income of

[23]Evan Schwartz, "Credit Bureaus: Consumers Are Stewing—and Suing," *Business Week*, July 29, 1991, p. 69.

$63.9 million on sales of $1.08 billion. Both TRW and Trans Union have engaged in similar practices, routinely selling mailing lists to junk mailers and other vendors.

A Socially Responsible Industry? The credit bureau industry is keenly aware of its deteriorating public image. The "big three" have been maligned by consumer groups and the media for its practices, which many see as an egregious invasion of privacy. Consequently, companies such as TRW and Equifax have begun to make some concessions; moreover, they are both considering further concessions to placate some of these angry stakeholders. For example, as we noted earlier, TRW has agreed to give its credit reports to consumers free of charge. Equifax and Trans Union defend their practice of charging consumers $15 by noting that no other company gives away its product or service free or charge. It seems likely, however, that they too will soon bow to public pressure on this matter.

Equifax, on the other hand, announced that it will put an end to the sale of data to junk mailers. According to an Equifax Senior Vice President, "Continuing the business just wouldn't be consistent with a socially responsible position."[24] However, the company will continue to send unsolicited credit card offers to credit-worthy customers. Also, as of 1993, TRW and Trans Union had no plans to follow Equifax's precedent.

It is clear, however, that as each company attempts to come to terms with what constitutes proper and responsible behavior, the changes in this industry are not nearly as rapid or comprehensive as consumer groups would like to see. So far, the "big three" have resisted calls to overhaul their practices in a major fashion. In the face of this slow response, one might expect the federal government to develop new regulations and play a more vigorous role in overseeing this industry. But thanks to the influential lobbyists representing credit bureaus, banks, and retailers, significant legislative reform appears unlikely at least in the short run. Unfortunately, the Fair Credit Reporting Act was written in 1971 and is woefully outdated.

Finally, there will undoubtedly be many new challenges in this industry as technology continues to evolve and companies develop even faster methods to deliver information to their clients. For example, all three companies are currently working on sophisticated electronic networks that will make credit reports automatically accessible at any of its customer locations. Obviously, this new service could lead to serious abuses. What is to stop companies from pulling up credit reports of individuals who have not applied for credit? The bureaus say that they will make their customers promise to pull up reports only for lawful reasons, but enforcing this well-

---

[24]Michael Miller, "Equifax to Stop Selling Data to Junk Mailers," *The Wall Street Journal*, August 13, 1991, p. B1. Reprinted by permission of *The Wall Street Journal*, © 1991 Dow Jones & Company, Inc. All rights reserved worldwide.

intentioned policy will be virtually impossible. Hence more careful consideration must be given to security issues *before* these changes are implemented. One thing seems certain: As credit data become even more easily accessible, it will be increasingly difficult to prevent a credit bureau's clients from checking up on their friends, enemies, or business rivals.

Credit is important to the American economy, and it cannot be provided without credit bureaus. Thus, the "big three" and their local counterparts *do* play a critical role in our economy. But there appears to be some need for a better balance between the demands for timely credit information and the privacy rights of consumers. Finding the right balance is one more challenge of the responsible use of information in the information age.

Questions

1. What is your general assessment of the credit bureau industry? Has it behaved in a socially responsible fashion? If not, which policies or practices should be modified?
2. One of the most controversial practices of this industry is the sale of credit data to data collectors for target marketing. Is this practice immoral? Why or why not? Which ethical theories/principles substantiate your position?
3. In your view, what constitutes "fair credit reporting"? In other words, how should the industry define the legitimate uses of credit data?

CASE 5.2

The "Marketplace: Households" Product Controversy

When the details of the Lotus *Marketplace: Households* software were made public in April 1990, no one at the well-known Cambridge computer company could have anticipated the resulting vehement protests about this product. Consumers and computer users besieged the company with letters and electronic mail messages, claiming that it would be an irresponsible intrusion into their lives and a violation of their personal privacy.

Lotus was working in conjunction with Equifax Inc., one of the three major credit bureau companies in the United States. The proposed software package would enable small businesses and other organizations with limited resources to purchase targeted mailing lists, which they could use to solicit new customers through direct mail campaigns. In the face of the firestorm of protest generated by this announcement, however, both companies had to reconsider the future of this innovative product.

Lotus Development Corporation Lotus Development Corp. was founded in 1981 by computer wizard and entrepreneur Mitch Kapor. Its objective was to produce business productivity software for personal computers. In 1983 the company introduced its most popular and successful product, *Lotus 1-2-3*, a spreadsheet software package. Despite many competitive products such as Microsoft's *Excel*, *Lotus 1-2-3* dominated PC spreadsheet products since its first appearance; in 1991 its share of this market was still 60 percent. Lotus also marketed business graphics and database products. It combined its three major application packages—graphics, database, and spreadsheet—in another popular product known as *Symphony*. The company's other major businesses included CD-ROM products, financial information products for personal computers, and electronic mail packages for local area networks.

Lotus was one of the fastest growing PC software companies during the 1980s. Its five-year (1986–1990) compound average growth rate in revenues was 28.8 percent. In 1991 Lotus reported healthy net earnings of $43.1 million and its revenues for that year were $828.9 million, a 19.7 percent increase over 1990.[25] But despite its financial success in 1991, Lotus stumbled in its introduction of *Lotus 1-2-3* for Windows, the popular new operating system for IBM's PC. As the market for spreadsheets became increasingly saturated, Lotus aggressively sought to market new products such as *Marketplace: Households* in an effort to sustain its high growth rate.

Equifax Equifax, a billion-dollar credit bureau, was founded in 1899 in Atlanta, Georgia, first known as the Retail Credit Company. Equifax grew quickly in the 1980s, thanks in large part to the acquisition of many smaller, regional credit bureaus. It was one of the "big three" credit bureaus which dominated this industry along with TRW and Trans Union.[26] In 1990 Equifax reported profits of $63.9 million on total revenues of $1.08 billion. (This was up sharply from net income of $35.6 million on revenues of $840 million in 1989.)

Equifax collected data on consumers from a variety of sources, including credit history from banks, employment history, and payment records from credit grantors. It also received data from the U.S. census bureau and periodically purchased drivers' license data from motor vehicle agencies. In this way, the company tracks information on approximately 150 million individuals and compiles it into a credit report that is sold to banks or other companies that are considering granting credit to an individual. The sale of such credit reports was the main source of revenue for Equifax and the other players in this growing industry.

---

[25]"The Datamation 100," *Datamation*, June 15, 1992, p. 96.

[26]For additional background on these companies and the credit bureau industry see Case Study 5.1, *The Credit Bureau Industry.*

A controversial practice of Equifax, TRW, and Trans Union was their participation in the mailing list business. At one time all three of these companies sold names, addresses, and limited financial data to direct mail organizations or companies initiating targeted direct mail campaigns. In 1990 the mailing list business for Equifax totaled only $11 million. This practice has been heavily criticized as a violation of personal privacy. The direct mail business fell under a gray area of the Fair Credit Reporting Act, according to which credit data can be sold only for "legitimate" business purposes, an obviously ambiguous term; according to the credit bureau industry, this law should not preclude the sale of such data to junk mailers.

Equifax played a pivotal role in the development of the *Marketplace: Households* software with Lotus, since it was the primary source of information on 80 million U.S. households. The company also used its extensive files on American consumers to compile the demographic and lifestyle information that became a vital part of the product's data base.

The Product   In April 1990 Lotus and Equifax announced the impending introduction of the new Lotus Marketplace product at the beginning of 1991. This CD-ROM (compact disk—read only memory) database would have two main components: *Marketplace: Households* and *Marketplace: Business. Marketplace: Households* consisted of the name, address, gender, age, marital status, shopping habits, and income level for 80 million households. The product was also to have 50 psychographic categories ranging from "accumulated wealth" to "inner-city singles," but both companies had reservations about using these categories.

Marketplace was "aimed at small and mid-size businesses that want to do inexpensive, targeted direct mail marketing."[27] Lotus sought to take advantage of CD-ROM's substantial storage capability and bring the direct mail marketing industry to the world of personal computers and desktops.

Marketplace: Households would enable small businesses to purchase targeted mailing lists with a minimum of 5,000 names for a direct mail marketing campaign. The categories of information listed above could be used as the basis of selecting the names. Thus, for example, a small luxury car dealer might want to do a local mailing to consumers with incomes greater than $60,000. The dealer might utilize the following criteria to generate the list: all the individuals in Farifield County (Connecticut) who are over 40 years, who have an income in excess of $60,000, and who have a propensity to purchase expensive cars and other luxury items. Unlike other

[27]John Wilke, "Lotus Product Spurs Fears about Privacy," *The Wall Street Journal*, November 13, 1991, pp. B1, B5. Reprinted by permission of *The Wall Street Journal*, © 1991 Dow Jones & Company, Inc. All rights reserved worldwide.

database mailing list products, which were rented to vendors for one-time use, this list, in CD-ROM format, would be the permanent property of the dealer, who would have unlimited use of the names. The projected cost of Marketplace was $695 for the program and the first 5,000 names, and $400 for each additional 5,000 names.

Privacy Concerns Both Lotus and Equifax steadfastly maintained that they had addressed consumers' concerns about privacy. Their lists did not include telephone numbers or personal financial data. They also made it impossible to query an individual name. One could not type in "Peter Brown" and expect to get his age, income level, and purchasing habits. Of course, if Brown is part of the targeted group selected according to broader criteria, then one would have this information. Lotus also promised that the product would not fall into the wrong hands, since it would be sold only to legitimate businesses. Businesses intending to purchase the product would be carefully screened, and the product would not be sold to individuals. Furthermore, a carefully worded contract would limit the product's use and prohibit the purchaser from reselling the names. Finally, consumers would be given an opportunity to have their names excluded from this database. Both companies felt confident that these safeguards would protect confidential information about a consumer and hence not violate his or her privacy.

Critics of *Marketplace*, however, were not satisfied by the announcement of these safeguards. If the product were widely disseminated, how could Lotus really control how it was used? Could the company monitor and enforce the contract prohibiting the resale of the data? There were also concerns that consumers would not be able to delete their names from the database or make corrections in a timely manner; by the time such corrections or deletions were implemented, inaccurate versions of the database might already be on the market.

Some of the criticism became vehement as thousands wrote strong letters of protest to Lotus' corporate headquarters in Cambridge. Many of these letters were transmitted electronically and copied on hundreds of networks, further fueling the controversy and provoking others to join in the protest. The thrust of most of the letters was that this CD ROM database was an intrusive transgression of personal privacy.

In response to these protests, Lotus agreed to delete immediately the names of anyone who contacted the company. In a short period of time it received over 30,000 such requests. However, this offer did not silence Lotus's critics, who seemed to be growing more militant. Organizations such as Computer Professionals for Social Responsibility added their voice to the chorus of protests; they were especially concerned that there would be no way to guarantee that everyone in the database had freely consented.

Finally Lotus and Equifax capitulated and agreed to cancel the product. It was reported that they made this decision in the interests of consumer privacy and economics; both companies feared that a consumer backlash would affect their core business. The *Marketplace: Business* software package, offering marketing information on 7 million American businesses, was not cancelled, however; under a licensing agreement with Lotus this product is being sold by a start-up company, the Marketplace Information Corporation in Cambridge.

The Aftermath   Despite the abrupt cancellation of *Marketplace: Households*, some of the product's supporters were surprised and confused by the hostility it generated. They pointed out that the product could be a significant benefit to small and mid-size businesses which need to use targeted direct mail campaigns to find customers. It should be noted that the same information is purchased by large companies for higher fees for DBM (database marketing) campaigns. *Marketplace* made the purchase of data less expensive for small businesses and hence gave them an opportunity to do their own DBM campaigns. Further, Lotus and Equifax did take great pains to address the privacy concerns. Thus, some in the industry felt that this was a valuable product with adequate protection against breaches of confidentiality.

An executive at a well-known consulting firm made the following observation:

> I'm quite sure that *Marketplace: Households* or a similar version of that product is not dead yet; it has only been postponed. Lotus or some other company will bring it back in some form or another. There is already a vast amount of this information for sale, and the data available in *Marketplace* is not that different from what is already available in other electronic databases of consumer information. With some minor changes and additional safeguards, this product could be quite successful.

Only time will tell if he is correct.

Questions

1. Discuss the pros and cons of this product. Do the benefits outweigh the costs or vice versa?
2. Did Lotus provide adequate safeguards to protect privacy? Is there any way to develop and market this product in a more socially responsible fashion?
3. Assume that the proposed *Marketplace: Households* product did not generate so much negative publicity. If you were an executive at Lotus, would you market this product? Provide an ethical justification for your decision.

CASE 5.3

The Topper Travel Agency[28]

> Too many employers practice a credo of "In God we trust
> others we monitor."[29]

Katherine Davis arrived early for work on a bright, sunny Friday morning to read over a long report and a petition from disgruntled workers documenting her company's alleged violations of their right to privacy. As she pulled into the empty parking lot of the corporate headquarters of the Topper Travel Agency, Katherine realized that the situation was quite volatile and must be handled with extreme care. She had only recently taken the job as Topper's Human Resources Director and this was her first major crisis. The company's president, Robert Donaldson, wanted her recommendations on the matter by the close of the work day. She had already discussed the situation at some length with the company's attorneys but they were not very helpful. After that conversation yesterday afternoon Katherine realized that the key issues in this dispute were not legal ones; rather, they were nettling ethical questions that defied easy answers.

The Company   The Topper Travel Agency was founded in 1962 by Gerald H. Topper and his brother William. The company began in a small suburban office with only four travel agents and a secretary for Gerald Topper, but within a few years the agency had added three new offices to handle its growing business. Because of its reputation for superior service, the Topper Travel Agency continued to attract new business, especially from corporate clients. As a result, the company expanded vigorously in the 1970s and 1980s and by 1992 its revenues had grown to almost $800 million.

Topper's corporate headquarters were located in a large Midwestern city. The company continued to specialize in providing fast, reliable, efficient service to many of the area's largest and most distinguished corporations. Its growing revenues were matched by high profits. Indeed, the company had shown a profit every year since its inception. But recently, because of the recession in the early 1990s and other forces, there were pressures on its profit margins. During the previous year Topper's profit margin declined from 6.7 percent to 5.5 percent. The company was forecasting little growth in revenues or profits for 1993 because of the slow economy and more competitive pressures in the Midwest market.

---

[28]This case is based on an actual situation; all names, dates, and other information have been modified.
[29]Marlene Piturro, "Electronic Monitoring," *Information Center*, July 1990, p. 31.

A Monitoring System   In response to these revenue and profit projections, company president Robert Donaldson decided to focus on improving efficiency and reducing costs in order to prevent any further erosion in profit. The company wanted to be certain that its travel agents were working at maximum efficiency, so it decided to install a sophisticated monitoring system produced by Rockwell International. Rockwell salespeople had emphasized to Topper the productivity gains that could be achieved by faithful use of this system. They pointed out that one second shaved off 1,000 agents' calls each year could save the company $1 million in labor costs.

The Rockwell monitoring system would be used primarily with the travel agents serving Topper's large corporate clients. The system measured the duration of each agent's phone conversation with a client. The company's standard for completing a simple airline reservation and processing the tickets was 108 seconds. If a client needed hotel reservations and car rental arrangements in addition, Topper used a different time standard but the same procedure for calculating variances. Variances were duly noted and summarized in a monthly report, which was sent to supervisors and the Human Resources Department. If an employee had a record of consistent negative variances, he or she received a reprimand from the department supervisor; a meeting was also scheduled with the employee in order to uncover an explanation of the problem and work out a tenable solution. If the problem persisted, a representative from Human Resources might be asked by the department to attend a follow-up meeting, at which time the employee would be given a warning that he or she would be dismissed if the problem were not corrected within three months. So far only one employee had received a warning, whereupon she resigned from the company.

The monitoring system had other features in addition to measuring the duration of phone conversations. It could also detect when an employee left his or her desk to go to the bathroom, take a break, and so forth, and could measure the duration of these "interruptions." Supervisors would thus know whether the employee was exceeding the "standard" time limits (3 minutes) for the bathroom, for a break (15 minutes), or for lunch (45 minutes). The travel agent could not leave the desk for any other reason. Finally, the system enabled supervisors to listen in on employee phone calls, so they could determine if employees were following the company's rigid instructions for booking reservations by phone. If employees failed to follow the correct protocol or if they received and made personal phone calls during company time, they could receive a reprimand and eventually a termination warning.

Employee Reaction   Electronic monitoring was not well received by most employees at the travel agency. Most of them regarded this computer system as an unwarranted and odious intrusion of their privacy. They felt it was especially unfair for the company to listen in on phone calls. Sometimes incoming or outgoing personal calls were a necessity, particularly in cases of an emergency or family crisis. And since the company monitored all phone conversations, managers were often privy to intimate details about an employee's personal life. Travel agents also complained bitterly that incessant monitoring of their phone calls was causing considerable stress and anxiety. According to one agent:

> This monitoring system is nothing more than a digitized whip to make us work faster. It produces incredible stress and I'm afraid sometimes that I'm going to crack under the strain.

One other long-time employee of Topper made the following observations:

> This new technology is terrible! It invades my privacy—this company knows everything I do, even how long I spend in the bathroom. Also, if the clients knew that they were being listened to, they wouldn't like it one bit. And they wouldn't be happy that we are under constant pressure to get the call over with and move on to the next customer. It makes it real difficult sometimes to be courteous and thorough with each of our clients.

Despite these complaints, Topper's management steadfastly defended its right to monitor its employees in order to ensure that they were performing up to company standards. Indeed, as Chairman William Topper observed at the most recent Board of Directors meeting, since Topper installed this system, productivity for the corporate travel agents had increased by almost 15 percent. If these productivity gains could be sustained, Topper would be able to eliminate several positions by attrition and thereby cut costs and improve its profit margins. When Katherine Davis pointed out the high level of employee dissatisfaction with the new system, Mr. Topper's response was peremptory and defensive:

> This company has a right and an obligation to shareholders to manage this workplace with the most effective tools available. No company can succeed unless it changes with new technology, and this means that the employees must learn to adapt. We need this technology to stay competitive, to maximize profits, and to deliver quality service to our customers with greater efficiency.

Ms. Davis's Dilemma Shortly after this meeting, Katherine Davis received the petition, signed by about 75 percent of the travel agents outlining their complaints and requesting that the monitoring system be removed. Since Katherine was seen as a manager with some humane empathy and had been sympathetic to various agents who had complained in the past, many saw her as their only ally among upper-level management. Thus Ms. Davis had a difficult decision to make. Should she become an advocate for the employees and press the issue with Donaldson, or defend management's right to monitor its employees and measure productivity?

Before deciding on a course of action, she had to weigh carefully some "philosophical" and practical questions. For example, does the employee's right to privacy take precedence over the employer's right to monitor its employees? Were the company's practices really unfair, or did employees simply resist the pressures to become more productive? Furthermore, was there a way to strike a balance between these competing interests? Also was the monitoring too intense? Should it be modified in some way to lessen the anxiety of the travel agents?

Regardless of how these questions were answered, something would have to be done. Katherine was apprehensive that the decline in morale would soon lead to other problems such as increased turnover or higher health insurance costs due to the enhanced stress level. These negative effects might in the long run offset the productivity gains achieved by the monitoring system.

As Katherine Davis arrived at her office on the fifth floor of the Topper building, she began to prepare her report and recommendations to company president Donaldson. She recalled the words that concluded the agents' petition:

> We used to enjoy working at this agency and helping its customers. Now we find this workplace to be an uncomfortable and hostile environment. We don't object to management checking on us, but we do object to this electronic straitjacket that has brought so much stress and anxiety into our lives.

Ms. Davis had to sort through many conflicting feelings and different perspectives in preparing her final recommendations to Donaldson.

Questions

1. Do you agree with the practice of using electronic monitoring in the workplace? If so, is it appropriate for this situation?
2. Does the use of electronic monitoring violate employee rights?
3. Evaluate Mr. Topper's argument that the company has the right and obligation to maximize productivity and profits for its shareholders.
4. Develop an action plan for Ms. Davis. What should she say in her report to the company president? Should she recommend that electronic monitoring be discontinued at Topper?

CASE 5.4

Incident at Saratoga International[30]

For about ten years Jeremy Prinn had been employed in various capacities at Saratoga International, a large manufacturer of metal and plastic containers located in a large northeastern city. He was now working in the Marketing Department as an analyst and market researcher. A week ago he was abruptly informed by the marketing director, Sheila Johnson, that his job was being eliminated because of budget cuts. Prinn was shocked since the company was doing reasonably well and there was never any indication that Saratoga was dissatisfied with his performance. On the contrary, his performance reviews had always praised his effectiveness, research skills, and "team spirit." Moreover, there were no other individuals being terminated at this time. When Prinn pressed Johnson for further explanation, she said that she could not elaborate on the decision.

Later that week he was having dinner with two colleagues from his department who were quite upset about his abrupt termination. During the course of the evening it became clear that one of them, Karen Devlin, was privy to the reasons behind Prinn's dismissal. At first she was reluctant to talk, but as the evening wore on, she felt increasingly sorry for Prinn and decided to tell him what she had learned about this unfortunate incident.

Apparently, Prinn had provoked the ire of the president's son, Roger Casper, at a meeting which had been arranged to introduce a new product line. Ever since this meeting the two individuals had had an antagonistic relationship. Although the company's president, William Casper, was aware of this conflict, he was not concerned and never held it against Prinn. Prinn was reluctant to criticize Roger Casper in public, but several weeks before he had taken the liberty of doing so in a long and candid e-mail message to a friend in the Manufacturing Department. Prinn told his friend that he felt Roger was high-handed and was "throwing his weight around" just because he was the president's son. Prinn made some other unflattering comments about both Roger and his father and then went on to discuss some business issues. He was unaware that electronic messages were sometimes screened by executives at Saratoga; the company's computer systems manager excavated these archived messages on an ad hoc basis when told to do so by Saratoga's senior managers. In this case the incoming and outgoing mail of Prinn's friend was being reviewed as part of his performance review. When the incendiary message from Prinn was uncovered it was turned over to the Vice President of Manufacturing, who

[30]This case study represents a hypothetical situation.

in turn felt obliged to contact the President. When William Casper was told of this communication, he demanded that Prinn be fired.

Karen had found this out somewhat inadvertently by overhearing a conversation. The company did not inform its employees that e-mail messages were sometimes screened. Prinn was dumbfounded at this disclosure, but at least the mystery of his termination had been solved. He was dismayed, however, that Saratoga had violated his privacy. As he remarked to Karen at the conclusion of the dinner: "I just assumed that electronic mail messages were the same as a regular mail message. Would the company open a sealed envelope to a fellow employee in another department? The more I think about this, the angrier I get. What about my right to privacy? And shouldn't the company at least have the decency to tell us that they would be reading our messages? Had they done so, I would have been more discreet and I would have still had my job!"

Questions

1. Has Jeremy Prinn been treated fairly? Was Saratoga right to fire him?
2. What do you think about the company's checking its employees' e-mail messages without any notice? Would you recommend any changes in that policy?

6

Intellectual Property

In this chapter we explore another pervasive and troublesome ethical problem in this era of new digital media and informational products: an apparent erosion of respect for intellectual property and the laws that protect such property. Unfortunately, borrowing, cloning, and copying software programs have become an unattractive reality in American society. These rampant copyright violations cause serious financial losses for many corporations and may well hinder the development of new technologies.

The problem is intensified by the nonchalant attitude exhibited by far too many computer users in the United States, where legal guidelines are fairly strict and unambiguous. Although it is illegal to make copies of software programs such as databases and spreadsheets, many users have no reservations about doing so. Some do acknowledge that using unlicensed software is a form of stealing, but they do it anyway because there is so little chance of getting caught. Others rationalize this behavior by arguing that software companies make such huge profits that they can easily afford to forgo a licensing fee here and there. According to computer analyst and commentator John Markoff, "these rationalizations and excuses reflect a widespread attitude that electronic information is, in effect, in the public domain and should not be protected as private property."[1]

---

[1]John Markoff, "Though Illegal, Copied Software Is Now Common," *The New York Times,* July 27, 1992, pp. A1, D3. Copyright © 1992 by The New York Times Company. Reprinted by permission.

But this issue is more complicated in many foreign countries such as those in the Far East, where the tradition of safeguarding intellectual property is especially thin. As we shall see, this situation can be attributed partly to a different philosophy in these countries that tends to treat intellectual property as communal or social property. Likewise, impoverished, developing countries are skeptical of intellectual property rights, but for somewhat different reasons. As Paul Steidlmeier has observed, these countries "shift priorities and define property rights first in a social and then in an individual way; the argument contends that the right to livelihood (development) takes precedence over other claims on which property rights are based."[2]

Regardless of the reasons for appropriating another's intellectual property, the situation seems to have steadily deteriorated. There are still no international standards or regulations that protect intellectual property beyond the boundaries of the United States, and American companies have paid an enormous price for this lack of comprehensive rules. It is estimated that lost revenues for 1990 amounted to about $2.4 billion.[3] This figure clearly underlines the magnitude of this problem and the urgency of reaching a commonly accepted solution that transcends country boundaries. It should be noted that there are now under way international negotiations to set worldwide standards for intellectual property, a move that may help to diminish the chaos that has characterized this area of international business.

These troublesome problems will probably continue to become more complex. For example, high-speed computer networks will allow users to retrieve books, files, and other sorts of documents. What's to stop them from reading that book or document and, by executing a simple command, transmitting it electronically to someone else? Indeed, as technology becomes more advanced, it becomes increasingly difficult to distinguish between software and information that is stored at different locations on a computer network. Many fear that unless solutions are found for these problems, there will be some serious impediments to the progress of the information age.

To be sure, the issue of intellectual property protection is not simple. For one thing, intellectual ideas have traditionally been viewed as belonging to the public domain—mathematical and scientific concepts are normally seen as public property which is shared by all members of society. But how should the algorithms and ideas incorporated into software programs be treated: as public property or as proprietary and therefore eligible for copyright and patent protection? Also, there is no doubt that it is wrong

[2]Paul Steidlmeier, *People and Profits: The Ethics of Capitalism* (Englewood Cliffs, NJ: Prentice Hall, 1992), p. 280.
[3]Markoff, "Though Illegal," p. D3.

to copy a software diskette, but other matters are fraught with ethical ambiguity. For example, is software with its multiple lines of command or source code analogous to a book or a magazine article? If so, should it then fall under the same copyright laws as these publications do? Or is software more like a machine or a process that should be afforded patent protection? The fundamental problem, of course, is that software is not like a tangible product and hence it is difficult to determine how it should be treated with respect to traditional patent and copyright law.

This chapter will turn its attention primarily to these issues and to the ethical dilemmas they can generate. We will focus on the software industry, where these issues have a particular urgency and complexity. We will consider, for example, the laws protecting software developers along with how far someone can go in mimicking another company's idea such as the concept of a spreadsheet or the use of clever icons and geometric figures in its user interface. We will also discuss the scope of a software developer's moral rights in this controversial area. These issues have serious implications for developers and users alike.

LEGAL PROTECTION FOR SOFTWARE

Before discussing the moral dimension of this problem, we must consider the various forms of legal protection for software programs. Computers themselves are protected under patent law since they are machines and therefore classified as inventions. It has been difficult, however, to define the parameters of such protection for software because of the unusual nature of this product. Nonetheless, there are three broad categories of this protection: trade secrecy laws, patents, and copyright laws. Let us discuss each of these in some detail.

Trade Secrecy Laws

The first form of legal protection for software programs and related forms of intellectual property places them under the category of trade secrets, which are covered by contract law. Such laws vary from state to state. Trade secrecy is a broad category that can include any ideas and information that have important economic value for a corporation. Hence trade secrets can include corporate assets such as R&D data, marketing strategy information, customer lists, and proprietary techniques or formulas. Companies make an investment of time and money in the creation of this information which gives the owner some advantage over the competition.

Unfortunately, trade secrecy theft is fairly common in the software industry, where employees are especially mobile and where intellectual assets have far more import than material assets. Recruiting practices often involve an implicit attempt to gain knowledge about one's competitors. Actual evidence is rarely found in trade secrecy cases so there are relatively few prosecutions. But consider the recent incident involving two prominent Silicon Valley software firms, Borland International, Inc. and Symantec Corp. Both companies produce database software and computer languages. When the manager of Borland's language software group defected to Symantec, he allegedly conveyed (via electronic mail) to this company information such as specifications for future products, strategic marketing plans, and other privileged communications. Despite the notoriety of this case, however, many software industry executives criticized Borland for pursuing the matter in a legal forum. They maintained that the theft of trade secrets has virtually become an industry norm and hence should not be seen as a serious legal offense but as a necessary cost of doing business.

However, the pervasiveness of this sort of activity does not mitigate its damaging consequences. Those who criticize trade secrecy laws maintain that they are often used to restrict employee mobility. In addition, they argue, companies cannot claim to own what's in an employee's head. These criticisms do have some validity and point to the need for balance and careful deliberation about just what constitutes a trade secret. Criteria for deciding this issue should be based in part on the following: How secretive is the information? How much time and money were expended to create this asset? How easily could it be duplicated? In other words, what is the nature of the investment, and does this secret really give its owner some distinct competitive advantage?

Now that we have discussed trade secrecy laws in general, we can treat their efficacy in protecting software as intellectual property. Software developers can classify their finished products and their works in progress as trade secrets. Doing so will prevent both insiders (such as engineers or programmers) and outsiders from copying these programs. Trade secrets usually include any kind of confidential formula, algorithm, or pattern of information that gives the corporation a competitive advantage in its business dealings. Most state laws allow software programs to be included under this general definition, especially if the program contains a unique algorithm or programming approach.

Trade secrecy protection is usually implemented by the use of nondisclosure agreements. Such agreements typically cover any information which the company considers to be confidential and valuable to its business operation. In the case of software programs, they are normally signed by developers, engineers, managers, and others who may be privy to the inner workings, formulas, and algorithms of a particular software product. The nondisclosure agreement prohibits the employee from using or disclosing this information should he or she leave the company. For example, it prevents an engineer or programmer from using source code from a former company in some related program at another company. An employee who violates the nondisclosure agreement could be subject to criminal prosecution and be held liable for damages.

The primary problem with relying on trade secrecy protection is that if the trade secret somehow becomes public, either intentionally or accidentally, it loses its proprietary status and becomes part of the public domain, so there is no way to stop other developers from using it. The bottom line, then, is that trade secrecy laws provide only partial protection for software developers. Also, trade secrecy laws and nondisclosure agreements are extremely difficult to enforce. It can be a formidable task to prove that a developer has appropriated an algorithm or a proprietary technique from a former employer, and it is even more difficult to prove decisively that a stolen source code has been incorporated into a competitor's software product. Most organizations could not afford the expensive litigation necessary to pursue such a claim.

Patents

A patent provides considerably greater protection than do trade secrecy laws. The federal government has established a fairly broad standard for which products fall under patency protection. According to the U.S. Code on patent:

> Whoever invents or discovers any new and useful process, machine, manufacture, or composition of matter, or any new and useful improvement thereof, may obtain a patent...[4]

But do software programs fall under this general definition? There has actually been a prolonged legal debate over whether these programs and their algorithms should be eligible for patents. In the 1972 decision, *Gottschalk v. Benson*, the Supreme Court ruled that an algorithm is unpatentable, but this ruling was reversed in the 1981 landmark case *Diamond v. Diehr*, when the Court ruled that a patent claim for a process should not be rejected merely because it includes a mathematical algorithm or computer program. In this case "the majority opinion of the Court concluded Diehr's process to be nothing more than a process for molding rubber products and not an attempt to patent a mathematical formula."[5] In other words, the process itself (in this case one for curing rubber) must be

---

[4]David Bender, *Computer Law: Evidence and Procedure* (New York: M. Bender, 1982), p. 4A-2.
[5]Henri Hanneman, *The Patentability of Computer Software* (Deventer, Netherlands: Kluwer Academic Publishers, 1985), p. 87.

patentable, and if computer calculations are part of the process, then they are covered by the patent *in this particular utilization.*

As a result of this decision, more and more companies are seeking this viable form of intellectual property protection. For a patent, a written application must be filed with the U.S. Patent Office; it must convincingly evince that the "invention" is truly novel or unique. Obviously, this process takes time, and the proof of novelty and innovation can be difficult. Nevertheless, software developers and other IT vendors have been eager to take advantage of this protection.

If a patent is obtained, it will protect the basic concepts incorporated in a software program, typically for 17 years. Securing a patent can have inestimable benefits for a software developer, since the patent creates a long, strongly protected monopoly around the program and excludes others from using or profiting from that program. Patents create a powerful incentive for developers, who can reap great financial rewards if their product is a commercial success. Many software firms claim that this sort of protection would be a significant stimulus to research and development and hence necessary for a steady flow of advanced, innovative products.

The use of patents to protect software programs is not without controversy, however, despite the 1981 Supreme Court decision. Currently, only the "programmed machine" or application programs are patentable, but it's not clear which application programs are patentable or which pieces of such a program are eligible for this protection. For example, it seems evident that mathematical formulae, algorithms, ideas, and other abstract principles cannot be patented, but, as we observed, a program containing a mathematical formula or algorithm as one of its pieces is still eligible for a patent, so long as "the algorithm is not the basis upon which the patent claim rests."[6] Also, as Deborah Johnson points out, although patent laws do not allow the exclusive ownership of a mathematical algorithm, they do allow "ownership of a utilization or application of a mathematical formula—as long as ownership of the utilization or application does not preempt use of the formula."[7] This distinction, however, is not always easy to make.

Another controversial issue concerns the use of patents to protect user interfaces. For example, should a company be allowed to get a patent for the way its product arranges windows on the computer screen or for the icons and commands that constitute the interface? The same question applies to computer interfaces, the programs that link different computer systems or different programs to one another. According to one observer, "such an interface patent in the computer industry could have devastating results, perhaps making it impossible to forge links between different com-

[6]Deborah Johnson, *Computer Ethics* (Prentice Hall, Englewood Cliffs, NJ: 1985), p. 94.
[7]Ibid., p. 100.

puter brands without first paying royalties."[8] Many experts, then, are apprehensive about this reliance on patent protection since it could actually stifle creativity. A patent, for example, could give a particular vendor a stranglehold over a critical technology to the detriment of innovative research.

Copyright Laws

The third form of protection for software programs and products is copyright laws. Copyrights are easier to obtain than patents and have a much longer duration (an author's lifetime plus 50 years). In the 1960s and 1970s there was much debate over whether software qualified to come under copyright protection, but in 1980 an amendment to the 1976 Copyright Act gave software developers the same protection enjoyed by other authors such as novelists, playwrights, and songwriters. This amendment clarified that federal copyright laws protect not only source code (the lines of computer code written by programmers in a high-level language such as COBOL, BASIC, or C) but also object code (the binary code created when the source code is compiled). According to the conventional interpretation of the Copyright Law, "the original written source code is the authorship, the program (consisting of the logic and design of the software) is the expression, and all forms of software (written, printed, ROM, or diskette) from which a version of the program can be produced or communicated with the aid of a machine or device are protectable copies."[9]

Thus copyright infringement could occur in many different ways. An unscrupulous developer could blatantly copy lines of source code and sell them as his own program. Or someone could make duplicate copies of the finished product instead of purchasing or licensing her own copy. For example, if I buy a spreadsheet for my personal computer and someone borrows the diskette with the program (i.e., the object code) and copies the software on to the disk of his or her personal computer, the copyright laws have been violated. Finally, copyright laws *might* be infringed if someone copies the logic, sequence, and general design of the program but embodies this in his or her own original source code.

This last form of infringement entails considerable ambiguity and is quite problematic. A basic principle of copyright law is that it protects against the illicit copying of an author's *expression* of an idea but not the copying of the idea itself. In short, concepts and ideas along with systems, procedures, and processes are not protected by copyright. It is often diffi-

[8]E. Schwartz, "The Coming Showdown over Software Patents," *Business Week*, May 13, 1991, p. 106.
[9]Robert L. Graham, "The Legal Protection of Computer Software," *Communications of the ACM*, May 1984, p. 424.

cult, however, to distinguish between a concept and its expression; herein lies a fundamental problem with copyright law that is still being worked out in the courts. Consider the simple example of a popular computer program such as an electronic spreadsheet. It is clear that one cannot copyright the idea of a spreadsheet, the rows and columns of numbers that can be automatically calculated and recalculated, but supposedly one can copyright its expression or the form this idea takes. Thus there are many versions of spreadsheets, such as *Lotus 1-2-3* and *Microsoft Excel*, which owe some debt of gratitude to the first such system, a product known as *Visicalc*. But is the command structure of a spreadsheet part of the idea or of the expression? The same question can be asked about the user interface: Is the sequence of commands subsumed under the idea or is this too part of the expression?

Several legal precedents have presumably helped to impose some clarity on this confusion, but these issues are still in some flux. In *Whelan v. Jaslow* (1984) the Court ruled that even if a program is not copied line by line, its basic structure cannot be duplicated. Therefore, according to this ruling, screen design and command sequence are under copyright protection. Clearly, this case shifted the balance in favor of program creators and against copiers. Moreover, it set the stage for many other cases dealing with the "nonliteral" aspects of a program such as its structure, logic, and sequence.

In a subsequent case, *Lotus Development Corp. v. Paperback Software International* (1990), a federal court judge held Paperback Software liable for copyright infringement because it copied the screen layouts, the command organization, and the entire menu structure of the *Lotus 1-2-3* spreadsheet program. Judge Keeton decided that under the copyright law this type of "expression" should be protected: "I conclude that a menu command structure is capable of being expressed in many if not an unlimited number of ways, and that the command structure of *1-2-3* is an original and non-obvious way of expressing a command structure."[10]

In its defense Paperback International argued that it had merely copied standard features of spreadsheet interfaces and that the Lotus interface had become a *de facto* standard for spreadsheet software. The company also contended that one purpose of copyright laws was to help advance technological progress and that as a consequence the law should permit the incremental improvement represented by its user interface. But Judge Keeton categorically rejected these arguments because "he perceived no basis in copyright law for the standardization argument."[11] Furthermore, he reasoned that although copyright law does support incremental advances, these advances should be based on the idea and not its underly-

---

[10]John Markoff, "Lotus Wins Copyright Decision," *The New York Times*, June 29, 1990, p. C3. Copyright © 1990 by The New York Times Company. Reprinted by permission.
[11]Pamela Samuelson, "How to Interpret the Lotus Decision (And How Not To)," *Communications of the ACM*, November 1990, p. 31.

ing expression. As a consequence the judgment held that the Lotus interface was fully protected by copyright law. Hence, if this decision is not overturned, once a program becomes a *de facto* industry standard, it will enjoy a virtual monopoly and therefore it will be difficult for rivals to introduce similar, competitive products at lower prices. According to attorney Anthony Clapes, "The *Lotus v. Paperback* contest was a loss for the clones, and even though the outcome of the case was predictable, it shifted the advantage in the conflict for control over the computer industry decidedly toward the innovators."[12]

For some observers of the legal scene, the *Lotus v. Paperback* case underlines the inherent problem of relying on copyright laws to protect software programs. To be sure, for traditional creative works such as poems, novels, or plays the legal distinction between ideas and their expression has been quite effective. But as legal scholar Pamela Samuelson has observed, copyright laws are poorly applied to software because of the functional nature of computer programs. According to Samuelson, such programs are functional in the same way that machines and human–machine interfaces are functional, and "copyright law has never before protected functional works of these sorts."[13] Hence there is little precedent for resolving a difficult case such as *Lotus v. Paperback*, which at its core involves an interface between the end user and a machine.

It could be argued, of course, that a user interface is an artistic creation and thereby deserving of copyright protection. But an interface is also functional, and copyright law has imposed limits on the protection allowable for works that are both artistic and functional. Unless the aesthetic aspects are completely separable from the functional, there is no protection available under copyright law. Hence the "intermingling of art and function in user interfaces can be expected to make it difficult for developers to argue for a broad scope of copyright protection for user interfaces."[14]

In addition, later court decisions moved toward narrowing copyright protection. In July 1992 a judge in the *Computer Associates v. Altai* case decisively rejected *Whelan v. Jaslow* and ruled that the basic structure, sequence, and organization of a software program is not copyrightable. Judge Pratt concluded that the *Whelan* decision, which interpreted the command structure, sequence, and general organization as an aspect of expression, was misguided. Instead, his ruling in the *Computer Associates* case essentially restricts copyright protection to the literal copying of source code. This case seemed to be a clear-cut victory for those advocating weak or narrow pro-

---

[12]Anthony L. Clapes, *SOFTWARS: The Legal Battles for Control of the Global Software Industry* (Westport, CN: Quorum Books, 1993), p. 54.

[13]Samuelson, "How to Interpret," p. 33.

[14]Pamela Samuelson, "Updating Copyright Look and Feel Lawsuits," *Communications of the ACM*, September 1992, p. 31.

tection for software. According to Pamela Samuelson, "The *Computer Associates* opinion regards computer programs as functional works having a thin scope of protection from copyright."[15] Obviously, thanks to this ruling, there are now some sharp contradictions in the law which will only lead to more confusion. Although experts predict that the trend toward narrow protection will continue, the future of copyright law is still unpredictable.

Finally, no discussion of this issue would be complete without some treatment of the Apple Computer lawsuit filed against the behemoth software company Microsoft Inc. and the well-known hardware vendor Hewlett-Packard. The key issue in this case is whether copyright law should protect the "look and feel" of a program. The complicated suit contends that Microsoft's popular Windows program and H-P's New Wave program infringed on copyrights for the visual images used in Apple's Macintosh software. Apple claimed that the "look and feel" of its popular software was illegally copied by these two companies, which allegedly used elements of the Macintosh user interface in their products . The case will probably turn on whether aspects of this interface are functional or aesthetic. For instance, one element in dispute is overlapping windows; is this feature expressive (as Apple has argued) or functional? If the overlapping windows are considered functional, the feature would not be eligible for copyright protection. This case, then, which was not yet fully resolved as of summer 1994, raises the vexing question of whether or not copyright laws can be used to protect the screen display attributes or "look and feel" of a software product. If Apple is successful (and this appears unlikely) the judgment will again shift the balance to broad, strong protection.

The present state of copyright law, then, is in considerable flux, since the full import of recent decisions is not yet evident. Despite the shortcomings and ambiguity of this law, however, such protection is certainly not otiose or useless. At a minimum, it offers protection against the blatant copying of a program's source code or object code. In addition, depending upon future litigation, the scope of such protection could extend to nonliteral aspects such as structure and sequence. Beyond any doubt, software vendors should take full advantage of copyright laws even as they wait to see the extent of their protection.

Current Status of Legal Protection for Intellectual Property

It should be obvious that the evolving law on intellectual property is in a state of disarray. Many dispute whether patent law should apply to software, and, if so, whether these patents should be extended to algorithms,

---

[15]Pamela Samuelson, "The Ups and Downs of Look and Feel," *Communications of the ACM,* April 1993, p. 33.

as others have suggested. As we have seen, copyright law doesn't fully protect software programs, and there are still serious legal and social questions about whether the law should extend to the "look and feel" or structure of a program. The fundamental problem is that software doesn't neatly fit into traditional categories. On the one hand it is similar to books or scripts, which are covered by copyright protection, and on the other hand it is a functional product, like a machine or process that falls under patent laws. Because of its unique status and the problem of applying traditional copyright and patent laws, some experts are calling for a hybrid intellectual-property laws that would replace copyright and patent protection. Even if such a scheme could be devised, however, it would be difficult to implement at this stage without generating even more confusion. Thus, sweeping changes in intellectual property laws are highly unlikely. But there will continue to be incremental changes in copyright laws and patent protection which will help to clarify the scope of these laws.

Further, one could argue that the trend toward narrowing copyright protection makes eminent sense. Beyond any doubt, copyright and patent laws should offer companies firm protection against the misappropriation of source code or object code. Nevertheless, they should not be used to constrain the creation of "clone" software products that might share the same user interface features or the "look and feel" of established products. Otherwise there will be a lack of fair and open competition, which will only serve to hurt the end user community by limiting the availability of alternative, competing products. Broad or strong protection will also have negative effects for the industry, since it might raise barriers to entry for small companies, which have often led the way in developing incremental advancements. Should a *de facto* industry standard such as *Lotus 1-2-3* or *Windows* be protected from the competition, as the strong protectionists would have it? One can surely sympathize with a desire to protect the nonliteral aspects of a user interface, but if that occurs, consumers will likely pay higher prices for this software because of the lack of competing products. Moreover, there will be fewer incremental innovations, less standardization, and a slower diffusion of technological advancements. There are certainly compelling arguments for establishing the parameters of copyright protection accordingly.

There are several final observations to be made. We have reviewed some significant public policy issues that deserve careful attention. We have emphasized that the challenge facing litigators and judges is to promote and reward continued innovation in software without stifling the diffusion of technology. A strict, broad application of copyright laws could inhibit the impetus to standardized interfaces, which are immensely beneficial for end users and the software industry itself. Also there would be formidable impediments to industry progress if a basic technology (such as the notion of a spreadsheet) were regarded as proprietary, since this discourages incremental advancements and restrains competition.

At the same time, however, a free exchange of ideas in software development is equally problematic. Beyond question, "protecting computer programs by *copyright*, and protecting them as literary works, is quite appropriate to the intellectual property inherent in them."[16] If substantial investments in software development are not protected and rewarded, there may also be a negative impact on the development of breakthrough products, since the incentives to develop such products would be diminished. Thus a lack of adequate protection could also impoverish the user community of radically new technologies. Consequently, the development of new copyright and patent laws or rulings must somehow incorporate a careful balance between these competing concerns.

ETHICAL ISSUES AND PROPERTY RIGHTS

We now turn from the legal dimension of this problem to the ethical issues at stake and the legitimate moral *rights* of software developers. From a moral point of view, what are the property rights to which developers are entitled? To begin this analysis we must address the issue of whether there are moral rights apart from legal rights. In other words, if we have no enforceable legal system to establish and uphold legal rights, are there any rights at all? In my view, there are such rights. As we observed in Chapter 2, a right is simply an entitlement based on some set of defensible, rational moral principles such as justice or fairness. Also, according to Virginia Held, "rights should be respected for their own sake, because they are yielded by valid principles; they need no further justification."[17] Given the reality of rights, how can we deduce or justify at least a *prima facie* right to property? And can we extend this right to intangible forms of property such as ideas or algorithms?

One philosophical justification for the right to private property is known as the *occupation theory*. It assumes that the original discoverer and occupant has a right to dispose of property as he or she sees fit. Although there are many flaws in this notion, there is some merit and value in this simple principle. According to Morris Cohen, "protecting the discoverer or first occupant is really part of the more general principle that possession as such should be protected."[18] He goes on to say that "continued possession creates expectations in the possessor and in others, and only a very poor morality would ignore the hardship of frustrating these expectations and rendering human relations insecure."[19] From a moral point of view, then,

[16]Clapes, SOFTWARS, p. 16.

[17]Virginia Held, *Property, Profits, and Economic Justice* (Belmont, CA: Wadsworth Publishing, 1980), p. 4.

[18]Morris Cohen, "Property and Sovereignty," in *Ethical Issues in the Use of Computers*, ed. Deborah Johnson and John Snapper (Belmont, CA: Wadsworth Publishing, 1985), p. 301.

[19]Ibid.

one who discovers or is the first to possess something in a legitimate way is entitled to a right of ownership. If this theory is applied to intellectual property or software, those who discover an idea and embody it in software would have a right to ownership by virtue of their discovery and possession.

Perhaps a more powerful argument for the moral right to property has been developed by the philosopher John Locke. His theory of property has been one of the most influential in the entire tradition. In Chapter 5 of *The Second Treatise of Government* Locke brings property to the center of political philosophy. If we strip Locke's theory to its essentials we can summarize it thus: The right of property emanates from labor, since one's labor transforms land or other goods from common useless property to private usable property. According to Locke,

> ...the grass my horse has bit, the turfs my servant has cut, and the ore I have dug in any place where I have a right to them in common with others, become my property without the assignation or consent of anybody. The labor that was mine removing them out of that common state they were in, hath fixed my property in them.[20]

Thus in Locke's analysis, "labor puts a distinction between the thing worked on and what is held in common,"[21] it adds value to the thing in question. Locke is arguing that people have a natural entitlement to the fruits of their labor. The only authority for owning property is having made or worked on the goods in question. Clearly, Locke's basic argument is that labor is unpleasant and hence people do it only to reap its benefits; as a result, it would be unjust not to let people have these benefits they take such pains to procure. In short, property rights are required as a return for the laborers' painful and arduous work.

Locke's theory of property assumes an abundance of natural resources and also conditions of fair access. He also emphasizes that what we appropriate has to be within the realm of our own need and ability to put to good use. There are real limits on acquisition, since we have a moral obligation to avoid waste. To be sure, there are numerous problems with Locke's theory, such as the assumption of plenitude. Also it seems outdated and irrelevant. We do not mix labor with nature but with a complex economic system; a person's labor is only a small input contributing to the production of goods.

Despite these flaws, however, Locke's view of property has played a key role in the formulation of other theories. Consider, for example, Hume's writings, which have also contributed to contemporary notions of property and justice. In *The Treatise on Human Nature* Hume articulates as

---

[20]John Locke, *Second Treatise of Civil Government* (New York: Bobbs-Merrill, 1964), p. 164.
[21]Ibid., p. 171.

the first principle of justice the idea "that every man is to be left undisturbed in the enjoyment of his proper possessions."[22] Everyone, then, is entitled to the right of ownership. One must simply settle on the valid criteria for deciding who is a rightful, legitimate owner. According to Hume, the right of ownership can be determined by five rules: present possession, occupation (i.e., labor), prescription, accession, or succession.

Both Locke and Hume, therefore, regard labor as the primary basis for justifying someone's right to property. Although this position has some defects, it can still be plausibly maintained that one is entitled to the fruits of one's labor. According to Lawrence Becker, who enunciates a careful revision of Locke's theory, people deserve a benefit for their labor "and when nothing but property in the things produced will do...then they deserve property in those things."[23] Of course, if substitutes will suffice, then the laborer deserves an equally satisfactory substitute.

Can we apply this notion of property rights based on labor to the intangible commodity of intellectual property? On the surface there does seem to be some merit in the argument that one is entitled to the fruits of one's labor regardless of whether they are real goods or more intangible things such as a software program. If a company or group of individuals invest time, money, and hard work in creating an elaborate piece of software, they should "own" the end result by virtue of this effort. If someone else copies this software and reaps some of the benefits, then from a moral standpoint such action is on the same level as stealing. Thus, for the sake of fairness and equity and as a reward for one's initiative and industry, one should have the right to retain control over one's intellectual property, to sell or license that property as one sees fit without the fear that someone will appropriate that property for their own profit.

The application of Locke's theory is not without problems, but it does suggest that software developers have a moral basis to at least a *prima facie* right in their creation, on the principles of fairness and equity as well as respect for the fruits of hard labor. Moreover, following Becker's criterion, there does not seem to be an adequate substitute other than a vested interest in this property.

It is also worth emphasizing that the right of intellectual property has significant social utility; without respect for this right, there would be less incentive for those who develop truly innovative software products. Creating powerful incentives by providing prolonged monopoly protection for innovations will result in significant breakthroughs which will be immensely beneficial to society.

This line of argumentation is based on utilitarian reasoning, which

---

[22]David Hume, *The Treatise on Human Nature* (London: Oxford University Press, 1978), p. 110.
[23]Lawrence C. Becker, *Property Rights* (London: Routledge & Kegan Paul, 1977), p. 49.

seeks to justify actions according to the consequences of those actions. There are other utilitarian reasons for supporting strong intellectual property rights in addition to the primary one of preserving the incentive to create innovative programs. These arguments would likely hinge on the important ideas of efficiency and competition. If people have a substantial personal stake in an invention or new technology, they will be motivated to exploit that invention or technology in the marketplace and maximize their profits.

But even if there is a moral basis for property rights, that fact does not mean that these rights are absolute or without some limitation. As Professor Cohen notes, "property, being only one among other human interests, cannot be pursued absolutely without detriment to human life."[24] The issue, then, is how should property rights be limited for the sake of the public interest or the common good? This issue seems especially important for software, which embodies knowledge and ideas that can benefit humanity. One such limit concerns the dichotomy between an idea and its expression. Recall that current copyright law protects the expression of an idea but not the idea itself. This constraint seems to be a reasonable way of balancing the *prima facie* right to private property with the common good.

As we have intimated, when a technology is fully owned by one individual or corporation, opportunities for others will be diminished. Broad copyright and patent protection could harm consumers and stifle competition. If one vendor becomes the sole gatekeeper of a critical technology, the consumer and society at large will be at a disadvantage. Monopolies are dangerous and costly, since they can restrict further evolution and diffusion of a technology; they can also lead to overpricing and underproducing. Narrow protection, on the other hand, can help bring about standardization and incremental innovations, which have social utility. For example, there would be a notable advantage for users if all user interfaces resembled the Apple interface in structure, functionality, and appearance. Given these arguments, it seems evident that there must be some reasonable limits imposed on the *prima facie* right to intellectual property in order to minimize the disutility that can be caused by a corporation's unwillingness to share a fundamental technology.

AN INTERNATIONAL PERSPECTIVE
ON INTELLECTUAL PROPERTY

It would also be instructive to consider here the practices and legal traditions of countries other than the United States. Many cultures take a much different ethical view of intellectual property rights. In Korea, for example,

---

[24]Cohen, "Property and Sovereignty," p. 305.

new ideas and technologies are considered to be "public goods for everyone to share freely."[25] There is an assumption in this culture that intellectual property of any sort should be shared in the public domain for the good of society. Many developing countries are far more concerned about extending technology throughout society than about providing incentives for major technological innovations. As a result, they support only a weak scheme of protection for intellectual property.

The same viewpoint prevails to some extent in Japan and was partly responsible for the historic conflict between two giant computer companies, IBM and Fujitsu. In this controversial case Fujitsu copied IBM's operating system software, which essentially controls the basic operations of the computer, in order to design an IBM-compatible mainframe. When confronted by IBM, Fujitsu acknowledged that some of its programs relied heavily on copyrighted IBM material.

The case, which was ultimately resolved by means of a complicated arbitration settlement, highlighted how legal protection for intellectual property differs between the United States and Japan. The key assumption underlying the Japanese approach is that knowledge of any sort is communal and belongs in the public domain, where it can benefit many different parties. As a result, the Japanese system of legal protection for intellectual property allows for the "laying open" or publicizing of patent applications after only 18 months, in contrast to the U.S. approach of strict confidentiality. According to a Harvard Business School case study on the IBM–Fujitsu dispute, some analysts "believe that Japan's 'laying open' of patent applications promotes a practice called 'patent flooding' because competitors can file multiple improvement patents to force the inventor to cross-license its technology rather than defend the patent in litigation."[26] In short, the Japanese approach emphasizes dissemination of knowledge and a more rapid extension of technology. It only loosely protects the rights of inventors, in order to foster incremental innovations or even more significant breakthroughs.[27]

An underlying assumption of developing countries and countries such as Korea and Japan is that intellectual property should be seen more as common property than as belonging exclusively to one individual or corporation. According to Paul Steidlmeier, "developing countries argue that individual claims on intellectual property are subordinated to more fundamental claims of social well-being."[28] He notes that these countries

---

[25]Steidlmeier, *People and Profits*, p. 247.

[26]"The IBM Fujitsu Dispute," in *Policies and Persons*, ed. Kenneth Goodpaster, John Matthews, and Laura Nash (New York: McGraw Hill, 1991), p. 507.

[27]For more background about this case consult Fenwick, Stone, Davis, and West, "Legal Protection of Computer Software in Japan," in *Intellectual Property Rights in High-Technology Products and Sensitive Business Information* (New York: Harcourt Brace Jovanovich, 1982).

[28]Paul Steidlmeier, "The Moral Legitimacy of Intellectual Property Claims: American Business and Developing Country Perspectives," *Journal of Business Ethics*, February 1993, p. 161.

also reject the so-called "trickle-down theory," the notion that technological developments will eventually be transferred to others despite a strong system of protections. Also these countries do not give much weight to the Lockean arguments concerning one's entitlement to the fruit of one's labor. Rather, they maintain that "while people may have a right to the fruit of their labor, they have a duty to reward society which practically made the very fruitfulness possible."[29]

This line of thinking is alien to the American conception of private property and its system of patent and copyright protection, but it does present some tenable arguments for the dilution of the strict legal protection for intellectual property that is consistent with the American legal tradition. It reminds us that even the technological innovators are indebted to society for the knowledge and ideas on which their innovations are based. It calls into question the notion of exclusive right to the fruits of one's labor for a certain duration, especially when the new ideas or technologies are more beneficial to society if they can be shared and improved upon by others. Rather, it emphasizes that these rights should be subordinate to the public good. Also, this moral viewpoint implicitly criticizes long monopolies that heavily protect inventions and new technologies, since they are exclusionary and impede society's intellectual and technological progress. In short, there are utilitarian arguments for loose copyright protection that conflict with the more rights-based approach used to justify the stronger protection supported by the American legal system.

A MIDDLE GROUND FOR INTELLECTUAL PROPERTY RIGHTS

As we have seen, there are divergent ethical arguments about the nature and scope of legitimate intellectual property protection. Some of these differences are cultural and reflect conflicts that are becoming more common in a pluralistic global society. There is probably no way definitively to resolve these conflicting moral arguments. Rather it is necessary to reach a balance between the principle of reward for labor and the need to share knowledge for the common good.

This middle ground for these polar viewpoints may eventually be embodied in the evolution of the U.S. legal system's interpretation of copyright and patent law. This network of laws and regulations seeks to articulate a nuanced moral position that protects individual inventor rights while not stifling the dissemination of new ideas and technologies. The objective is to protect the form of expression but not the underlying idea of the work, to limit the scope of copyright and patent protection in order to foster the

---

[29]Ibid., p. 162.

free exchange of ideas, while still restricting the blatant copying of source code or object code and perhaps even nonliteral aspects of a program.

There is, however, a great deal of moral and legal ambiguity in this middle ground. As we have already observed, it is not an easy task to differentiate an idea from its expression. After all, as philosophers such as Wittgenstein would remind us, there is no such thing as an idea apart from its expression; concepts and ideas must of necessity be embodied in some sort of human or computer language. Also, defining the exact scope of copyright protection represents a major legal and *moral* challenge. By now, the controversial questions should be familiar: Which elements of interfaces should be protected? And should such protection be extended to the "look and feel" or basic appearance of a software product?

These questions are extremely difficult but are worth pondering. As the information age matures, one of the enormous challenges will be maintaining this tenuous balance between the inventor's rights and the public interest. As we attempt to resolve the ethical issues revolving around intellectual property such as the ones in *Apple v. Microsoft*, we might bear in mind some of the nettling moral questions that have been raised in this chapter:

- How and where do we draw the line between theft of original ideas and the use of those ideas as a stepping-stone to a new level of technology, that is, an extension or enhancement of a basic technology?
- What are the limits (if any) on the rewards one should legitimately expect from a software program? To what extent do software developers have the right to benefit from their creations?
- What are reasonable moral limits to the duration of monopoly power associated with patents and copyrights? Should we consider software patents that have duration of only 6 to 8 years (instead of the standard 17 years)?
- Do companies have a moral right to property created by their employees? Does assuming risk and investing resources automatically bestow property rights? Or should such rights be shared with the employees who engage in the actual labor?
- Should copyright protection be extended to computer interfaces? If so, should it include the user interface layout or sequence of commands? Should it include the interface's functionality or the "look and feel" of the interface?

These and other questions must be dealt with in any treatment of the legal and moral issues that arise in disputes over intellectual property.

SUMMARY

We began this chapter by describing the widespread borrowing, cloning, and copying of software which flout current American copyright laws. There must be greater recognition that illicit copying of software programs is simply stealing, at least in the context of the U.S. legal tradition. However, the protection of a corporation's other forms of intellectual property is more complicated. There are multiple problems in defining protection for software programs, since they do not fit into the traditional categories that have been used as a basis to determine the applicability of patent and copyright laws. For example, if software were a machine, it would clearly be patentable.

The three current legal methods of protecting intellectual property are trade secrets, patents, and copyright laws. A trade secret can include any intellectual asset in which the firm has an investment and which provides some sort of competitive advantage. Companies can classify their software programs as trade secrets, a status usually enforced by nondisclosures agreement. Patents provide more secure protection, and since a 1981 Supreme Court ruling it has been possible to obtain patents for software. But there are controversial issues regarding the suitability of using patents to protect algorithms, user interfaces, and so forth.

The current status of copyright laws as they pertain to software is in a state of evolution and some disarray. Although object and source code are clearly protected, the scope of protection regarding the nonliteral aspects of a program (command sequence, structure, etc.) is in question. The basic distinction is that copyright laws do not protect ideas but only the underlying expression of those ideas. There have been several conflicting legal rulings about the scope of copyright protection. As a result, one finds two factions among intellectual property lawyers and software developers: those who favor weak or narrow protection and those advocating a strong or broad scheme of protection.

There are several moral issues at stake in intellectual property issues. Do those who develop complex software programs have a moral basis for property rights in those products? A right is an entitlement based on moral principles such as fairness or justice. Traditional arguments based on the occupation theory and Locke's seminal analysis of labor state that possession and labor engender property rights. Hence there is justification for claiming that those who invest time and energy in such products do have a *prima facie* property right. In addition, there are utilitarian arguments for supporting such property rights, since respect for intellectual property as manifested in rewards for initiative and industry is a powerful incentive for future developers. But a utilitarian perspective on this issue is not so conclusive, since there are tenable arguments on behalf of the position that intellectual property should be only loosely and narrowly protected to ensure the dissemination and sharing of ideas and technical knowledge.

In some developing and Far East countries intellectual property is only loosely protected to ensure incremental innovations and the more rapid extension of technology. The rights of inventors or creators are seen as subordinate to the common good; also knowledge is seen as a social good rather than a private one. We have argued here that somehow there must be middle ground between the principle of reward for labor and for assuming risks and the need to share basic technologies for the social good.

Finally we posed some critical questions that should be addressed in further analysis of intellectual property issues. One basic question revolves around the distinction between stealing an idea and using it as a stepping-stone to a new idea or innovative technology. Other questions concern the reasonable limits to the duration of patents and copyrights and the extent to which such laws should be invoked to protect user interfaces or the so-called "look and feel" of software programs.

CASES FOR DISCUSSION

Introduction

The first of these two cases looks at the famous dispute between Microsoft and Apple. It considers explicitly property rights in software and raises the issue of when those rights have been transgressed. The second case, *Agrico, Inc.—A Software Dilemma*, examines a problem facing an information systems executive who must decide whether or not to copy a software program that has been inadvertently left on his firm's computer system. If he does so, Agrico will be protected from an unreliable software vendor; but can we justify such "theft" even under these compelling circumstances? This case raises issues that are also relevant to the central themes of Chapter 4 concerning vendor–client relations.

CASE 6.1

The Microsoft Windows Lawsuit

The Microsoft Corporation   The Seattle-based Microsoft Corporation was founded in 1979 as a small upstart software company by computer wizard Bill Gates. Gates, a Harvard University dropout, realized early on the tremendous potential of the personal computer and decided to concentrate his energies on this lucrative market. Thanks to Gates's remarkable foresight, Microsoft was able to exploit the revolutionary technology of the PC.

In 1980 Gates and his company were asked by computer giant IBM to write an operating system (OS) for its new personal computer. An operating system consists of an integrated set of software programs that control the basic operations of a computer. It invokes various end user applications such as word-processing software, and it manages the programs needed to produce output such as reports and other listings of data. Thus the operating system directs the hardware to handle these different tasks that are requested by the user.

Gates agreed to IBM's request and for $50,000 he purchased an outdated operating system known as 86-DOS from a small company called Seattle Computer Products. Gates rewrote 86-DOS and renamed it MS-DOS. He licensed this product to IBM in 1981 but wisely retained ownership. Consequently, when other hardware vendors such as Compaq decided with IBM's blessing to clone the IBM PC, they had to go to Microsoft to license MS-DOS. As one observer noted, "the IBM–Microsoft surge inspired the software industry to devote most of its energies to writing applications for IBM-compatible machines rather than for the scarcer Apple-manufactured ones."[30] The availability of applications software for these machines made them far more attractive in the marketplace. Ironically, Apple turned to Microsoft to write applications for the Macintosh, thereby providing another major source of revenues for the company.

Thanks to MS-DOS, Microsoft has completely dominated the market for personal computer operating system software. Presently MS-DOS is used in approximately 70 million IBM and IBM-compatible computers. As a result, Microsoft has 90 percent of the world market for operating system software; the remaining 10 percent belongs to Apple, which uses a proprietary operating system for its line of personal computers such as the Macintosh.

Microsoft's domination of this fast-growing market has enabled the company's revenues to grow at a phenomenal pace. For fiscal 1993 Microsoft earned about $1 billion on $3.8 billion in revenues. Microsoft has 8,100 employees and has become the world's largest supplier of PC operating systems and applications software (spreadsheet products such as *Excel* and word-processing software such as *Microsoft Word*).

MS-DOS and Windows   For all its popularity and success, MS-DOS came under much criticism because it is "character based" or command driven. This means that users must type in commands to execute various functions. For example, to delete a file from a directory, the user might have to type:

DELETE filename

The user must memorize these commands along with each command's plethora of options in order to avoid heavy reliance on the manu-

---

[30]Fred Moody, "Mr. Software," *New York Times Magazine*, August 26, 1991, p. 56.

als. MS-DOS has also been assailed because it does not support *multitasking*, the ability to use one application such as a word processor while another is working in the background (e.g., a spreadsheet or data base). Multitasking has become a very popular feature with personal computer users.

These problems were avoided by Apple Computer when it introduced its popular and user-friendly Macintosh PC. The Macintosh relies on windows with various icons that can be manipulated by a mouse. It thereby insulates the user from cumbersome commands that are difficult to recall. For example, in order to delete a file, the user simply drags that file into an icon that looks like a trash can. The Apple interface has become extremely popular because of these features, and some would argue that it has also become the *de facto* industry standard. Apple's approach is known as the *graphical user interface* or GUI (pronounced "gooey").

As a result of these shortcomings of MS-DOS and because of the easier-to-use Apple operating system, Microsoft decided in 1984 to build a new operating system known as Windows. In 1985 Windows 1.0 was shipped. Unfortunately, this initial version had some problems and did not meet with positive market acceptance. But in May 1990 Microsoft released a much-improved version known as Windows 3.0, which has been exceptionally successful. Within a short time sales for this new operating system were steadily increasing, and by the end of 1991, 9 million copies had been sold.

In reality, Windows isn't a new operating system but rather a convenient interface or shell that makes DOS more functional and easier to use. Windows is not command driven; instead, like the Apple interface, it is graphical and lets users choose between applications or functions by manipulating icons and pictures on the screen with the aid of a mouse. Thus it too spares users from the need to master arcane commands. It also supports multitasking and allows several programs to run simultaneously. The reaction to Windows has been highly positive by many users, who say that "Windows is alluring because it offers a single, intuitive interface from which they can execute many applications."[31] Corporate clients have raved about Windows since it appreciably increases user productivity by making it easier to work with different applications, access the network, and so forth.

Microsoft is also rapidly developing application software for the Windows environment. This includes *Word for Windows*, which is a sophisticated word-processing package, and a new version of *Excel*, Microsoft's spreadsheet product that competes with *Lotus 1-2-3*. Although Microsoft

---

[31]Linda Bridges, "Users' Windows Outlook: Sunny, a Few Clouds," *PC Week*, April 6, 1992, p. S17. Copyright © 1992, Ziff-Davis Publishing Company, L.P.

will realize tremendous revenue gains from the sale of these products, its huge share of the Windows applications market will be reduced by competitive software programs. Nevertheless, the potential for Microsoft is enormous. In 1993 there were approximately 18 million users of Windows—and in order to take full advantage of Windows, all of these users will need new applications software. Thanks in part to its Windows technology, Microsoft seems well poised to continue its record pattern of growth in both revenues and profits.

The Apple Computer Lawsuit   There has been, however, a dark cloud over this bright horizon. In January 1988 Apple Computer Inc. filed suit against Microsoft for copyright infringement. This lawsuit could cost Microsoft as much as $5.5 billion. As we have noted, Apple Computer pioneered the graphical user interface, which relies on manipulating pictures and icons rather than on using commands. Apple charged that Microsoft copied the "look and feel" of the Macintosh interface. Apple alleged in this lawsuit that Windows is a blatant infringement of its Macintosh copyrights, especially the copyright covering the on-screen display of overlapping windows. Apple contended that the "look and feel" of its interface is valuable and hence should be afforded protection from being copied. The key issue in the case has been whether the total appearance or "look and feel" of the Macintosh graphic user interface is a protectable expression.

Apple also sued Hewlett-Packard at the same time, claiming that H-P's *New Wave* program bore substantial similarity to the Macintosh interface. *New Wave* has not been a great commercial success, so there is far less at stake for Hewlett-Packard.

The outcome of this closely watched case is obviously critical for both companies. A loss or significant setback in this case could jeopardize the future of Windows. It could also lead to a substantial settlement for damages that will hurt Microsoft's cash flow. Apple, on the other hand, is relying on this case to maintain control over the concept of the graphical user interface technology that includes the use of icons and overlapping windows. Because of setbacks at the hands of Judge Vaughn Walker, Apple has decided to abandon its efforts to get a jury trial and moved the case to an appeals court, which it hopes will be a more receptive forum.

There is clearly a resemblance between the Apple's popular graphic interface and the Windows product. But are the interface and its various visual elements protected by copyright law? In essence, this is the nub of the case from a legal point of view. How much of a program's "look and feel" is protected by copyright law? The *Lotus v. Paperback (1990)* decision is a key precedent. The ruling in this case was that software developers cannot copy screen layouts, menu structures, or the way in which commands are organized. However, the courts seemed to back off from this position in

Computer Associates v. Altai (1992), when they stipulated that the basic structure of a software program was not eligible for copyright protection. The Microsoft case could break new legal ground by extending copyright protection to the screen appearance of a program, or it could decisively limit the parameters of such protection.

Apple has argued in this case that its Macintosh screen was a unique expression of an idea, and hence can be copyrighted, and that cloning that screen should be a violation of that copyright. Its copyright infringement suit is based on "the copying of the gestalt—or overall 'look and feel'—of the Macintosh interface and the unique combination of elements it employs."[32]

Microsoft's counterarguments have centered on the fact that "individual elements of the Macintosh's screen lacked originality or were pioneered by such companies as Xerox Corp. and International Business Machines Corp."[33] Microsoft has also contended that the use of desktop objects (e.g., a trash can) in the interface to suggest different functions (e.g., discarding a file) is an analogy that cannot be copyrighted. Moreover, geometric shapes in the interface are not eligible for copyright protection. Microsoft and Hewlett-Packard further have held that there is only a small number of ways to perform the functions encompassed in the interface. For example, there are only a limited number of options for iconically representing certain functions, such as deleting a file by depositing it in a trash can. Apple concurs that copyright protection cannot be provided for geometric shapes in an interface, but, according to the company's attorneys, one can arrange those shapes in a unique way and this pattern of arrangement should be eligible for a copyright.

Ethical Issues in the Dispute   There are many legal nuances to this case that make it extremely complex and difficult to resolve. Clearly, the major significance of the Apple–Microsoft controversy is the precedent that will be set in the court's delineating the parameters of copyright protection for software programs. The question of whether property rights have been infringed upon is especially difficult to ascertain in these circumstances. It is true, perhaps, that Windows does incorporate some ideas and visual elements from the Apple interface. On the other hand, virtually all artistic works that are covered by copyright law do have some unoriginal content (for example, consider a drama such as *West Side Story*, which is a recreation of Shakespeare's *Romeo and Juliet*). To a certain extent all creative

---

[32]Pamela Samuelson, "Updating Copyright Look and Feel Lawsuits," *Communications of the ACM*, September 1992, p. 31.

[33]Stephen Yoder, "Microsoft and Hewlett-Packard Win Ruling over Apple, *The Wall Street Journal*, April 15, 1992, p. B1. Reprinted by permission of The Wall Street Journal, © 1992 Dow Jones & Company, Inc. All rights reserved worldwide.

endeavor is a re-creation, a developing of a fresh perspective on some previous accomplishment. Nothing can be created or developed in a total vacuum.

But this analogy raises another vexing issue that is at the center of this case: Is the Macintosh interface the equivalent of a true artistic creation (i.e., a kind of Mona Lisa, as Apple's lawyers have maintained) which deserves copyright protection, or is it composed of utilitarian elements and everyday ideas that do not deserve such protection? The case raises many other questions of rights, fairness, and the legitimate bounds and ethical propriety of borrowing from another's work. Specifically, should a company such as Apple be entitled to *property rights* in basic interface elements such as icons and overlapping windows? Should there be protection for the "look and feel" of the Macintosh interface despite the unprotectability of its individual elements? Is copying various aspects of such an interface tantamount to pilfering intellectual property? Or can it be ethically justified as the use of a *de facto* industry standard that becomes the basis for incremental innovations?

Questions

1. Assume that you are an attorney representing either Apple or Microsoft. Develop a cogent set of arguments that support the position of your client.
2. Should Apple have any property rights in this interface?
3. Should any consideration be paid to Apple's huge financial investment in the Macintosh interface? Does this investment of time, money, and labor engender property rights, and is this notion consistent with Locke's conception of these rights?

CASE 6.2

Agrico, Inc.—A Software Dilemma[34]

George P. Burdelle, vice president of information systems at Agrico, Inc., walked into the computer room with his systems and programming manager, Louise Alvaredo, at 6:30 P.M. on Wednesday, May 27, 1987. Alvaredo typed a few keystrokes on a systems computer console and turned to

[34]Copyright © 1988 by the President and Fellows of Harvard College.

Harvard Business School case 189-085.

This case was prepared by H. Jeff Smith under the direction of Professor F. Warren McFarlan as the basis for class discussion rather than to illustrate either effective or ineffective handling of an administrative situation. All identities have been disguised. Reprinted by permission of the Harvard Business School.

Burdelle. "So, as you can see, Jane Seymour [the software engineer for Agrico's new AMR system] left the source code on our computer when she left for dinner." She paused and then asked, "Should I copy it to tape and ship it to our off-site storage facility?"

Agrico's $500 million portfolio of farm management properties was set for conversion to the new computer system over the upcoming weekend. AMR, a vendor of farm management software, had been selected to provide the software for the new system. The previous summer AMR had agreed to supply the object code for the system but had been quite reluctant to release the source code to Agrico.[35] The software purchase agreement between Agrico and AMR provided that the source code be placed in escrow to provide protection in case of a natural disaster or in the event of AMR's bankruptcy or inability to provide adequate support for the software. But, despite repeated attempts, Burdelle had been unable to reach an acceptable arrangement with the software company regarding the escrow of the source code.

Burdelle and Alvaredo knew that Agrico would have certain access to the most recent version of the source code should they choose to copy it now and secure it. Given his experience with AMR over the past year, Burdelle was not confident that AMR's proposed arrangements to escrow the source code were adequate. And if Agrico's $500 million portfolio were converted to the new computer system and something happened to the existing object code, the possibility existed that the object code could not be reproduced.

Furthermore, Burdelle had an operational concern. He wanted to be sure that any future modifications to the software were made using the most recent version of the source code, which included all previous modifications. Otherwise, there was a risk that the portfolio data could be altered—or corrupted—without anyone's knowledge.

He recalled the words of Agrico's attorney from a discussion held earlier that week:

> What if you *could* get a copy of their source code through some means? The contract states we cannot have a copy of the software without AMR's written permission. On the other hand, the agreement clearly calls for an escrow

[35]*Source code* contained a computer program's statements written by programmers in high-level programming languages like BASIC, COBOL, FORTRAN, PL/I, C, etc. It could be printed out on paper or shown on a display terminal and read much like text. A compiler (a special computer program) translated the source code into *object code*, which was in a binary format executed by the computer. Usually, object code could not be read by programmers or easily modified. To make changes to an existing program, programmers usually changed the source code and then recompiled the program, thus creating a new version of the object code. (Most computer software packages purchased by consumers, such as Lotus 1-2-3, contained only the object code. The source code was seldom distributed in such packages.)

agreement that is acceptable to both AMR and Agrico. If it ever got to court that we took their source code, the judge or jury could well side with us, especially when we explained the trouble we have had with AMR and their unsatisfactory response to our concerns. Still, a lawsuit would be bad publicity and would consume a lot of everyone's time, even if we won. If we lost, it is not clear what the impact might be.

Now, because of an AMR employee's oversight, Burdelle had access ton the source code.

"When do you need a decision?" Burdelle asked his systems manager. "Jane said she'd be back from dinner by eight o'clock," Alvaredo replied, "so I need to know in an hour or so."

"I'll give you an answer at 7:30," responded Burdelle as he walked to his office.

Agrico Company Background   Agrico, Inc., started by two farmers in Des Moines, Iowa, in 1949, provided farm and ranch management services for 691,000 acres of land in several Midwestern states. With market value of its portfolio at $500 million by 1987, Agrico ranked as one of the nation's larger agricultural management firms. Maintaining four regional offices housing an average of five farm managers each, Agrico was able to provide cost-effective management services for more than 350 farms and ranches. The company, acting as an agent, bought equity interests in farms and ranches for their clients (usually pension funds) and managed them to provide operating cash flow and capital appreciation.

Agrico had three different arrangements for the properties. Under crop-share lease arrangements, which represented 47 percent of their portfolio, tenant farmers would agree to farm land managed by Agrico in return for a portion of each year's crops, which Agrico would ultimately sell in commodity markets. Under cash-rent leases (51 percent of the portfolio), farmers made cash payments for use of the land. Agrico also directly managed a few properties (about 2 percent of its total). (See Exhibit 1 for selected data on Agrico and Exhibit 2 for an organizational chart of the company.)

Agrico's New Computer System[36]   During their 1985 business planning process, Agrico's executives decided that their existing arrangement for computer services—an agreement with a nearby commercial real estate concern that provided all services for a yearly fee—was not adequate for their present or future needs. The same year they also identified a need for

---

[36]See Exhibit 3 for a summary of Agrico's experience with its new computer system.

office automation to improve productivity. Their local contract for computer services expired on September 30, 1987, and as summers were traditionally slow (buying, selling, and leasing of farms took place in the winter and spring and supervising of crop harvests in the fall), June 1, 1987, was set as the target conversion date.

Since Agrico had no internal computer systems staff, they contracted with a large computer consulting firm for recommendations on their computing needs and responsibility for them. The consulting firm assigned several of its employees to the project, including a project manager—George P. Burdelle, a mid-1970s graduate of Georgia Tech who had received his MBA from the Harvard Business school shortly thereafter. The results of the systems planning project indicated that Agrico should do in-house data processing. But as they had little expertise, and to minimize cost and installation lead time, it was recommended that they use a software package rather than attempt to develop a custom-coded system. Thus, a software selection and systems design project was begun in March 1986.

Exhibit 1   Selected Company Data

	1987
Acres under management	691,000
Market values of properties	$500 million (approx.)
Number of farms	250
Number of ranches	130
Number of employees	83
Number of clients	170
Tenants	
Crop-share lease	175
Cash-rent lease	<u>197</u>
Total tenant leases	372

Other Data	1986	1985
Revenues	$5,272,000	$5,157,000
Net income	487,000	436,000
Total assets	3,027,000	2,691,000

Exhibit 2 Organizational Chart

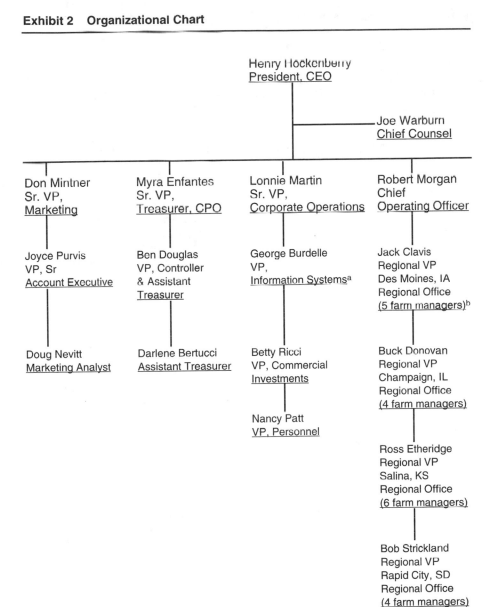

[a]One systems and programming manager, two programmers, and two computer operators reported to Burdelle

[b]In addition, for directly managed properties, other employees were often included in reporting relationships through the farm managers.

Exhibit 3   Experience with New Computer System—Major Events

Date	Event
1985—Business Planning Process	Executives set June 1, 1987, as target conversion date.
March 1986	Software selection and systems design project started; consulting team in place (including Burdelle).
July 1986	Work on system installation project begun. Burdelle accepts job at Agrico; resigns from consulting firm. AMR agreement signed.
September 1986	New computer hardware delivered; systems staff on board.
October 1986	AMR delivers object code.
October 1986–January 1987	Software acceptance testing; Agrico team (staff and consultants) work at AMR's Omaha offices.
March 1987	Significant software flaws corrected. Jane Seymour (AMR's software engineer) begins work on Agrico's computer in Des Moines.
May 26, 1987	Burdelle speaks with Agrico attorney.
May 27, 1987	Seymour leaves source code on computer.

Functional requirements for the system were very complex, since it was expected that a single software package would be used for all three property arrangements under Agrico management. The cash-rent leases offered few problems—that accounting was fairly straightforward. The directly managed properties, though few in number, required a different focus—"all the logistics of running a farm or ranch," according to Burdelle. As for the crop-share leases, since Agrico not only shared all expenses and revenues from these farms but also often received part of the crops for payment, it was heavily involved in farm commodity markets. So, in addition to the program requirements needed to manage the receiving, selling, and delivering of its portion of the crops, the software had to accommodate the commodity market information.

Agrico insisted that these software requirements be met by a single vendor offering an integrated package. From an initial list of more than 40 potential vendors, only two were identified; each was asked to submit a bid in a "request for proposal" (RFP) process. Agrico selected AMR for their software. As Burdelle later explained:

> When you came down to it, it was a relatively straightforward decision for Agrico. AMR had twelve clients up and running, and they had excellent references. we visited two clients and saw demonstrations of features we knew we needed. The software ran on a minicomputer that also provided excellent office automation capabilities. The only major risk we saw was the fact that AMR was a small company.
>
> Our second-choice vendor—a mid-sized software house with about 120 employees—sold software that met most of our functional requirements, but they had sold only three copies, none of which were in production yet. Their software ran on a mainframe, with heavy systems support and operations expertise requirements. In addition, the mainframe had very limited ability to support office automation.

A number of modification and enhancement requirements were identified for the AMR software during the selection process, and the cost and completion schedule were included in the RFP response from the vendor. Work on the system installation project began in July 1986.

Throughout this period Agrico was impressed with Burdelle's grasp of their complex system needs; they offered him the position of vice president of information systems, and Burdelle accepted on July 11, 1986. He said:

> Agrico had a need for someone to build a systems department, and I enjoyed working with company personnel. The june 1, 1987, conversion target date allowed us adequate time for the installation, and we had the ability to run parallel with the old system before cutting over.

The AMR Relationship   AMR, a small software outfit headquartered in Omaha, Nebraska, had been founded in 1977 by A. M. Rogers. It sold only one software package—a system for managing farm and ranch portfolios. With twelve clients in nine states, AMR appeared to hold the solution for Agrico. Burdelle described them:

They were a small company with ten employees, including Rogers himself. We called every one of their customers and got the same story: positive experiences. Rogers was the core of AMR and had his hand in everything, from marketing to software design and programming. The other employees were systems people, but they were more "carpenters" than "architects."

Also in July, Agrico and AMR signed an agreement stating that AMR would provide software consistent with Agrico's needs; AMR would be required to make modifications to its software package. The total purchase price for the software, including modifications, was approximately $200,000. Agrico would also pay one percent of this amount monthly as a maintenance fee. The modified object code was to be delivered to Agrico no later than October 1, 1986; the agreement stated that Agrico's access to the source code was limited to "viewing listings reasonably necessary to test the system." Only AMR was allowed to make modifications to the code. Commented Burdelle:

We realized that a good percentage of Rogers's revenue came from modifying the software to meet unique client requirements, so we offered to pay more to buy the source code. We acknowledged that if we modified his source code he would not be responsible for retrofitting our changes to his new software release. However, he was apparently afraid that someone would steal a copy of his software. We offered to sign nondisclosure agreements, whatever, but Rogers was really irrational about keeping the source code.

The software purchase agreement required AMR to maintain the software in escrow with a third party to ensure adequate backups. (See Exhibit 4 for excerpts from the agreement, which was prepared primarily by Agrico's attorney.)

The Software Experience   AMR delivered the object code, as promised, by October. It was installed on Agrico's new computer, which had been delivered in late September. During this same time, Burdelle completed the hiring of his systems staff, which included a systems and programming manager, two programmers, and two operators.

The software acceptance test followed. Both the new Agrico staff and the consultants were involved in the testing. Burdelle related the experience:

We quickly discovered that all was not right. There was no standard software, as AMR had installed twelve versions—one for each of its clients—

around the country. No two were the same—the AMR programmers added or deleted code based upon the needs of each client. We wanted to use practically all of their options, and apparently none of their clients had used them all together. While the individual options worked, they did not always work correctly when combined. We also found out that a number of functions had never been thoroughly tested anywhere.

As it turned out, AMR usually installed and converted the software and then fixed bugs when they were discovered by the client. We were not willing to live with that approach.

Given this situation, we rearranged our schedule to provide more time for software acceptance testing. Our purchase contract required us to pay 20 percent of the software price upon contract signing, 60 percent of it 30 days after completion of software acceptance testing, and the remaining balance 90 days after system conversion. We had AMR's attention, because they did not get most of their money until the software passed our acceptance test. I was not going to jeopardize our clients assets with bug-filled software. Furthermore, I began to see that the escrow of our software was very important, since a standard version literally did not exist.

From October through January, the Agrico team worked at the AMR offices in Omaha. Significant flaws were identified in the software, but AMR had successfully corrected them by March, and Jane Seymour from AMR had begun working on Agrico's computer in Des Moines. But this testing and repair process had exacted its toll on the relationship between Rogers and Burdelle. A contentious tone had crept into their correspondence, which was frequent. On one occasion Rogers complained about the Agrico project team's "tiger testing" of the software, and Burdelle noted: "I instructed the team to be ruthless in identifying bugs. I refused to sign off on the acceptance test until the software was perfect. It was not a pleasant experience."

Off-Site Escrow   During this same period, Burdelle began lengthy discussions with Rogers to define the specific arrangements for the escrow of the object and source code. Burdelle explained:

When we realized that every one of AMR's installations was unique, we understood just how important it was to have copies of the unique source code for our system stored for backup purposes. Without source code, there was potential for our being forever locked into the existing system with no chance for enhancements or modifications. It was possible we would have to go through the detailed software acceptance testing process again if any changes were made. Given our experience with AMR to date, I was not willing to take it on faith that our source code was adequately protected.

Rogers claimed that we should be satisfied with his backup plan, in which he occasionally took tapes to his bank's vault in omaha. However, we had no independent way to verify that the source code AMR stated was our escrow copy was in fact the source code that generated our object code. There are companies that store computer tapes in special facilities, like the one we employed in Des Moines for our data tapes, and we wanted that kind of security. Plus, we wanted an independent third party to ensure that the latest version was available. The easiest way: escrow the source in the off-site facility we already used.

But Rogers was afraid that we would modify or sell his source code if it was in the same off-site facility we use, and he was paranoid about keeping control. We talked and talked with him, but our discussions came up empty. He said he thought our concerns about backup procedures were overblown.

Concerned that the June 1 conversion date was fast approaching with backup procedures for code storage still unclear, Burdelle discussed the situation with Agrico's attorney on Tuesday, May 26:

The attorney said that we had a classic problem of ambiguity. The contract did require AMR to provide us with access to the source code so that we could understand it, but only AMR had the right to copy and store it. Yet AMR was supposed to store it in a "satisfactory" manner; apparently, we each defined "satisfactory" differently. The attorney felt that if we could get access to the source code we might have a good court argument for storing it ourselves. but technically, getting and storing the code did violate the contract.

Burdelle had also considered other solutions, such as discontinuing the relationship with AMR and looking for other vendors. He said:

Many times along the way, I thought about telling AMR "thanks but no thanks." I realized that the expenses we had incurred were really sunk costs: things like our consultants' bills for debugging the software, which by then had accumulated to $75,000. The biggest problem was that there were few other options: We already knew there was only one other vendor that had even a remotely similar software package, and it used different hardware.

Time was of the essence; any delays in converting to the new system would cost Agrico dearly. we did not want to start over and develop a custom system; that would have been a monumental project. I was confident that the software now worked as it should, but I was concerned about future modifications.

We had also created much ill will with Rogers, and he was becoming even more irrational as the days went by.

In contrast to the deteriorating relationship with Rogers, Agrico had developed great rapport with Jane Seymour. On Wednesday, May 27, Alvaredo said, in fact, that she believed Seymour may have "looked the other way" in leaving the source code on the computer when she went to dinner. "I think Jane knows the bind we are in with Rogers," she told Burdelle.

Burdelle's Decision   Burdelle, alone in his office, pulled the AMR contract from his file cabinet and read again the words concerning access to source code. He thought once more about the attorney's advice, and he quickly reviewed the ramifications of the potential need for modifications to the software. "While we've had more than our share of disagreements, I have always been honest with Rogers, and I've tried to prove that he had no reason to distrust us," Burdelle mused. "I want to abide by the terms of the contract, but I don't want to jeopardize Agrico's clients' assets."

At 7:30 P.M. Burdelle walked to the computer room to give Alvaredo his decision.

Exhibit 4   Excerpts from AMR Agreement

Agreement made and entered into this 10th day of July 1986, between AMR Software Company, Inc. ("AMR"), a Nebraska corporation with its principal place of business in Omaha, Nebraska, and Agrico, Inc. ("Agrico"), an Iowa corporation with its principal place of business in Des Moines, Iowa.

[Specifics of the sales agreement followed in items 1–14. Included was an agreement that Agrico could examine the source code listings "reasonably necessary to test the system." Item 15 described the monthly maintenance fee—one percent of the purchase price—and defined the support services to be provided.]

16. AMR PROPRIETARY MATERIAL

a)   The software may not be copied or reprinted in whole or in part without the prior written permission of AMR.

b)   Agrico shall not allow anyone other than Agrico or AMR personnel to copy any code or documentation manuals. Agrico shall not give, sell, or allow access to any person not employed by Agrico or to any other company a copy or listing of any of the programs contained in the software, except to *bona fide* consultants of Agrico who, prior to such access, execute with AMR a nondisclosure agreement.

c)   The software, including the programs therein and the documentation manuals, is proprietary information of AMR and Agrico shall not disclose any of this proprietary information to any other parties except as otherwise provided in 16.b above.

d)   The source code listings shall not be copied or duplicated.

e)   Agrico or Agrico's consultants shall not disclose the fact that AMR has provided the source code listings to Agrico hereunder.

f)   The source code listings shall not be removed from Agrico's premises.

[Items 17–22 referred to responsibilities of the parties.]

23. ESCROW OF SOURCE CODE: AMR shall place a copy of the source code for programs comprising the software in the custody of a third party (in escrow) that is satisfactory to both Agrico and AMR. AMR warrants and represents that it will update the source code in the possession of the custodian on an annual basis at no cost to Agrico. AMR shall charge Agrico for the cost of escrowing the source code.

AMR warrants that in the event AMR commences a voluntary case or other proceeding seeking liquidation, reorganization, or any other relief with respect to itself or its debts under any bankruptcy, insolvency, or other similar law now or hereafter in effect or seeks the appointment of a trustee, receiver, liquidator, custodian, or other similar official for AMR or a substantial part of AMR's property; or an involuntary case or other proceeding shall be commenced against AMR seeking liquidation, reorganization, or other relief with respect to AMR or its debts under any bankruptcy, insolvency, or other similar law now or hereafter in effect or seeking the appointment of a trustee, receiver, liquidator, custodian, or other similar official for AMR or any substantial part of its property, and such involuntary cases or other proceeding shall remain undismissed and unstayed for a period of 60 days; or an order for relief shall be entered against AMR under the federal bankruptcy laws as now or hereafter in effect; or AMR discontinues marketing or support of the software, and upon Agrico's reasonable belief that AMR is no longer able to provide maintenance of the software, after demand has been sent to AMR at their current address by registered mail, the custodian shall deliver to Agrico the source code and all technical documentation.

Agrico reserves the right to test the escrow disk pack at AMR's office to ensure the software is an exact duplicate of the current version of the Agrico software.

24. WARRANTY: AMR hereby represents and warrants to Agrico, such representation and warranty to be in effect as of the date hereof and for so long thereafter as Agrico pays the monthly fee described in item 15 hereof, that the software delivered hereunder is free from defects in manufacture or materials and will continue to meet the specifications and requirements as described in the proposal, the RFP, and this agreement after installation, and AMR will, without charge to Agrico, correct any such defects and make such additions, modifications, and adjustments to the software as may be necessary to keep the system in good operating order and performing in accordance with the foregoing representation and warranties. In addition, AMR warrants that all modifications made to the software meet the business objective of the modification, will be fully unit tested, system tested, documented, and will not adversely affect the system.

[Item 25 detailed several general clauses regarding payment agreements and official addresses.]

IN WITNESS WHEREOF, the parties hereto have executed this agreement under seal in duplicate originals as of the date first written above.

[Signatures followed.]

Questions

1. Analyze the ethical and management issues confronting Mr. Burdelle in this situation. What makes this case so difficult and complicated?

2. What would you advise Burdelle to do?

3. Is it *ever* legitimate for a customer to copy source code from a software vendor (such as AMR) without the vendor's permission?

7

Ethical Issues
and Information Security

The location of this final chapter following the sections on privacy and intellectual property is deliberate. These two chapters have implicitly highlighted the security needs of organizations that rely on sensitive data or various forms of intellectual property. The issues of privacy and security are especially interrelated since the best intentions to respect privacy mean very little without the implementation of proper security methods.

As we have seen, information is a critical corporate asset that must be carefully managed. Classified, proprietary information as well as other forms of intellectual property need to be protected. Purloined technological or strategic secrets can give a powerful competitive advantage to one's adversaries. A corporation's IT strategy would be seriously deficient without attention to securing the information that is at the center of its applications.

In addition, those individuals who are the subjects of that information have a significant stake in security issues. If their personal information falls into the wrong hands because of an organization's carelessness, the results could be disastrous. If, for example, a person's confidential medical records were accessed by unauthorized users, the effects might lead to unfair employment decisions or other forms of discrimination or harassment. Such possibilities make the moral obligation to protect information all the more critical.

Security breaches have two general sources. They can originate from technical deficiencies, since even the most secure system is not impregnable. They can also result from poor corporate policies or questionable practices regarding the dissemination and disclosure of data. The IT systems may be quite secure, but perhaps those who manage those systems share sensitive data too readily or thoughtlessly. Our main concern here will be the technical dimensions of the security problem, but we will also consider the role of corporations and individuals as owners and custodians of information.

In addition, our primary but not exclusive focus is on *information security*. Those who use computers describe the need for information security in terms of three requirements:

1. Confidentiality: controlling who gets access to information
2. Integrity: ensuring that information is updated and altered only by authorized individuals
3. Availability: ensuring that information is constantly accessible to authorized users[1]

The porosity of our environment in this era of "digital disclosure" and networked computers does pose a real challenge for those responsible for information security. The problem of safeguarding valuable information along with protecting computers and networks is compounded by the proliferation of personal computers, which are not nearly as secure as their ancestors, the minicomputer or the mainframe. Personal computers have an open architecture which makes them especially vulnerable to security breaches. In addition, client/server applications, new operating systems, and more complex networks have made PC security a much more difficult task.

In the past, computer equipment was usually confined to one or two rooms, so security was not a great problem. Today, however, corporations do not have this centralized control over their computer equipment and the information that that equipment manages, and so both physical security and system security are more difficult. Now managers must worry about securing thousands of PC's, workstations, terminals, and servers in a myriad of locations that are often part of sprawling networks. Of course, it is easier to secure a network of personal computers than individual standalone machines; many organizations have implemented networking partly in order to increase centralized control.

To be sure, there are tremendous benefits to decentralizing informa-

---

[1]Report of the National Research Council, *Computers at Risk* (Washington, DC: National Academy Press, 1991), p. 49.

tion and many advantages in the flexible, open architecture of personal computers. But the downside of this expanded accessibility and flexibility is increased security risks. Companies must strive to balance "the rewards of letting PC users share data more widely and more easily against the risks of unwanted data access and data corruption."[2]

This migration to networked personal computers, then, is one of the technical issues that has complicated efforts to secure information systems. In this chapter we will consider this complication and other technical aspects of security. We will also discuss the types of security problems that organizations must contend with, and consider some reasonable precautions. But the main axis of discussion here concerns the moral obligation of corporations to ensure that their IT systems are as protected as possible and that sensitive, proprietary information is carefully safeguarded. When companies or individuals are negligent or indifferent about security issues, they are clearly acting irresponsibly. The risks of an insecure system are quite grave.

TYPES OF TECHNICAL SECURITY PROBLEMS

Security problems within an organization can occur accidentally or they can be perpetrated deliberately. Let us first consider internal mishaps—users' inadvertently accessing confidential data or destroying data accidentally. Data integrity problems of this sort plague every corporation despite the most elaborate precautions. A recent survey of Digital Equipment's VAX users found that the primary cause of security breaches is still user accidents and careless mistakes.

Users may be unintentionally given the wrong view of the data or be provided access to documents which they shouldn't see. Also there are still many ways for a user to corrupt or destroy data accidentally. Fortunately database management systems and other software are becoming increasingly sophisticated in maintaining data integrity. But if a system is poorly designed from a security standpoint, unauthorized access and corrupted data may occur easily.

The more disturbing type of security problems are those that are intentional and malicious. There is a wide spectrum of deliberate computer misuse, ranging from simple pranks to serious crimes such as theft and sabotage. Examples of such computer misuse include unauthorized electronic break-ins, bank and credit card fraud, and the use of worms and viruses that wreak havoc on a computer system and sometimes destroy

---

[2]Sheila Osmundsen, "Security in a PC Network Age," *Digital News*, June 8, 1992, p. 1.

vital information. Estimates of the monetary value of these losses vary widely, but some claim that the total is as much as $5 billion a year. More realistic accounts show losses to be at least $1 billion a year.[3]

One of the most serious forms of computer crime is theft, either of money or of information. Analysts have noted two primary techniques for monetary theft. The first is the *Salami*, "which involves spreading the haul over a large number of transactions like slices of salami." For example, a perpetrator might create a program that takes a small sum of money from a number of bank accounts and credit it to his or her own account over a period of time. The second technique is the infamous *Trojan Horse*, whereby one inserts corrupt information into a program so that it makes bogus payments to a phony account or otherwise profits the culprit.[4] Theft is undoubtedly the most common and costly form of computer crime.

In addition to this distinction between deliberate computer misuse and accidental errors, we can also distinguish between computer crime that is perpetrated by *outsiders*, such as competitors or "hackers," and *insiders*, such as employees, ex-employees, and independent contractors. The computer hacker phenomenon is well-known in America since hackers have been involved in some ingenious forays into supposedly secure computer systems.

In the insiders group we often find employees or ex-employees who have a grudge against the company or who have discovered clever ways to line their own pockets. According to most security experts, although hackers and other outsiders have been guilty of violating many susceptible computer systems, they are not the major problem. Rather, the most serious and costly transgressions are executed by employees, consultants, and others who have authorized access to the system.

Indeed, employees who know the intricacies of their company's computer system have proven to be especially resourceful in exploiting its vulnerabilities. As an illustration, consider three senior AT&T employees who worked at the company's British headquarters. They established their own outside company with a 900 number that charged a fee to the callers. They then programmed the company's computers to call that number incessantly, running up high bills which were paid to their company by AT&T. When this ingenious plot was uncovered by AT&T officials with the help of Scotland Yard, the three individuals were summarily dismissed. They were also charged with tampering with computers and conspiracy to commit fraud. Unfortunately, the criminal case was dropped by the prosecution because of certain legal technicalities.

---

[3]Richard S. Rosenberg, *The Social Impact of Computers* (San Diego, CA: Academic Press, 1992), 170.

[4]Tom Forrester and Perry Morrison, *Computer Ethics* (Cambridge, MA: MIT Press, 1990), p. 11.

In addition, employees have been known to sabotage computer systems at their own companies. A recent incident at a small printing company in Athens, Georgia, Southeastern Color Lithographer, Inc., underscores the high costs of such deviant behavior. At Southeastern, Marshal Williams, a job price estimator, allegedly damaged computer files and in the process tormented his fellow workers. For example, users might be working on customer files which would suddenly vanish. Or they might get a screen full of undecipherable data, such as customer names spelled backwards. As one might expect, this mischievous activity frustrated Southeastern's employees and debilitated operations. Some employees were so demoralized by the need to restore data which would then disappear again that they simply resigned from the company. Finally, through a sophisticated monitoring scheme, Williams was caught executing a program to destroy some data. In 1990 he was convicted of corrupting data files and sentenced to five years in jail.[5]

There are other forms of computer abuse besides theft, embezzlement, and deliberate sabotage. One of the more insidious problems has been the growing popularity of parasitic, destructive programs. In particular, time bombs, virus attacks, and worms seem to be on the increase.

A logic bomb or *time bomb* is a piece of erroneous software coding designed to cause damage in some way. It is usually inserted in a normal program and set to detonate at a particular time. A typical time bomb might be programmed to crash a computer or to erase hard disk drives.

A *virus* is a parasitic program that can insert copies of itself into other programs and replicate itself incessantly. It continually copies itself until it has consumed large portions of a computer's memory, thereby causing the system to malfunction. It can also permanently erase or corrupt information. A virus is contagious; it can be passed on to other computers and it can be transmitted over telephone lines by means of networks. In some situations, then, a virus can quickly infect a whole network of computer systems. One analyst has observed "that most mainframe computers can be successfully subverted within an hour, and that networks—even an international network with thousands of computers spread over continents—can be opened up to illicit intrusion within days."[6]

A *worm* is a destructive, self-replicating program that infects idle workstations or terminals on a network. It might, for example, be pro-

---

[5]For more detail on these incidents see William Carley, "Rigging Computers for Fraud or Malice Is Often an Inside Job," *The Wall Street Journal*, August 27, 1992, pp. A1, A7. Reprinted by permission of *The Wall Street Journal*, © 1992 Dow Jones & Company, Inc. All rights reserved worldwide.

[6]Rodney O. Andrews, "Computer Crime: The Worm in the Apple," in *The Information Web: Ethical and Social Implications of Computers*, ed. Carol Gould (Boulder, CO: Westview Press, 1989), p. 231.

grammed to delete what has been stored in the computer system's memory. The key difference between a worm and a virus is that the former tends to seek out idle machines while the latter is usually designed to prey on active systems. Both of these perverse programs can cause untold damage for organizations both large and small.

There have been many incidents involving worms, viruses, and time bombs, but two of the more notorious and well-publicized incidents are worth mentioning here. In the spring of 1992 there was a great deal of publicity about the infamous Michelangelo computer virus, which was cleverly designed to wipe out the hard disk drives of infected computers. This virus affected over 65,000 computers worldwide. Although most major organizations escaped danger, the Michelangelo virus focused international attention on the problem of protecting equipment and software from these insidious viruses.

Also, in one of the most famous computer break-ins, the Internet, a network of computers used by government agencies, military sites, corporations, and universities, was plagued with a worm that ultimately infected about 6,000 machines and disrupted their operations for some time by denying access to the network. Fortunately, the worm was not designed to destroy data, or this incident would have been a tremendous calamity. Nevertheless, the Internet worm and similar intrusions have dramatically illustrated the inherent vulnerability of computer systems and the need for tight security and constant vigilance. (See the second case study at the end of this chapter.)

SECURITY TECHNIQUES

What can be done about these different types of security problems? How can companies prevent theft and catastrophe or guard against intrusions of a nefarious worm or virus? To some extent security techniques have lagged behind the development of computer technology. Nevertheless, there are many tools, programs, and strategies available to protect systems from these security breaches.

To begin with, a secure environment requires an unambiguous security policy that is uniformly enforced throughout the organization. According to experts, "a security policy is a concise statement by those responsible for a system (e.g., senior management) of information values, protection responsibilities, and organizational commitment."[7] Once a security policy has been established, management controls and proce-

---

[7]National Research Council, *Computers at Risk*, p. 50.

dures (both administrative and technical) must be put in place to implement that policy. A complete, well articulated security policy supported by top management is essential for effective security measures. It is also necessary that key management personnel be given the responsibility to maintain security. Security enhancements and programs cannot substitute for the managerial skills needed to plan as impregnable an environment as possible. Moreover, a sound security system must include user education and training; all users must be made cognizant of controls, educated about security compliance, and informed about the consequences of violations. The policy must also be strictly enforced or it will have little effect.

A corporation's security procedures should generally include at least three main objectives: to maintain access control, to preserve the integrity of the system and its data, and to provide recovery and backup if the system should fail. In other words, a *secure* IT system limits access to authorized users, prevents any corruption of software programs or data, has resources to restart a computer in the case of failure, and has a reliable backup copy of important data.

Security analyst Donn Parker elaborates on these objectives and recommends that a comprehensive security system involve the following functions:

1. *Avoidance* of loss or damage by removal of corporate assets from threatening situations
2. *Deterrence* by preventing people from initiating unauthorized activities (whether deliberate or accidental)
3. *Prevention* of unauthorized activities
4. *Detection* of loss or damage in a timely fashion so that damages can be minimized
5. *Backup/recovery* to allow for the retrieval of lost or impaired data
6. *Correction* of any security gaps to prevent future problems.[8]

Parker's approach is to divide security into its component parts, to consider each part in isolation, and then to assess the total solution.

It is instructive to consider at least some of the specific measures that can be adopted to implement Parker's strategy and achieve the three broad objectives of controlling access, preserving integrity, and providing backup and recovery should the system fail.

The front line of any security system is the control of access—keeping out unauthorized users while letting authorized users access only the files, data, and programs that they are entitled to see.

[8]Donn B. Parker, "The Many Faces of Data Vulnerability," *IEEE SPECTRUM*, May 1984, pp. 46–48.

Authorization and authentication techniques usually involve an identifying username and a corresponding password. When users log in to a mainframe or network, they must enter these identifiers or they will be denied access. Since systems can be especially vulnerable to outside intruders, many corporations put emphasis on remote access security. Multiple passwords and modem call-back are most commonly used to provide the extra security.

Passwords in many cases are at the core of computer security, and password policy should be given the most scrupulous attention. Passwords and usernames should be carefully guarded and should be as unobvious and esoteric as possible. Simple, obvious passwords render the computer system more vulnerable. According to Clifford Stoll, there are only a few basic requirements for a quality password: "passwords must be nonguessable, not in a dictionary, changed every few months, and easily remembered."[9] Despite these simple rules, the problem of poor passwords persists in many organizations. Even machine-generated passwords are problematic because they may be difficult to remember.

Another key tool in security systems is encryption software, which scrambles data being transmitted over a network. There are several encryption technologies available, but in 1977 the National Bureau of Standards and the National Security Agency established the first national data encryption standard, known as *DES* (Data Encryption Standard). This system encrypts data that is to be transmitted over public channels; it is also used by the government for its own unclassified data.

Clearly, encryption is an important security technique for transmissible data. Security-conscious companies should be utilizing encryption algorithms to prevent proprietary information from being intercepted. For example, without encryption, electronic mail is highly vulnerable to security leaks as messages repeatedly pass across local area networks. Most security experts contend that encryption is vital for securing the network itself. They extoll the technique of "end-to-end data encryption, which encodes information and places it in an electronic envelope…that cannot be forced open until it reaches its destination."[10]

Another important tool is audit control software that details and monitors transactions on the system. If the first line of defense fails and someone does break into the computer system, there should be mechanisms that will provide some tangible evidence of the break-in and might enable the company to trace the identity of the culprit. If an audit system is to be effective, users should be trained to be alert to any strange transac-

[9]Clifford Stoll, "Stalking the Wily Hacker," *Communications of the ACM*, May 1988, p. 493.
[10]Jeffrey Rothfeder, "Holes in the Net," *Corporate Computing*, May 1993, p. 118.

tions or activity in their accounts. For example, if it is Monday morning and the user has not used her computer since Friday afternoon, she should be suspicious if she gets a message indicating her last log-in was 4:00 Saturday morning. This should be reported immediately as a potential break-in. Audit control software provides audit trails and accounting logs that can provide evidence that a problem has occurred or is occurring. For example, an audit trail provides evidence of who gained access to the system and exactly when; once again, log-ins at strange hours may indicate a break-in. Audits can also reveal an abnormal number of false entries, which is often an indication that someone is using a trial-and-error approach to entering the system.

Since some electronic trespassing can be done by employees who have access to the system but not to all its files and applications, it is essential to have applications-level audit trails in addition to operating system audit trails. Each database should have its own trail. One common type of application-level audit is the "terminal session log," which provides a complete record of a user's input and the system's output. This log will generally indicate to the system-level manager any unusual or fraudulent activity.

If systems are penetrated and tampered with, there will be a need for backup and recovery mechanisms. Because computer systems and data are vulnerable to break-ins, user accidents, and other phenomena, there is a need to back up the files and programs that reside on the system. A backup is simply a copy of the data that is maintained on a separate system or is kept off-line on another medium such as magnetic tape or an optical disk. If the data on the computer system are destroyed or compromised, the backup file can be loaded on to replace the original. Companies must determine how often to back up files and other programs. Some organizations do daily backups while others back up their files more infrequently, perhaps once a week. The frequency should depend on the volatility of the files and the importance and sensitivity of the information they contain.

It is also important to have the facility of recovery. Recovery allows the system to be restarted or "rebooted" in case of a crash or failure. According to Peter Keen, "recovery...can be either quick, involving a 'hot' restart that is automatic and so fast that users may not notice loss of service, or lengthy, requiring a 'cold' restart in which the entire system is reloaded using the backup data files."[11] Obviously, an efficient backup and recovery system will minimize the risk of damage from an intruder or other disasters and provide for continuity of service for end users.

---

[11]Peter G. W. Keen, *Every Manager's Guide to Information Technology* (Cambridge, MA: Harvard Business School Press, 1991), p. 39.

Backup has become more complicated in a heterogeneous networked hardware environment. Most hardware producers now offer packages that back up different systems over a network, thereby allowing the network manager to dictate backup schedules or let users rely on their own schedules. The manager can also control which files are backed up in a centralized area and which files the users must back up for themselves. Many companies have learned the hard way that avoiding backup nightmares requires investment in the right tools and carefully thought-out policy decisions.

Finally, we should consider how organizations can protect themselves from the effects of parasitic programs. The most viable protection against viruses, worms, and time bombs is heavy reliance on anti-virus packages. Most companies now require that software packages, data files, and other programs brought in from the outside be examined by specialized virus detection software. In addition, many large organizations scan hard disks periodically for any signs of a virus. Anti-virus programs normally have a scanner which looks for computer code that matches certain "signatures" characteristic of a virus. Sometimes they include a program that will extirpate the virus from the software. In addition, these programs are designed to seek out new viruses that do not possess a "signature"; they do this by looking for any mysterious activity such as notable changes in size of files or other programs.

Obviously, none of these packages can offer a foolproof method of detecting and correcting viruses; a clever virus could elude the scanning mechanism. Indeed, as hackers learn more about these anti-virus packages, they will undoubtedly develop a new breed of viruses that will be harder to detect. Thus there will likely be a constant game of wits between hackers and developers of anti-virus software. Unfortunately for users caught in the middle, the stakes are high, given the destructive potential of most viruses. Nevertheless such software should be a vital component of any comprehensive strategy for protecting corporate data.

We have considered the various types of security problems as well as methods that can forestall or at least minimize damage. Above all, it is imperative that one manager in the organization have security as a primary responsibility and constant focus. That person should ensure that security procedures be organized and standardized. We should not lose sight of the fact that security is a management issue, which should be taken seriously by every organization. It also requires the commitment of senior management, which must be instrumental in establishing and enforcing the high-level policies that will outline the goals and objectives to guide information and system security.

ETHICAL ISSUES AND SECURITY

Moral Responsibility for Secure Systems

Now that we have presented an overview of security issues and the elements of a comprehensive policy, we must consider the ethical aspects of maintaining a secure environment. As in other areas considered in this text, there are important social and ethical questions along with some potentially intractable dilemmas. Some of these involve the intrusions of hackers, the debate over whether copying information is akin to other forms of theft, and the scope of the corporation's ethical responsibility to protect sensitive and proprietary data. An additional challenge is the need to provide security without restricting the free exchange of information and possibly violating the First Amendment's guarantee of freedom of speech.

A reasonable place to begin is the moral responsibility to ensure that systems are secure and that data are adequately protected. This responsibility falls first on individuals such as the IT professionals who develop or manage these systems. They are obliged to construct applications with robust security functionality. They must eschew any temptation to cut corners on security in order to expedite development or cut costs. Some managers rationalize weak security by extrapolation from previous experience ("We haven't had any trouble, so why be so concerned about the future?"). Or they may conclude that security would be nice to have but must be traded off to stay cost competitive. But such thinking is myopic, dangerous, and grossly irresponsible.

Obviously, the more sensitive the data, the more attention must be paid to the security and integrity of the environment in which those data are collected, stored, accessed, and distributed. Some databases contain highly sensitive information—medical records, credit and financial histories, etc.—and if it is not carefully protected, innocent people could be victimized. Hence the moral obligation to provide sufficient security is based to some extent on the principle of nonmaleficence, the general moral duty to prevent injury to others. Also, failure to protect information because of carelessness or indifference manifests a lack of respect for the right of privacy. Moreover, this obligation to provide for adequate security falls squarely on application developers and other IT professionals because of two key factors: proximity and capability. In effect, these individuals have the keenest awareness of where the security risks might be along with the expertise and resources to minimize those risks.

Managers who are so-called owners of the information contained in IT systems must likewise regard themselves as custodians of that information. They too have a clear moral responsibility for ensuring that data are disclosed only to those who are authorized to have it and those who will use it conscientiously. They must consider the legality and ethical propriety of requests for this information. Adequate information security thus goes beyond sophisticated technological safeguards and entails the way employees handle and divulge the information contained in the databases they manage.

This responsibility to monitor the access to information raises many problems. For example, there is great potential for abuse in the direct mail industry, where many large mailing lists and consumer databases are bought and sold every day, usually through so-called "list brokers." How can adequate security be provided in such an environment? Should these brokers be responsible for checking up on their customers? Should they attempt to determine how those customers will use the data, and are they partially responsible if their customers misuse those data in some way? In general, where does a company's responsibility for its product end?

At a minimum, these brokers and other information handlers should not be selling to disreputable firms, especially those that have a reputation for misusing mailing lists or exploiting vulnerable customers. It should not be that burdensome to determine which direct marketers are legitimate and to screen out irresponsible ones. They should also make some effort to ascertain how the data will be used; a brief description of the marketing campaign or a sample of the mailing would suffice. These simple precautions might save some consumers from becoming the prey of unscrupulous marketers. In many respects information is no different from other products that have the potential to be misused by customers. And as with other consumer products, companies must be held liable for that misuse when it could have been prevented by their taking reasonable precautions.

Information, then, must be viewed as much more than a mere commodity that can be sold to any customer who has enough money to buy it. Rather, it must be seen as a protectable asset, to be shared with others only with the utmost care and vigilance. Thus information brokers must have a high regard for the proprietary nature of most information, even simple names, addresses, and zip codes. This concern in turn will increase appreciation for security consciousness at all times. In short, those who control information must see themselves as the guardians of that information.

In addition to the individual's responsibility for security, there is also a *corporate* responsibility. In some organizations the corporate structure and culture may tolerate shoddy security practices, flawed, and poorly executed policies, and a general lack of security consciousness. In these cases the corporation is as much to blame for security breaches as those staff members who design, implement, or manage its IT systems. Like individuals, organizations are moral agents with a fundamental ethical duty to prevent injury and to respect the rights of those affected by their actions. This duty requires them to invest the necessary resources to ensure that their systems are as secure as state-of-the-art security technology will allow. Furthermore, the need for security must take precedence over financial considerations or convenience. Security should be as unobtrusive as possible, but companies simply cannot afford to trade off security for the sake of convenience and openness.

Obviously, the level of security necessary will depend on the company, the nature of its business, and the sensitivity of the data in question. For example, a hospital needs greater security to protect patient data than does a manufacturer whose data are primarily inventory or accounts payable information. Every company, however, must be diligent in safeguarding its data. A morally responsible organization, one with a thorough *security net* for all its IT systems, is manifesting more respect for its stakeholders than an organization that is indifferent to this imperative.

But how far companies should go is a considerably more ambiguous and problematic question. Should those who are at risk from lax security have some input about the security of these systems? Should representatives of the stakeholder groups review these systems? Also, should managers and users be held liable for choosing poor passwords that leave the system vulnerable to sophisticated hackers? Should vendors who provide weakly protected software share in the liability for a security breach? Or does the responsibility of securing these systems reside solely with an organization's systems manager? Given the complexity of protecting computer systems in a networked environment, how do we decide when security is adequate or when a company has been remiss in this critical area? In essence, how do we assess when a company has not exercised its full responsibility? (It is worth noting that the National Academy of Science has been calling for a set of Generally Accepted System Security Principles—GSSP—as a general guideline. This would go a long way toward facilitating such an objective assessment.)

One last word. As far as the law is concerned there are currently no explicit criminal liability statutes for failing to provide adequate security for an IT system. It is possible, however, that a corporation could be sued for negligence if its security system were seriously flawed and other parties suffered losses as a result. According to Richard Barker, to avoid liability, "the first requirement is that you observe the accepted standards of your field."[12] The industry's established security practices and procedures con-

---

[12]Richard Barker, *Computer Security Handbook*, 2nd ed. (Blue Ridge Summit, PA: TAB Reference Books, 1991), p. 218.

stitute a frame of reference for judging whether one has done an adequate job of securing an IT system. Obviously there is some vagueness here which will probably work to the advantage of the defendant. But as we have been at pains to insist, regardless of legal liability there is certainly an ethical liability for failing to secure systems adequately. Also, companies that are lax in this area will soon see a loss of confidence among many of their stakeholders, including their customers. This pragmatic reason alone should be a real incentive to treat security matters with the diligence they deserve.

Related Ethical Issues

We have been considering security from the viewpoint of the potential victim. It is also instructive to examine this issue from the perspective of the perpetrator. As was noted earlier, many security breaches are caused by hackers, and some have maintained that most of their intrusive activities do not pose a serious ethical problem. Is there any merit to this popular argument? In addition, how do we measure the damage caused by such intruders? Do we consider only the files or data that have been corrupted or also the resources that have been squandered? If no files or data have been corrupted, should the intrusion be dismissed as insignificant? Finally, what is an appropriate punishment for electronic trespassers and hackers?

There have been numerous arguments put forth to defend break-ins by hackers, especially when there is no deliberate destruction of property. Among these arguments we find the following: Break-ins actually serve a valuable purpose because they uncover security flaws that would otherwise go unnoticed; moreover, the intruder is probably utilizing only idle resources so there is really no cost for the victim. There is also what Eugene Spafford calls the student hacker argument: "Some trespassers claim that they are doing no harm and changing nothing—they are simply learning about how computer systems operate."[13]

On the surface some of these arguments may appear plausible. If, for example, a hacker is able to penetrate a secure environment and search through programs and files but does no damage, where is the harm? This action might be analogous to walking through someone's property but leaving everything intact. Thus one could argue that unauthorized access that leaves the environment undisturbed is only a minor ethical transgression. Also it should be pointed out that most state laws against electronic trespassing stipulate that the trespasser have malicious intent, so they are

---

[13]Eugene Spafford, "Are Computer Hacker Break-ins Ethical?" *Journal of Systems Software*, January 1992, p. 45.

usually not invoked against hackers who are engaged in merely "exploring" another's computer system.

On the other hand, it is generally recognized that it is simply wrong to trespass even if no direct damage is caused. When one trespasses, one violates respect for property rights, which is an important ethical and social value. And beyond doubt, a computer system is a form of property; one is trespassing when one enters an operating system fully aware that only privileged individuals are authorized to use that system. To be sure, the distinction between public and private space may be difficult to establish in cyberspace, the complex environment of networked computers, but that fact does not mean that the distinction should be ignored.

Furthermore, the hacker may intrude into a system not intending to do any harm but may inadvertently cause damage to a file or program. The more complex the system, the more likely the occurrence of accidental damage. Finally, unauthorized use of a computer system wastes valuable CPU resources, which does amount to a form of theft.

Thus, a strong case can be made from a moral viewpoint that electronic trespassing is a serious offense because it violates property rights, wastes computer resources, and could lead to unintended negative consequences. It should be noted, however, that our legal system must be fair in dealing with exploratory hackers and make sure that the punishment is proportionate to the particular offense.

To some extent our legal system has not yet sorted out all of the issues involved in this new breed of criminal activity. There is some confusion over where to draw the line between responsible and irresponsible behavior in the use of computer systems. According to Richard D'Ippolito:

> Our view of computer crimes has not yet merged with society's view of other property crimes: while we have laws against breaking and entering, they aren't widely applied to computer crimes.... There still seems to be the presumption that computer property, unlike other property, is fair game.[14]

The question of unauthorized access becomes even fuzzier when the issues of ownership are ambiguous. Recall that this is the basic ethical issue in *Revlon v. Logisticon* (Chapter 4). Logisticon justified its surreptitious access of Revlon's system because Revlon had not yet paid for its inventory control software. Logisticon's disabling of this sophisticated software was tantamount to repossessing a product that had not been paid for by the customer. Repossession is usually not regarded as immoral even if it does require the trespassing of another's property. However, in Revlon's view

---

[14]Richard D'Ippolito, "AT&T Computers Penetrated," *Internet Risks Forum*, September 1987, p. 41.

this was an act of "commercial terrorism," since there was no moral or legal basis for Logisticon's furtive electronic trespassing.

But there are many complex issues in this case. For example, who really owned the software installed at Revlon? What about Revlon's investment of resources in this program? Does the company's extensive labor investment confer a greater property right or is this point really irrelevant?

The ethical question of security raises important issues about the nature of property in the information age. The primary question is this: Do we need a redefinition of the concept of property, since information can be copied and replicated without limits and without affecting in any way the original information? When an intruder has copied a file without disturbing the original data, therefore, has there really been a theft? The data are still available for use by its original owner; it has only been reproduced, albeit illegitimately. Is any unauthorized reproduction tantamount to theft?

Perhaps such action does not correspond to the legal definition of theft, but one could surely argue that it is unethical, since at the very least there has been a flagrant violation of privacy. Moreover, it manifests no respect for the proprietary nature of some information. The point is that I do not have the right to copy or even examine information that is considered private and proprietary by another party, even if I can do so by leaving that information intact.

From a legal viewpoint, however, should we consider the copying of information as theft or just as an invasion of privacy? According to legal scholars, if copying or misappropriating information is to be regarded as theft, then information must be classified as private property. There are, however, complex issues raised in doing so. The traditional legal rule has been that one could not be prosecuted for the theft of information if the victim still had the use and possession of that information. But there is a recent trend in U.S. courts to reverse this tradition and consider information as property. From a moral point of view, the categorization of information as private property and its misappropriation as theft must be weighed against the important social value of information's unencumbered dissemination. There would be a serious social cost if the free flow of information were impeded by strict laws. Consider, for example, the negative ramifications that would result if medical or scientific information became the discoverer's private property; restricting the free exchange of that information could ultimately be detrimental to society.

The issue of whether someone's informational resources are private property is not simple and cannot be answered unequivocally. Rather, as Pamela Samuelson has observed, there is a pressing need to develop criteria that will help us to determine under what circumstances information ought to be classified as property. These criteria should address the questions of whether there is an investment in the information, the originality of the ideas, the information's value to society, and so forth. To be sure, such criteria will be difficult to establish, but the alternative is intolerable. As Ms. Samuelson has perceptively noted, "a world in which all information is its discoverer's property under all circumstances is unthinkable."[15]

Still another ethical concern is the need to balance the investigation and prosecution of computer crime with respect for everyone's civil liberties. Many civil libertarians and others in the computer industry argue that the crackdown on computer crime has threatened constitutional freedom. Government officials have sometimes used questionable tactics in the pursuit of computer criminals, which have raised some important moral and public policy questions. For example, should a company be liable to legal action and the seizure of its equipment and data if a single employee has used that equipment to engage in some fraudulent activity? This has happened in several instances, most notably the case of the Steve Johnson Games company of Austin, Texas. While some maintain that such aggressive action is necessary to forestall the growth of computer crime, others are deeply concerned that the corporation's rights are being violated because of one employee's criminal behavior. It is perhaps worth considering the following analogy: If an unscrupulous employee used a company's truck to traffic in stolen property, does that mean that the company's whole fleet of trucks should be subject to seizure? Such action does seem extreme and may well be a violation of constitutional rights such as protection from search and seizure.

Many critics point to the celebrated case of Craig Neidorf as an example of how government's zealousness has led to the trampling of constitutional rights. Neidorf was a college student accused of fraud and interstate transport of stolen property. He made the fatal mistake of publishing a document about Southwestern Bell's Enhanced 911 system in his newsletter known as Phrack. Niedorf was charged with ten felony counts for misappropriating this information from Bell South. The company contended that the E911 information was proprietary and confidential; moreover, according to Bell South, the information was worth approximately $23,900. It was alleged that the document was stolen by a friend of Niedorf, Robert Ripp, who electronically sent the E911 text file to Niedorf. Niedorf admitted publishing an edited version of this document in Phrack with names, telephone numbers, and some other sensitive data deleted. The government's case against Neidorf was based on the claim that "the E911 text file

---

[15]Pamela Samuelson, "Is Information Property?" *Communications of the ACM*, March 1991, p. 18.

and the Phrack version contained highly sensitive and proprietary information that provided a road map to the 911 system and could be used to gain access to the system and disrupt service."[16]

One of the key controversial issues to emerge in this case centered on the constitutional right to freedom of the press. Defenders of Neidorf claimed that the government indictment was a blatant infringement of that right. After all, they argued, Niedorf did not steal anything or intentionally misappropriate information. Rather, he published sensitive information that was obtained by questionable means. However, this is a common and acceptable practice in the news media; the Pentagon Papers incident is one of many examples of the press's publishing a document that was misappropriated or leaked by a third party. The media have never been held legally liable for such activity. Indeed publishing such material is protected by freedom of the press. Isn't the prosecution of Niedorf, then, a violation of his civil liberties? The irony of this case is that the charges were ultimately dropped after it was revealed that Bell South included the same document in a booklet that was sold to the public for $13!

Nevertheless, the critical issue remains: Do electronic communications and publications enjoy the same First Amendment protection as traditional printed documents? Likewise, do private messages sent by electronic mail enjoy the same protection as correspondence sent through the U.S. mail? And what about electronic bulletin boards; are they analogous to electronic meeting places that are also protected by the Constitution? Finally, should computer networks be regarded as mere carriers of information with no restrictions on the content, or can network service providers control the substance of electronic messages? For example, would the suppression of incendiary messages or obscene communications be consistent with the principles of freedom of speech? These difficult questions must be dealt with if society is to strike the right balance between its efforts to control computer abuses and the civil liberties of all parties.

Although we cannot attempt to answer all of these questions in this chapter, it should at least be pointed out that if First Amendment rights are extended to electronic publications and communications and even computer networks, there must be definite limits on those rights. Free speech is not an absolute right and should not be invoked to protect all forms of electronic communication. For example, copyright infringement, libel, dia-

---

[16]Dorothy Denning, "The U.S. vs. Craig Neidorf," *Communications of the ACM*, March 1991, p. 27.

logues bordering on criminal conspiracy, and similar forms of communication represent an irresponsible use of one's right to free speech no matter what the medium. But where to draw the line here will always be an extremely difficult issue to resolve.

SUMMARY

In this chapter we have elaborated upon the issue of computer system and information security. It is very difficult to secure systems in a heterogeneous, networked hardware environment. This problem is further compounded by the proliferation of personal computers and laptops, which do not lend themselves to centralized control, as do mainframe systems. Security concerns not only the deployment of the technology necessary to protect computer systems and information but also the development of comprehensive policies regarding the dissemination of sensitive data.

Security problems can be caused by outsiders such as hackers or by insiders, namely, employees and consultants. For the most part, the more costly security breaches have been caused by insiders, such as dissatisfied or mischievous employees. Employees have manipulated computer systems for their own personal gain or sabotaged those systems as a means of vengeance against their employer. In either case the cost to corporations has been especially high.

Several types of security problems can occur, ranging from unauthorized access and electronic trespassing to more sophisticated and expensive computer crimes such as theft, sabotage, and bank and credit card fraud. Corporations must also contend with perverse parasitic programs such as viruses, worms, and time bombs, which can do substantial damage if they are not detected and extirpated from the system.

Given all these threats, corporations must develop a cohesive and comprehensive security policy, with at least three major objectives: to protect against unauthorized access, to maintain system and data integrity, and to provide adequate backup and recovery. One or more managers must have security concerns as a primary ongoing responsibility.

Some specific measures that can help to make systems less vulnerable include unobvious passwords, user IDs, and other restrictions to prevent unauthorized access. Security precautions should also include encryption to protect the transmission of information, audit trails and accounting logs to help track an electronic trespasser, and anti-virus software programs. Backup and recovery capabilities are also critical and essential aspects of computer system management in case of an intrusion that causes system failure or the deletion or corruption of valuable data.

Finally, we discussed in some detail the ethical issues provoked by the question of security. The main purpose of security is self-protection, but other parties often rely on that protection as well. Hence both companies and individuals have a serious moral obligation to protect the information that is entrusted to them, because the leakage of sensitive information can cause irreparable damage. If an organization is a custodian of sensitive data, it has a duty to invest the necessary resources to ensure that its computer systems are as secure as state-of-the-art technology will allow. Companies should not sacrifice security on behalf of financial expediency or for the sake of open systems or the convenience of their end users. There is some ambiguity in determining just how far corporations should go in protecting the security of its systems and data, and who should be liable for security breaches. Also, should those stakeholders who are most at risk from lax security have some input about security issues, or would this participation carry the principle of "informed consent" a bit too far?

We also considered the ethics of security from the viewpoint of the perpetrator. Several questions were raised. For example, how harmful is unauthorized access by hackers and what constitutes appropriate punishment for transgressions such as electronic trespassing? We have argued here that these offenses should not be treated lightly even if no ostensible damage has been done, since valuable resources have been squandered and respect for property rights violated.

Another issue peripherally related to security concerns the nature of information. Is information property and, if so, is someone criminally liable for theft if he or she reproduces that information without permission? Of course, as we observed, even it such an action is not strictly speaking "theft," it is still a serious violation of privacy.

A third ethical issue that should not be overlooked is the need to balance security concerns with respect for civil liberties and the important First Amendment right of free speech. This issue raises questions such as whether networks should be value-neutral regarding the content of the information they carry, and whether electronic publications enjoy the same protection as the publication of documents in more traditional media.

CASES FOR DISCUSSION

Introduction

The first of these two cases considers the ethical implications of a deliberate act of sabotage by an ex-employee. It includes several themes that have been addressed in this chapter. Specifically, it underscores the responsibility of organizations to provide adequate security and raises questions about liability and integrity when security is compromised. The second case describes another security breach, the Internet worm. In this case the perpetrator was an outsider who could be characterized as a sophisticated hacker. How should we weigh the severity of this action from a moral viewpoint and what is a fitting punishment for this incursion?

CASE 7.1

The Disgruntled Consultant[17]

Donald Chase had just celebrated his tenth anniversary at TTI Consulting when he received the bad news. Because of declining revenues and a shrinking customer base, he was one of seven consultants who were being dismissed. His boss, Dr. Phillip Bluestein, informed Mr. Chase at 11:00 A.M. on Tuesday that his services were no longer needed. Dr. Bluestein was customarily rather abrupt in his dealings with subordinates, and unfortunately this situation was no different. Chase was told to pack his things and clear out of the building by noon.

Crestfallen, Chase returned to his small office on the third floor of the TTI building. He struggled to suppress his anger and resentment. He had given his heart and soul to this company during the last ten years and felt betrayed by this sudden dismissal. These feelings were perhaps accentuated because he had just recently completed a major project for one of TTI's established clients, The Northwest Commerce Bank. He had worked long hours and weekends to finish its complex cash management application on schedule. Chase had completed this sophisticated program only several days before, and during a brief internal demo he had received considerable praise from upper management, including Dr. Bluestein. Managers at Northwest Commerce were eagerly awaiting delivery, since they estimated

---

[17]This case is based on an actual incident. The identity of all individuals and organizations has been disguised.

that this new system would save the bank about $60,000 a month thanks to more efficient cash management.

However, at the time of Chase's dismissal the application had not yet been delivered to the client. It remained on the server, which was linked to Chase's IBM PC. Chase kept the only backup copy of this system in his briefcase, so that he could work on the application at home at his convenience.

As Chase began packing his belongings, Dr. Bluestein appeared at the doorway. They briefly discussed the Northwest Commerce application, and Chase pointed out to Bluestein how the application could be accessed on the company's client/server network. This discussion was followed by a cursory overview of the programs that comprised this system. It appeared to Chase that Bluestein wanted to make sure that everything was intact for the system's imminent delivery to the Northwest Commerce Bank. Bluestein remained with Chase as he finished packing a few boxes of books and other materials. Chase then put only a few additional items in his briefcase and left his office, followed by Bluestein He did not return the backup copy of the Commerce Bank system. After saying goodbye to a few friends, Chase left the building and drove home.

Upon his return home, Chase decided to seek revenge on his ungrateful employer. He used his PC to connect to the company computer system, entered his user ID and password, and accessed the only copy of the Commerce Bank application. He proceeded to disable several key programs by inserting a code that subverted the display of menu screens and corrupted data. Chase also had the presence of mind to cover his tracks by erasing the audit file that accompanied the program; thus there was no record of this unauthorized access.

Executives at TTI were not aware of what had happened until two days later when an associate of Chase did one final quality assurance test before final delivery of the program to the bank. When she logged in to the application, she quickly realized that it had been tampered with and called Dr. Bluestein, who strongly suspected sabotage. He immediately and repeatedly called Chase's residence but there was no answer; also Chase's large severance check had already been cashed.

As Commerce Bank waited patiently for its cash management system, the company quickly launched an internal investigation. It was apparent that the layoffs represented a chaotic situation within TTI, and as a result, there was inadequate communication between certain departments. For example, the company's security manager was not informed about the layoffs until the day after they occurred. At that point user ID's and passwords for the discharged employees were revoked. However, this was too late to save the Commerce Bank application from this deliberate act of sabotage. When asked by the Executive Vice President about this communication failure, the Human Resources Manager informed her that his department had never coordinated layoffs and dismissals with the security manager. "We've never had the sense in this company that we should lock the gates and put up barricades when people leave," he said; "our employees are trusted colleagues even after they've been let go."

As the investigation continued, Dr. Bluestein faced a difficult decision about how he would deal with his contact at the Commerce Bank, who was eagerly awaiting the now overdue cash management program. Chase was an especially clever programmer and consequently Bluestein estimated that it would take at least several weeks to unearth the bugs and fix the system. Also, all of the other consultants were assigned to high-priority projects, so there might be some delay in getting started on this work.

Bluestein wondered what he should tell the people at Commerce. Should he be candid about the company's untimely security lapse? Commerce was one of TTI's most security-conscious customers, and hence this revelation might jeopardize lucrative future contracts. But Commerce had been told the previous week that the project was done and that they would receive it on time. How, then, could he explain what could have gone wrong to delay delivery by several weeks and maybe longer? Also Bluestein wondered about the corporation's legal and moral responsibility for what happened. Chase was clearly the main culprit here but to what extent was the corporation also liable for his transgression? And if the company was liable, should it make some restitution to its customer, whose business would be adversely affected by this mishap? Bluestein began sorting through all of these questions as he stared at the pink phone messages in front of him.

Questions

1. How could TTI improve its security policies and its procedures for dismissing employees?
2. What should Dr. Bluestein say to his client, the Commerce Bank? Should he be open and truthful about what went wrong or tell the executives at Commerce something else?
3. Is TTI liable, that is, responsible, for Chase's reckless actions, or is TTI the victim in this case? Should it compensate the bank in some way for the delay in delivering the cash management application?

CASE 7.2

The Internet Worm

In early November 1988, Americans witnessed a shocking example of the vulnerability of networked computer systems. A destructive virus infected Internet, a widely used national computer communications network. This virus temporarily denied service to many computers at various academic, military, and business sites. It is estimated that about 2,000 computers across the country were affected in some way in a matter of only a few hours.

The Internet Worm incident raises some difficult practical and ethical issues. For example, can we tolerate electronic trespassing if it brings about positive results by exposing security flaws? Was the worm really malicious or just an innocent experiment that got out of hand? How should the perpetrator be punished? Finally, how can this incident be prevented from happening again? These and other questions will be raised in this case study of the infamous Internet Worm.

The Internet Network   The Internet is a massive web of hundreds of computer networks that span the entire world. Internet allows its users to access scientific and government research archives and also to exchange electronic messages with colleagues, view bulletin boards, and so forth. Many universities, corporations, and government agencies are connected to Internet in order to share research information and other data. It is also available to the general public through on-line information services such as CompuServe and Dow Jones. Despite this expanded accessibility, the network is still used predominantly by government and university researchers and private businesses. Individuals connected to Internet can communicate with as many as 5 to 10 million users worldwide. Users cannot be easily identified because of the system's vastness and complexity.

Internet's rapid growth has produced many benefits for its users. However, it has grown in a random, piecemeal fashion, with no centralized control. Thus there is no central index or centrally offered services. Some have compared Internet "to a library where all of the books are dumped on the floor in no particular order."[18] Anyone who uses Internet must have

---

[18]Robert E. Calem, "The Network of All Networks," *The New York Times*, December 6, 1992, p. D12. Copyright © 1992 by The New York Times Company. Reprinted by permission.

some familiarity with how to navigate through the network and retrieve the information they are seeking.

A Summary of Events Sometime after 5 o'clock on the evening of November 2, 1988, Internet was beseiged by an insidious worm program. The activity actually began on ARPANET, a computer network for academics. It then spread to MILNET, a Defense Department network, and ultimately to the Internet. (These networks are all connected by gateways.) This clever program was executed on a host machine connected to the network, and it used network and user information to break into other machines. This process was abetted because of security flaws in the system software of these machines. Once these computers were entered, the program replicated itself incessantly. It did not modify system files or destroy any information.

The performance of systems infected by the worm deteriorated rapidly, and some infected computers simply crashed, because the uncontrollable replication of the worm clogged the computers' memory. In addition to the estimated 2,000 computers infected by the worm, many more had to be tested for infection. All of these systems had to be taken off-line in order to apply the remedial and preventive measures necessary to destroy the worm and prevent its recurrence.

The worm exploited well-known weaknesses in the UNIX security system. The basic strategy of the worm was repeated attempts to uncover user passwords which would allow it to penetrate the system at hand. It succeeded in this effort because in the UNIX system software the encrypted password of each user was in a publicly readable file. According to one observer, "UNIX password authentication works without putting any readable version of the password onto the system, and indeed works without protecting the encrypted password against reading by users on the system."[19] Thus, lax systems security was a major contributing factor in this break-in.

Although many computer systems on Internet were infected by the worm, those of major universities seemed to be the hardest hit. Universities affected included MIT, Purdue, Stanford, and The University of California at Berkeley, among many others.[20] Two of the research agencies affected

[19]Donn Seeley, "Password Cracking: A Game of Wits," *Communications of the ACM*, June 1989, pp. 700–701.

[20]For a description of MIT's experience with the worm see Jon A. Rochlis and Mark W. Eichin,"With Microscope and Tweezers: The Worm from MIT's Perspective," *Communications of the ACM*, June 1989, pp. 689–98.

include the NASA Ames Laboratory and the Rand Corporation. Several of the universities affected pooled their intellectual resources to help solve this crisis. By 5 o'clock Thursday morning, approximately twelve hours after the first system was infected, the Computer Systems Research Group at Berkeley had developed a program to halt the worm's spread. The final tally: 2,000 computers infected in some way and a clean up cost of about $1 million.[21]

The Culprit   Shortly after the incident occurred, Robert Tappan Morris, a first-year graduate student in computer science at Cornell, was identified as the author and creator of the worm. A Cornell University report indicated that Morris worked alone; the report described Morris's behavior as "a juvenile act that ignored the clear potential consequences."[22] The Cornell Commission also reached the following conclusion regarding Morris's intention in unleashing the insidious worm: "It may simply have been the unfocused intellectual meandering of a hacker completely absorbed with his creation and unharnessed by considerations of explicit purpose or potential effect."[23] The Commission concluded that Morris had no intention of destroying data or interfering with normal computer operations. Moreover, the Commission opined, the young student did not intend for the worm to replicate itself uncontrollably. However, it also noted that "given Morris' evident knowledge of systems and networks, he knew or clearly should have known that such a consequence was certain, given the design of the worm."[24] It is worth mentioning, however, that Morris did not make any measurable effort to impede the worm's progress and did not inform anyone of this transgression and its apparent consequences.

The Cornell Commission unequivocally condemned the actions of Robert Morris. According to the Commission, "the act was selfish and inconsiderate of the obvious effect it would have on countless individuals who had to devote substantial time to cleaning up the effects of the worm, as well as on those whose research and other work was interrupted or delayed."[25] Shortly after this incident occurred, Morris took a

---

[21]Anne Branscomb, "Rogue Computer Programs and Computer Rogues: Tailoring the Punishment to Fit the Crime," *Rutgers Computer and Technology Law Journal*, 16:1, 1990, p. 7.
[22]Ted Eisenberg et al., "The Cornell Commission: On Morris and the Worm," *Communications of the ACM*, June 1989, p. 706.
[23]Ibid.
[24]Ibid.
[25]Ibid., p. 709.

leave of absence from Cornell. He was indicted for violating federal laws that prohibit electronic trespassing and tampering with computer systems.

Ethical Considerations   For many observers, the Internet Worm scandal is not as ethically unambiguous as the members of the Cornell Commission had supposed. Some have argued, for example, that the Internet Worm was not really malicious, that it was simply an experiment that inadvertently got out of hand. There is some evidence that this was a development version of the worm which accidentally got loose and caused havoc on Internet. But others point to evidence that "the worm was designed to reproduce quickly and spread itself over great distances."[26] Some sympathetic members of the press pointed out that Morris did the computer community a service by highlighting the security flaws in UNIX. Many have argued that the worm was designed to reveal security problems to complacent system administrators whose machines were connected to the Internet. Indeed, Morris's defense attorneys argued that because the worm did reveal these flaws, Morris's action had some positive social benefits which should lessen the gravity of his offense. Still others maintain that this event was analogous to trespassing on someone's unlocked property without the intention of doing any damage; the damage caused by this runaway worm was simply the unfortunate result of unanticipated and uncontrollable interactions.

Lastly, there are some cultural issues to consider. Computer pranks and intrusions by sophisticated hackers are relatively commonplace in our society, though few cause the commotion of the Internet Worm. As Eugene Spafford observed, many computer professionals "started their careers years ago by breaking into computer systems at their colleges and places of employment to demonstrate their expertise and knowledge of the inner workings of the systems."[27] But are such transgressions graver and more costly now that so many organizations depend so heavily on the smooth functioning of their computers and the networks to which they are linked? If this is so, aspiring computer wizards will have to find new and legitimate ways to hone their skills and develop their expertise.

---

[26]Seely, "Password Cracking,"p. 703.
[27]Eugene Spafford, "The Internet Worm: Crisis and Aftermath," *Communications of the ACM,* June 1989, p. 686.

Questions

1. What do you think about electronic trespassing by hackers such as Morris? Are there conditions under which these actions might be justified?

2. Do you accept the argument that hackers do the community a service by exposing security flaws in computer systems. Do these positive results justify the action of trespassing?

3. What is a fitting punishment for someone like Robert Morris? Does it matter if he did not intend to do any damage to the computer systems linked to the Internet, or is this consideration irrelevant?

Annotated Bibliography

This bibliography does not include general works on ethical theory. Rather it encompasses books and articles that deal explicitly with the moral and social dimensions of managing information. Readers interested in background material on ethics should consult some of the sources cited in Chapter 2.

BOOKS

Barker, Richard. *Computer Security Handbook.* Blue Ridge Summit, PA: TAB Professional Reference Books, 1991.

> This is a practical "how to" treatise that covers a broad range of topics on computer security. It does, however, consider some of the ethical concerns raised in Chapter 7. It also contains a brief section on the legal ramifications of shoddy security practices or the failure to protect information adequately.

Bynum, Terrell W. (ed.). *Computers and Ethics.* New York: Blackwell, 1985.

> A collection of provocative essays on computers, information technology, and ethics. This volume includes an excellent introductory essay to this topic by James Moor entitled "What Is Computer Ethics."

Moor argues that new technologies demand a rethinking of many public policies and ethical standards.

Clapes, Anthony Lawrence. *Softwars: The Legal Battles for Control of the Global Software Industry*. Westport, CT: Quorum Books, 1993.

An articulate, lucid overview of recent legal cases (such as *Lotus v. Paperback Software*) that determine the nature and extent of intellectual property protection for software. According to the author, this book takes a "traditional protectionist" point of view which assumes that traditional principles such as copyright and patent protection are essential for the vitality and continued growth of the global software industry.

Dejoie, Roy, George Fowler, and David Paradice (eds). *Ethical Issues in Information Systems*. Boston: Boyd & Fraser Publishing Company, 1991.

An anthology of readings on traditional ethical issues such as intellectual property, privacy, and access. This book has an entire section dedicated to artificial intelligence and ethics which considers issues such as responsibility, ownership, and machine decision making. Some of these essays on AI also address the question of who owns the knowledge in an expert system.

Ermann, David M., Claudio Guitierrez, and Mary B. Williams (eds). *Computers, Ethics and Society*. New York: Oxford University Press, 1990.

The major asset of this book is its interdisciplinary set of readings and essays which address the numerous social and ethical problems of the computer age. The authors illuminate both the positive and negative aspects of new technologies. In the preface they write that the purpose of this book is to provide students "with a greater desire to discover what they will have to do if their work in the computer field is to contribute to creating a better society."

Forrester, Tom, and Perry Morrison. *Computer Ethics: Cautionary Tales and Ethical Dilemmas in Computing*. Cambridge, MA: MIT Press, 1990.

A witty and insightful treatment of issues such as privacy, intellectual property, security, and the impact of computers in the workplace. This book is punctuated by many hypothetical and engaging scenarios that pose difficult and intractable ethical dilemmas for managers.

Gould, Carol (ed.). *The Information Web: Ethical and Social Implications of Computers.* Boulder, CO: Westview-Press, 1989.

A collection of essays dealing with the profound ethical implications of networking and networked computer systems. The primary issues covered in this anthology include privacy, security, free speech in cyberspace, and the social ramifications for those who lack access to various services. The essays on privacy and computer security are especially noteworthy.

Johnson, Deborah. *Computer Ethics*, 2nd ed. Englewood Cliffs, NJ: Prentice-Hall, 1994.

This book was one of the first to deal with the key ethical problems caused by computer systems. This updated edition provides a comprehensive discussion of issues such as intellectual property, privacy, computer crime, responsibility and liability, and the social implications of computers.

Johnson, Deborah, and John Snapper (eds.). *Ethical Issues in the Use of Computers.* Belmont, CA: Wadsworth Publishing Company, 1985.

Although this book is now a bit dated, it does contain some classic essays on computer ethics such as Jim Prince's "Negligence: Liability for Defective Software." The first section presents codes of conduct that have been adopted by various professional computer associations. Besides discussions on privacy and liability it also includes a section entitled "Computers and Power," which concerns how computers affect the distribution of power in society.

Penzias, Arno. *Ideas and Information.* New York: W.W. Norton & Company, 1989.

This book discusses what its title implies: the pivotal role of information in our computer society. It considers the critical importance of deriving usable information from masses of data. Although it does not explicitly discuss ethical issues, it does serve as an enlightening backdrop to many of the topics treated in this text.

Rosenberg, Richard. *The Social Impact of Computers.* New York: Harcourt Brace Jovanovich, 1992.

A timely examination of the broad spectrum of social issues generated by computers and information systems. One of the primary advantages of this book is the depth and breadth of its coverage. It considers, for example, the expanding role of computers in education, government, medicine, and so forth. It also examines some of the incidents discussed in this book, such as the Internet Worm.

Rothfeder, Jeffrey. *Privacy for Sale: How Computerization Has Made Everyone's Life an Open Secret*. New York: Simon & Schuster, 1992.

This book elaborates upon many of the privacy abuses that have been presented in Chapter 5. For example, Rothfeder discusses the laxity of credit bureaus and the government's loose policies for safeguarding information. The author does not discuss the philosophical dimensions of the right to privacy but he does provide many disturbing examples of how that right is under increasing pressure thanks to advances in information technology.

Schoeman, Ferdinand. *Philosophical Dimensions of Privacy: An Anthology*. Cambridge, England: Cambridge University Press, 1984.

A collection of essays on privacy which underscore the fundamental importance of this basic right. Although none of the essays addresses the threats to privacy posed by computer technology, they do provide many arguments that support the need to be constantly vigilant in the face of those threats. The article by S. I. Benn on the connection between privacy and freedom is especially relevant.

Zuboff, Shoshana. *In the Age of the Smart Machine: The Future of Work and Power*. New York: Basic Books, 1988.

A seminal work on the impact of computers in the workplace. Although ethical issues are not explicitly discussed, they are constantly on the periphery of Ms. Zuboff's brilliant discussion.

ARTICLES

Cespedes, Frank, and H. Jeff Smith. "Database Marketing: New Rules for Policy and Practice," *Sloan Management Review*, Summer 1993, pp. 7–22.

An incisive treatment of how database marketing (DBM) campaigns can pose threats to privacy while allowing for more efficient target marketing. The authors observe that most managers have given little reflection to the social issues implicated in DBM programs. Their response to this problem is a series of carefully crafted rules that in their view provide for DBM fairness.

Chalykoff, John, and Nitin Nohira. "Note on Electronic Monitoring," *Harvard Business School Publications*, 1990.

A provocative discussion on the use and abuse of electronic monitoring in the workplace. This Note includes a detailed description of the technical aspects of these systems along with a discussion of the negative impact on employee morale and other problems.

Clarke, Roger. "Information Technology and Dataveillance," *Communications of the ACM*, May 1988, pp. 498–512.

A comprehensive treatment of the use of data systems to monitor the activities of employees. The article discusses in some detail the benefits and costs of these sophisticated systems.

Collste, Goran. "Expert Systems in Medicine and Moral Responsibility," *Journal of Systems Software*, 17 (1992), pp. 19–24.

A careful examination of the use of expert systems in the medical profession which explains how these systems could threaten the autonomy and responsibility of doctors. It also considers whether expert systems can incorporate moral considerations into the decision-making process.

"Communications, Computers and Networks," Special Issue, *Scientific American*, September 1991.

An excellent array of articles on networking, including several that deal with public policy and social issues such as respect for civil liberties and the need to rethink the laws that govern information and ownership. Of particular interest are articles by Mitch Kapor ("Civil Liberties in Cyberspace") and Anne Branscomb ("Common Law for the Electronic Frontier").

Gentile, Mary, and John Sviokla. "Information Technology in Organizations: Emerging Issues in Ethics and Policy," *Harvard Business School Publications*, 1991.

An overview of the ethical and public policy issues generated by information technology. This article serves as a practical guide for IT managers and vendors who must face these issues periodically. Issues considered include privacy, accuracy, security, control and ownership. This is one of the few publications to consider ethical issues involved in the relationship between IT vendors and their customers.

Johnston, Russell, and Michael Vitale. "Creating Competitive Advantage with Interorganizational Information Systems," *MIS Quarterly*, June 1988, pp. 153–65.

This article covers the various competitive advantages to be gained from IOS systems as well as some of the technical aspects of these systems. It also briefly but incisively considers some of the social ramifications of an IOS.

Manson, Richard. "Four Ethical Issues of the Information Age," *MIS Quarterly*, March 1986, pp. 46–55.

The author discusses four fundamental issues concerning "intellectual capital" in the information age: privacy, accuracy, property, and access, which he summarizes in the acronym, PAPA. This brief article is a concise introduction to these critical issues.

Marx, Gary T., and Sanford Sherizen. "Monitoring in the Job: How to Protect Privacy as Well as Property," *Technology Review*, November–December 1986, pp. 63–72.

This well-written article provides a probing discussion of the monitoring systems that are available to keep tabs on employees. It considers some of the ethical implications of the growing use of these systems and recommends that companies develop codes of responsibility to help safeguard the rights of employees.

Mykyntn, Kathleen, Peter Mykyntn, and Craig Slinkman. "Expert Systems: A Question of Liability," *MIS Quarterly*, March 1990, pp. 30–37.

An excellent guide to the ethical and product liability issues that are provoked by the use of expert systems. The authors provide some concrete guidelines for minimizing liability such as avoiding excessive product hype regarding the product's decision-making capabilities.

Samuelson, Pamela. "How to Interpret the Lotus Decision (And How Not To)," *Communications of the ACM*, November 1990, pp. 30–33.

A brief but perceptive explication of the landmark *Lotus v. Paperback* decision. In the course of her discussion of this famous case Professor Samuelson also explains how copyright laws are poorly applied to software because of its functional nature.

Samuelson, Pamela. "Is Information Property?" *Communications of the ACM*, March 1991, pp. 15–18.

An important and well-argued article addressing the question of whether information should be classified as property. The author demonstrates the many difficulties with this particular viewpoint.

Spafford, Eugene. "Are Computer Hacker Break-ins Ethical?" *Journal of Systems Software*, January 1992, pp. 41–47.

The author strongly believes that these break-ins are indeed unethical. He refutes the "hacker ethic" that defends break-ins on the basis of arguments such as the following: Hackers are simply making use of idle machines, or unauthorized break-ins serve the useful purpose of pointing out security gaps. Spafford illustrates the flaws in these and other arguments normally invoked by hackers to justify their unorthodox activities.

Steidlmeier, Paul. "The Moral Legitimacy of Intellectual Property Claims: American Business and Developing Country Perspectives," *Journal of Business Ethics*, February 1993, pp. 157–64.

The theme of this article is that many developing countries do not recognize the monopoly claims of patents and copyrights which are at the heart of America's legal system for protecting intellectual property. The article does a good job of presenting the viewpoint of developing countries, which support only weak protection of intellectual property. It elaborates upon many of the issues discussed in Chapter 6.

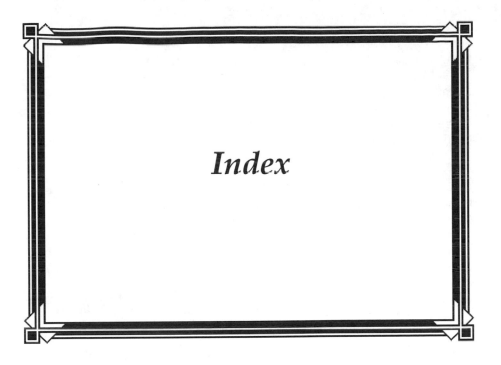

Index